The best of
Mrs BEETON'S
Kitchen Garden

The best of Mrs BEETON'S Kitchen Garden

WEIDENFELD & NICOLSON

This edition produced for The Book People Ltd, Hall Wood Avenue,
Haydock, St Helens WA11 9UL

First published in 2006 by the Orion Publishing Group Ltd
5 Upper St Martin's Lane
London
WC2H 9EA

Text selection © Orion Publishing Group Ltd 2006

Designed by seagulls and cbdesign
Index prepared by Chris Bell
Produced by Omnipress Ltd, Eastbourne
Printed in China

CONTENTS

1

A BRIEF HISTORY OF THE GARDEN

From the ancient world onwards, a brief history of the ornamental garden.

THE traditions of this art, as opposed to the cultivation of soil for mere existence, refer to periods of remote antiquity. Egyptian tomb paintings from 1500 BC depict row-planting around selected sites in royal gardens. Ancient legends celebrate the gardens of the Hesperides and of Alcineus, and history tells us of the hanging gardens, by means of which the mighty King Nebchadnezzar of Babylon sought to reconcile his Medean queen to the flat and relatively barren country of her adoption. The Persians cultivated gardens from the earliest period. Darius had a 'paradise garden', and Xenophon, the historian, says of Cyrus: 'Wherever he resides, or whatever place he visits in his dominions, he is careful that his gardens shall be made to produce.'

The ancient Grecians followed Persian steps, forming gardens not merely for fruit and vegetables but for the cultivation of flowers with them. The narcissus, the violet and the rose were in high repute; myrtles and box trees were clipped into fantastic forms; and things out of season were produced in their forcing pits; for violets in profusion could be bought in the markets of Athens while the snow was thick upon the ground. From Ptolemy's gardens at Alexandria to Hadrian's villa, the ancient Romans left us plenty of information. When Tarquin the Proud was planning with the 'false' Sextus the betrayal of the city of the Sabines, he took the messenger who was sent to him into his garden, and, without a word spoken, cut off the heads of all the tallest poppies growing there, to show that their end could be gained only in removing, one after another, the chief men in the city to be betrayed. The wealthy Lucullus had gardens of an immense extent, and imported from Persia the apricot, the cherry and the peach in about 60 BC. The gardens of Sallust are also much praised, as well as those of the Emperors Nero and Hadrian. Flowers and fruits, we learn, were placed by the Romans under the guardian care of special Deities, and floralia or flower festivals instituted; indeed, to such a pitch of extravagance was the passion for flowers carried that at one period it became necessary that sumptuary laws should be enacted to restrain it. At one single supper, given by the luxurious Cleopatra, the roses alone are said to have cost an Egyptian talent (about £200 of Victorian money and over £12,500 today). The prodigality of Heliogabalus reached an even higher pitch, allegedly smothering his dinner guests to death with rose petals. Pliny, the naturalist, enumerates in his history about one thousand plants of all descriptions; but of these, according to his testimony, only a very few were in general cultivation.

Mr Loudon[1] expresses the opinion that the following lists include all the culinary plants and fruits in use at the time of the fall of the Roman Empire.

🖝 CULINARY PLANTS Peas, beans, vetches, lentils, kidney beans, gourds, cucumbers, melons, cabbages of several sorts, turnips, carrots, parsnips, beet, skirret (white roots similar to sweet potatoes), radishes, sorrel, asparagus, onions, garlic, and some few other alliaceous plants; also endive, lettuces, succory (chicory), mustard and other salads, parsley, celery, orach (red leaves like spinach), alexanders (like celery), elecampane (a bitter aromatic herb), fennel, and chervil.

🖝 FRUITS Figs, almonds, citron, peach, pomegranate, apricots, plums, and cherries, 22 sorts of apples, 36 sorts of pears, quinces, and medlars, many kinds of grapes, mulberries, walnuts, chestnuts, stone pines or pignons (pine nuts) and olives.

During the unsettled times which were consequent upon the breaking up of the Roman Empire, the art of gardening would seem to have fallen into disuse. Its revival was due to the monks. In the great religious institutions which rose and increased so rapidly during that period of European history which is usually called the Dark Ages, the arts of peace and civilisation were maintained and cherished. The enclosure of every monastery embraced a piece of ground which, for exercise as well as utility, was cultivated by the inmates; and even the hermit's cell had its little plot for the growth of a few herbs, and perhaps a few choice flowers for the chaplets and garlands of some favourite saints.

A separate horticultural tradition in China around this time, in which highly-controlled landscapes were built around ponds and hills to emulate river and mountain landscapes. Japanese gardens, designed to suggest nature rather than to copy it, and to be viewed from inside buildings, grew out of this influence and became the stylised Zen gardens of Buddhist temples.

The chief step, however, taken in the way of general gardening was in the time of Charlemagne. That wise monarch, in his *Capitularies*, commanded the formation of gardens throughout his dominions, and gave special directions for the cultivation of certain plants most useful for diet and for medicinal purposes. At a later period the Italians became noted for their exertion in this respect. Alfonso D'Este, Duke of Ferrara, established botanical gardens in several places – the chief of these being known as Belvedere, on the banks of the Po. Naples, Florence, Pisa, Padua, and other large Italian cities soon followed the fashion so extensively, as to give rise to what we describe as the Italian style.

---

1 John Claudius Loudon (1783-1843) did much to educate the Victorian middle class gardening. His designs for Birmingham's Botanic Gardens became synonymous Gardenesque movement (see page 8).

In our own country, gardening as an art, and especially as a science, is of comparatively very modern date. Our ancestors in all probability derived their first notions of gardening from the Romans. Strabo, writing in the first century, tells us that the people of Britain were ignorant of the art of cultivating gardens. The continual wars in which Britain was engaged from the fifth century, when the Romans vacated the islands, probably rooted out all traces of an art so civilising as that of gardening, although there are indications that vineyards planted in the third century, under the Emperor Proteus, existed in the eighth century, where they are mentioned by the Venerable Bede. William of Malmsbury also, writing in the twelfth century, commends the vineyards of the county of Gloucester; and Pliny tells us that cherries, which Lucullus had introduced into Italy about a century before, were grown in Britain in the first century. The opulent Earl of Northumberland, whose household consisted, in 1512, of a hundred and sixty persons, had but one gardener, who, according to the 'Household Book', attended 'hourly in the garden for setting of erbes, and clipping of knottis, and sweeping the said garden clene.'

Towards the end of the fifteenth and in the early part of the sixteenth century, Henry VII had nearly succeeded in rooting out the feuds of the Roses, red and white, and a long period of interruption no doubt prepared the people for the revival of gardening with the other arts of civilization, which took place in the succeeding reign of Henry VIII. The royal gardens of Nonsuch were laid out by this monarch with the greatest magnificence.

In Elizabeth I's reign Holland and Hatfield House were both laid out. Mazes and labyrinths and concealed pipes, by means of which visitors might find themselves lost one minute and deluged with water at the next, seems, indeed, to have been the taste of that day – a jocular sort of hospitality, 'more honoured in the breach than the observance.'

During the reign of James I, Theobalds was planned and erected. 'A large square, having all its walls covered with phillyrea, and a beautiful *jet d'eau* in the centre, the parterre having many pleasant walks, part of which are planted on the sides with espaliers, and others arched all over. At the end is a small mount, called the Mount of Venus, placed in the midst of a labyrinth, and which is, upon the whole, the most beautiful spot in the world.' It was now that this subject engaged the comprehensive mind of Bacon, with little immediate result. However, the contempt he expresses for 'images cut out of juniper and other garden stuff' was not without its weight a few generations later, when a purer taste came to prevail. Hampton Court, Chatsworth, Wooton, and many other of the finest gardens in England, were laid out in Charles II's reign. Garden structures also began to be erected. André Le Nôtre planted Greenwich and

St James's Parks, under the immediate directions of Charles, Versailles being the model, although only at a humble distance. Clipped yew trees and other Dutch tendencies, enclosed by the magnificent gates and iron railings now introduced, became the rage in the reign of William and Mary – 'terraced walks, hedges of evergreens, shorn shrubs in boxes, orange and myrtle trees in tubs, being the chief excellences.' In 1696 an orangery with a glass roof was erected at Wollaton Hall, Nottinghamshire, said to have been the first structure of the kind in England, until William Kent and 'Capability' Brown ushered in a vogue for botanic gardens, such as at Kew, a century later.

The Dutch at an early period became noted for their love of flowers, and their skill in the cultivation of them. Their wealth, and their commerce with the Cape of Good Hope, the East Indies, and other remote parts, gave them extraordinary facilities over other nations in the acquisition of plants, and to them we ourselves are indebted for the introduction, not only of many beautiful flowers, but of vegetables now in common use. For a long time their gardens at Leyden were considered the richest in the world. Through the zeal of the wealthy Dutch merchants, in less than a century – that is, between the years 1633 and 1720 – the number of the different species of plants in these gardens was raised from 1104 to upwards of 6000, as shown by the catalogue of Boerhaave, who was at the time Professor of Botany there.

There is with us a growing taste for gardening, which has both created a great commercial enterprise, and is itself fed from the same source. The invention of the lawnmower by Edwin Budding in the 1830s did much to bring gardening within common public reach. The demand for flowers has kept alive the popular appetite by the continual introduction of something new. And even more than this can be effected; for the skill of our florists can increase, by hybridizing and other processes, the specific varieties of such plants as are placed under their care, until their number becomes almost endless.

Our historical sketch must of necessity be brief; but we must not fail to mention among the chief operating causes which have made gardening an art so popular in this country, the great encouragement given by garden allotments, and village flower shows.

DIFFERENT STYLES OF GARDENING

National styles and peculiarities in most things, especially throughout the European Continent, are now rapidly passing away. Still, for all this, there are generally said to be four characteristic gardening styles viz., the Italian, the French, the Dutch, and the English, or, as it is frequently called, the 'natural style'.

The Italian style is probably a continuation of that of the Romans, with whom it was an amplification of the house itself:

'A pillar'd shade,
High overarch'd
And echoing walks between'[2]

Broad paved and sunny terraces and shady colonnades connected in their style with the house. Marble fountains, statuary, and vases, and other vestiges of ancient art found in the ruins, out of which they have been raised, are the chief characteristics of the magnificent gardens of Italy, and nothing can be nobler than this style when the accessories are all in keeping; 'In spite of Walpole's sneer,' says Mr Bellenden Kerr, 'about walking up and down stairs in the open air, there are few things so beautiful in art as stately terraces, tier above tier, and bold flights of stone steps, now stretching forward in short, steep descents – each landing affording some new scene, some change of sun or shade: a genial bask-ing-place or cool retreat – here the rich perfume of an ancestral orange-tree, which may have been in the family three hundred years – there the bright blos-soms of some sunny creeper; while at another time a balcony juts out to catch some distant view, or a recess is formed, with seats for the loitering party to "rest and be thankful." Let all this be connected, by means of colonnades, with the architecture of the mansion, and you have a far more rational appendage to its incessantly artificial character than the petty wildernesses and picturesque aban-don, which have not been without advocates even on an insignificant scale.' Yet it is only a few gardens of the wealthy that can be so fitted up.

The French style is theatrical. Even at Versailles in its best days, though representing two hundred acres in extent, and we believe something like 8 million Sterling in value (approximately 500 million pounds), the geometric style Le Nôtre recommended largely by its extent and magnificence. In the elaborate productions of this school there is much formality:

'Grove nods at grove, each alley has its brother,
And half the garden just reflects the other.'[3]

A grand effect and display may be produced by a labyrinth, in which thirty-nine of Aesop's fables are represented by means of copper figures of birds and beasts, each group being connected with a separate fountain, and all spouting water.

---

2 John Milton, *Paradise Lost* (bk. IX.)
3 Alexander Pope, Epistle VI, to Richard Boyle.

The Dutch have less picturesque scenery in their own country to imitate, so these practical and industrious cultivators of the soil make no attempt at producing an effect which the eye of every beholder would at once detect as being unnatural to them. Their skill has shown itself in the arrangement of beds, terraces, and grassy slopes. They are fond of large broad spaces, filled with beds in geometrical figures, separated by lines of well-clipped box edgings. Different portions of their gardens are also shut off from view by hedges of evergreens, frequently cut into fantastical forms. The Dutch style exhibits a profusion of ornament of this sort, mostly on a small scale. They have, moreover, canals and watercourses made to accommodate the bridges thrown across them, caves, fountains, and the never-failing 'lust-haus', or summer-house, with a profusion of trellis-work and green paint. There is neatness everywhere. Whatever is seen in a Dutch garden, we may rest assured – be it fruit, flowers, or vegetables – is worth growing, and is taken care of accordingly.

All these different styles have at times been introduced into our own country, and found advocates. Happily, we have raised a style for ourselves.

John Loudon and Henry Wise were among the earliest innovators, and they are highly praised for the manner in which they laid out Kensington Gardens. Charles Bridgman followed, hewing down many a verdurous peacock and juniper lion. Kent, the inventor of the ha-ha (a boundary ditch instead of a fence or a wall), came next, and broke up the distinction of garden and park; and Lancelot Brown ('Capability' Brown, as he was called) succeeded him with round clumps and boundary belts, artificially winding rivers and lakes, with broad drives terminating in summer-houses.

It is not surprising that when taste revived, the opponents of the old style rushed, at a very early period, to the opposite extreme; many fine old gardens were recklessly pulled to pieces; in the words of Sir Walter Scott, 'Down went many a trophy of old magnificence – courtyard, ornamented enclosure, fosse, avenue, barbican, and every extensive monument of battled all and flanking tower.'

Brown is admitted by everyone to have been a man of genius, and he astonished the gardening world by the skilful manner in which he arrested the river and formed the beautiful lake at Blenheim; but he could not be everywhere, and he found many ignorant imitators. Sir Walter Scott tells an amusing story of one of these conceited pretenders, who was employed by Lord Abercorn in laying out the grounds at Duddingston. The house embraces noble views of Craigmillar castle on the one side, backed by the Pentlands; on the other, by Arthur's Seat and the Salisbury Crags; and, on a third, the eye is carried past the precipitous rocks on which stands the castle of Edinburgh, across the rich plains of Midlothian: the improver conceived it to be his duty to block out every glimpse of this noble land-

scape. Duddingston Loch is a beautiful piece of water, lying at the foot of Arthur's Seat: he did the same for this, and would have done as much for the surrounding hills, but they were too grand objects to be so treated. Lord Abercorn laughed at his absurdities, but he was too indolent to interrupt his vagaries.

Sir Uvedale Price, who went a certain length with the prevailing mania, which he afterwards was still more active in arresting, expressed bitter regret for the destruction of an ancestral garden on the old system which he condemned before he found out his error. He was afterwards led to write strongly in favour of the preservation of the remains of ancient magnificence still untouched, with modifications calculated to redeem them from the charge of barbarism.

The Gardenesque style, which may be described as a skilful disposition of trees and shrubs, in regular or irregular figures, or singly and at equal or unequal distances, preserves, amid apparent irregularity, a certain degree of uniformity. The chief feature of this style is, that no two plants shall be planted so close together as to touch each other, and that flowers of the same species are kept distinct. It forms a tasteful gradation between the geometric and the picturesque style. The latter Mr Loudon defines as imitating nature in a wild state, according to art. Thus the picturesque style may be said to consist of irregular groups of figures, masses, or clumps, disposed at regular intervals; for in this style the grouping is everything.

Lately, English domestic gardening has become more relaxed and 'wild'. Gertrude Jekyll's mixed herbaceous borders from the 1890s, and Vita Sackville-West's romantic gardens at Sissinghurst, of the late 1930s, have been strong influences. A seemingly effortless garden is now the most commonly desired, with heed paid to a broader ecological framework as well as the creation of 'a room outside' – a multi-purposefulness that allows kitchen gardening to coexist with flower gardening, wildlife and family leisure areas.

In addition, modern technology has enabled giant steps to be taken, such as in Cornwall, both to restore fine old gardens, such as twelfth-century Heligan, and to create repositories of international plant specimens, such as the extraordinary glass biomes and ambitious landscapes of the Eden Project.

THE GARDENER'S YEAR

A month-by-month guide with advice for planting traditional varieties of flowers, fruit and vegetables, and helpful expert tips.

JANUARY

❧ FLOWER-GARDEN AND SHRUBBERIES: The moment that flower-beds are cleared of their summer occupants, they should be dug up as roughly as possible. It would be difficult to say whether the mechanical or chemical influence in enriching the quality of the soil is the most important.

Shrubberies on poor soils would be much benefited by manuring during this month. When once shrubberies are properly established on good soil, no rake should ever cross their surface; and every leaf that falls upon them should be merely dug in, any time from December to April – the earlier the better.

All newly-planted shrubs and trees should have their roots protected during the first winter by mulching. The next point of most importance in planting trees or shrubs, especially of large size, is to secure firmly the top to a strong stake, or by any other method, so as to keep it immovable.

During January, plant crocuses and any other hardy bulbs for succession: the main crops should have been planted in October or November.

All bedding-plants will bear a much stronger heat while they are striking in the spring than in the autumn; verbenas will root in a week, placed in a close pit, with a bottom-heat of from 26–32°C / 80° to 90°F.

Prepare a good stock of soil, clean pots, sticks, labels, stakes, &c., in bad weather, so that there may be no hindrance during the busy season. No soil is better for the majority of bedding-plants than equal parts of loam and leaf-mould, and a sixth part of sand.

In very severe weather, autumn-sown annuals should be protected by having some boughs stuck among them, or by being covered with mats, canvas, &c. Give beds a liberal dressing of two-year-old cow-dung, and lay them up rough, ready for planting next month.

In the rose-garden, proceed with planting and pruning hardy roses, and protect tea and China roses with boughs, mulching the roots. Procure stocks for budding; liberally manure all the ground occupied with roses, and take care that their roots are not injured during the process of digging. Water flowers in frames, with care; remove early blooms from polyanthuses and if any of the plants are heaved up by the frost, press them firmly down in the soil.

Sweep up leaves; roll grass and gravel; remove all litter of dead or dying plants.

❧ KITCHEN-GARDEN: The crops to be got into the ground this month are peas and beans, in the open ground or in cold frames; also in frames, radishes, lettuces (the black-seeded cos does well if sown early), Walcheren or early Cape broccoli, cauliflower; on a slight hotbed, early horn-carrots and potatoes: of course, these will be earlier and better for the assistance of a slight hotbed of 60 cm / 2 ft or so in height. A little parsley sown now on a slight hotbed will be useful for planting out early. A little celery for an early supply, and a little cabbage also, should these be scarce, so as to fill up the main crop, if thinned out by severe frosts.

Early peas may be got in any time that the weather permits. Where the ground is tolerably porous and well drained, and a warm border, well sheltered on the north, is available, nothing more is required than to sow in rows, 150 cm / 5 ft apart, the rows running north and south. Sow spinach apart, and leave the spaces between the peas till the time for planting potatoes, French beans, and other open-ground crops.

About the beginning of January, let some middling-sized potato tubers be laid in a warm and moderately dry place, well exposed to the light: here they will make short plump shoots by the time the bed is ready. Prepare a quantity of dung sufficient to make a bed 1 m / 3 ft 6 in in depth. When the bed is in order, lay on 8 cm / 3 in of soil, and place in the potatoes 40 cm / 15 in apart, covering them with 15 cm / 6 in more of soil. Some seed of the scarlet short-top radish may be scattered over the surface. The radishes will be ready in March; the potatoes early in May. Sow mustard and cress.

❧ FLOWERS UNDER GLASS: Protect plants thus; a trench 60 cm / 2 ft deep, dug in the ground if the soil is dry, will suffice, if covered. A vacant frame, cold pit, greenhouse or conservatory will also serve the purpose. On the other hand, where plants of a warmer climate are to be forced into early bloom, artificial heat must be applied. The temperature should not fall below 10°C / 50°F; and as the days lengthen, the temperature should be increased until it attains a minimum temperature of 15°C / 60°F, and a maximum of 21°C / 70°F; giving air daily, and keeping the atmosphere always moist and genial by spraying.

The Greenhouse: Soft-wooded plants may be moved into the larger pots in which they are to flower; while those which are more advanced and showing bloom, may be introduced into a warmer place. Cinerarias in bloom may be removed to the window or conservatory; those reserved for blooming in May and June should still be kept in cold pits or frames. If large cinerarias are required, shift a few into larger pots, and pinch off the tops to produce a bushy head, tying or pegging down the side-shoots to keep them open.

Fuchsias may be started, and large early-flowering specimens produced by cutting down the old plants and shaking the roots out of the old soil as soon as they have broken, repotting them in a good rich compost, with sufficient drainage. Strike cuttings for bedding-plants as soon as the shoots are long enough. Calceolarias and pelargoniums require great attention as to watering. Remove all decaying leaves as they appear, peg down the shoots to the soil, that they may root up the stems, and thus strengthen the plant. As seedlings advance, shift them into larger pots, and prick off those sown for late blooming. In potting, use a compost of light turfy loam, well-decomposed manure and leaf-mould, and a liberal portion of silver-sand, with an ample drainage of potsherds and charcoal, and keep them free from insects.

Should frost appear, or the weather prove damp, light the fires in the afternoon, and shut up the house before the sun disappears, keeping the heat as low as is consistent with keeping out frost and dispelling damp. Water those plants which have become dry, but water them copiously. To camellias and other plants of similar habit advancing into bloom, occasional doses of manure-water in a tepid state should be given, and the plants sprayed with tepid water every other day, until the flowers begin to expand.

Azaleas should be growing freely, if they were shifted and promoted to a warm place last month.

The Conservatory: To preserve bloom for the longest possible period is now the object. Water regularly when necessary, especially the bulbs, giving as much water, of the same temperature as the house, as they can assimilate; keep the temperature about 4°C / 40°F, rising a few degrees from sun-heat during the day, ventilating daily but avoiding cold draughts of air.

Vines, where they form a feature in the cultivation, are usually cultivated on some principle of succession. Supposing the plants to have been started in October, they would break last month with a temperature in houses of about 21°C / 70°F during the night. Later sections may follow for succession, beginning at a lower temperature, and increasing the heat gradually as the vines break and advance. The plants showing fruit should be assisted by occasional applications of manure-water in bright weather.

FEBRUARY

❧ FLOWER-GARDEN AND SHRUBBERIES: Where the beds are filled with shrubs in winter, they should be hoed deeply several times during the month, to expose a fresh surface to the air. Beds occupied with crocuses and snowdrops should have the surface broken with a rake occasionally, before the plants appear.

If the bedding system is to maintain its ground, the garden must be filled with flowering plants by the end of May. To effect it, verbenas must be planted 10 cm / 4 in apart, and geraniums from 15–20 cm / 6–8 in. With the exception of calceolarias, and probably geraniums, nearly all other bedding plants grow and flower as well, if not better, when propagated in the spring than in the autumn. Boxes of geranium- and dahlia-roots that have been stored in cellars through the winter may now be brought out into the light of day, and, if they have been carefully managed, the whole surface will be alive with buds and shoots. For this purpose, however, they must be placed in bottom-heat until the shoots are 5–8 cm / 2–3 in long. Then thin the stools by heeling off the cuttings; that is, taking them off quite close to the old stems. Place the cuttings in small pots: place them in a house or frame with a temperature of 15°C / 60°F, and in three weeks they will be well rooted. For verbenas, ageratums, and calceolarias, in the spring, no place is better than a pit or frame with top-and bottom-heat of from 15–21°C / 60°–70°F. If any or all of these have been gradually hardened off in the winter, the store pots ought to be now plunged into a temperature of 10–15°C / 50°–60°F, for a week or fortnight before the tops are removed for cuttings.

Sweep and roll turf and gravel; finish laying turf; top-dress, turn, renew, and relay the edgings of walks.

Shrubberies: Where digging is necessary, it should assume the character of pointing. Among shrubs, this operation should be performed by running the spade along the whole length, about 8 cm / 3 in beneath the surface, and inverting it. This process buries the leaves and rubbish, without injuring the roots. The growth of shrubs should also be regulated by pruning and training.

If the weather continues open, the hardy annuals listed overleaf should be sown during the month.

There are many other beautiful hardy annuals, some of which, such as the lupins, had better not be sown till March. Only half the packets of the above seeds should be sown in February, and the other half reserved for a second sowing. If the weather continues mild, autumn-sown annuals may be transplanted during the month: 5–10 cm / 2–4 in square. With the exception of ten-

HARDY ANNUALS TO SOW IN FEBRUARY

Alyssum calycinum (Sweet
Alyssum)
Bartonia aurea
Calandrinia speciosa
Calliopsis Drummondii
— bicolor atrosanguinea
Chrysanthemum coronarium
Collinsia bicolor
— grandiflora
Erysimum Peroffskianum
E schscholtzia califonica
— crocea
— alba
Eutoca Manglesii
— viscida
Gilia tricolor
— alba

Iberis coronaria (Candytuft)
—umbellata
— alba
— odorata
Leptosiphon androsaceum
— flore albo
— densiflorum
Limnanthes grandiflora
Nemophila atomaria
— insignis
— discoidalis
— maculata
Schizanthus porrigens
— pinnatus
— Priestii
Silene pengula
Sphenogyne speciosa
Viscaria oculata

week stocks, which should be sown in pots or a frame at once, the sowing of all other tender or half-hardy annuals may safely be deferred to next month; material, however, should be collected, and frames got in readiness for this purpose. A bottom- and surface-heat ranging from 10°–12°C / 50°–55° F will generally be amply sufficient for the germination of most flower-seeds.

▶ FLORISTS' FLOWERS: Auriculas, carnations, and other florists' flowers in frames, must be carefully attended to. Never water unless absolutely necessary, and then do it thoroughly, taking care to keep the leaves dry, and not allow a drop to fall on the crowns of the plants. During mild weather, too much air can hardly be given; but avoid cutting draughts of cold air.

Top-dress auriculas and pinks with rich soil, and re-pot all pansies that are intended to be bloomed in pots.

▶ KITCHEN-GARDEN: The operations in the kitchen-garden this month depend very much on the weather. In mild open weather, a sowing of radishes is made, and to protect them from birds and frost, cover lightly with straw or fern, uncovering the beds occasionally in mild weather. Netting stretched over the beds will admit light and air, and exclude the birds.

Cauliflowers under frames of bell-jars, should have all the air, sun, and light possible, and gentle showers in mild weather, where they are protected from frost, cold winds, or heavy rains. Dust them also occasionally with lime, to destroy slugs, and stir the earth about the roots.

Peas which are advancing should be earthed up, both to protect and to strengthen them. A dusting now and then with lime will protect from birds and mice.

Dwarf peas may be sown closer together. The Bishop dwarf, long-podded, is a good cropper, and may be grown without sticks. The taller sorts, which grow 1.8–2.4 m / 6–8 ft high, bear most enormously if in good soil and mulched. During this month it is advisable to get in some of the medium sorts, as Auvergne, Imperial, Scimitar, or Champion; the later sorts had better be left till next month.

Broad Beans of any sort may be got in for succession.

Cabbages: Dust with lime when the ground is wet, or early in the morning, to destroy slugs. Replace all the plants that have been destroyed by frost or otherwise, and draw earth up to the stems. Sow under frames or bell-jars a little cabbage, of some quick-heading kind, as early York or Eastham: they will follow those which have stood the winter, and be very useful in July, August, and September. Some Brussels sprouts may be sown; also purple Cape and Walcheren broccoli for autumn use.

Parsley may be sown in drills, or broadcast, or as edgings or between dwarf or short-lived crops. It takes several weeks to germinate at this season of the year.

Carrots of the short-horn sort, if sown on a warm border now, will come into use in May. Sow rather thickly, and thin to 5 cm / 2 in apart.

Onions for salading may be sown on a warm border. A small sowing of leeks may be made at the same time and in the same manner, but not quite so thick.

Red Beet if sown now, will be very useful late in the summer. Sow in drills 25 cm / 9–10 in apart, or broadcast, and thin to the same distance. The white beet may be sown for the leaves, which are eaten like spinach in summer.

Early Potatoes may be planted on a south border, or under a wall having a sunny aspect. At this time it is well to plant middling-sized tubers whole.

Salading and Potherbs: Lettuces should be sown now for succession; mustard-and-cress also, under frames or glass.

☞ FRUIT-GARDEN: **Strawberries:** If it is desirable to make new plantations of strawberries at this time, it may be done by taking up runners with a trowel, and planting them 45 cm / 18 in apart. After planting, mulch with dung. Old plants should be cleaned and mulched.

Bush Fruit should be pruned without delay, if not done before.

15

Apples and Pears: Finish pruning all fruit-trees this month. In pruning these, the main object is to produce short fruiting-spurs; but the stronger the shoots the less they should be cut; for too close cutting throws them into the production of wood and leaf, and not fruit. Figs on walls should scarcely be cut at all, and no trees should be cut in frosty weather.

FLOWERS UNDER GLASS: Keep a night temperature of from 4–7°C / 40°–45°F, allowing a rise of 10° with sun-heat. Unless during very severe frost or cutting winds, give air daily, if only for an hour at noon. Prune, and destroy scale and other insects on climbers and other permanent plants. All plants should be carefully examined before they are introduced in order to prevent all importation of insects.

Water with care, examining carefully the balls of the plants, which sometimes become so hard and dry that the water refuses to penetrate. If found in this condition, they should be plunged into a pail of water for twelve or twenty-four hours, until the ball is thoroughly soaked.

One of the chief things to be attended to before placing any plant, and especially any hard-wooded plant, into a larger pot, is to see that the old ball is in a nice healthy growing state. The extremities of the roots should also be carefully untwisted or unwound, to induce them to start at once in the fresh soil. The new soil must also be pressed firmly into the pots, or the water will pass through it, instead of penetrating through the old mass of roots.

Pelargoniums, calceolarias and cinerarias now delight in a temperature of from 7–10°C / 45–50°F. The sun's rays striking upon plants with any drops of condensed moisture on the leaves, is certainly one cause of the spot on these plants. Shifting the young successional stock should now be completed. Greenflies are particularly fond of these plants: they must be destroyed on their first appearance.

Fuchsias, after re-potting, thrive best if plunged in a gentle bottom-heat. Water carefully until fresh roots are emitted; shade in bright sunshine to prevent flagging. Never cut down and shift fuchsias at the same time, nor shake them out for re-potting before they have again begun to grow.

FRUIT UNDER GLASS: **Vines:** A few leading principles seem to form the basis of the successful culture of the grape-vine. It should be planted on a dry bottom. The soil should be light, rich, and need not exceed 1 m / 3 ft in depth. The roots should be kept at the same or a few degrees higher temperature than the branches. The best mode of feeding vines during their growing and fruiting stages, is either by a liberal application of manure-water or a rich top-dressing of the very best manure. Vines in houses, started in October, will now be swelling their fruit. Thin in time, and maintain a steady growing temperature of 18°C / 65°F. Those started in January will show their bunches this month, and a temperature from 12–15°C / 55°–60°F will be suitable. Some prefer leaving the disbudding until the bunches show, so as to leave the best.

Figs may be started at 10°C / 50°F. The terminal buds of the young shoot should be removed, to insure a good crop. Maintain a moist atmosphere, and water copiously when necessary.

☞ HOT-BED AND FRAME CULTIVATION: Cucumbers in full growth require every attention. See that the heat of the beds does not fall below 21°C / 70°F: apply fresh linings as soon as this is the case. Attend to stopping and setting; allow no more than two or three cucumbers to grow at the same time on one plant; give all the light possible, but cover at night with mats or straw, and add fresh earth if required. If it is desired to start more beds, the dung may be got ready, and during this time the seed may be sown in pots and placed in a bed in full operation. Peg the bines down as they grow: if a proper temperature and sweet dewy atmosphere pervade the frame, they will never be troubled with insects or mildew; but if they are chilled or over-heated, these will soon follow.

Water of the same temperature as the bed is absolutely necessary. Always water over the leaves, as well as at the roots, about twice or three times a week, which is as often as the plants are likely to want it. For asparagus and kale, a little salt, about a teaspoonful to the gallon, may be advantageous: it is better to water effectually at once, than to water little and often, because the latter is apt to keep the surface slimy and sodden.

February is also a good time to put some potatoes in a little heat. An excellent plan is to pare the soil off an old cucumber-bed: add 8 cm / 3 in of fresh earth, then set the potatoes 40 cm / 15 in apart, and cover with 15 cm / 6 in more earth; put on the windows, and then give a good lining of prepared dung.

French beans may still be sown: they may be placed in an old hotbed fresh lined. Radishes, if sown now on a slight hotbed, will come in much earlier than those in cold frames.

Now is the time for making a hotbed for sowing vegetable marrows, tomatoes, capsicums, and such plants. Those who have hotbeds in operation may sow these seeds in pots, and put them in the frames; otherwise it is necessary to make a bed for them. Although it is advisable to get the dung, and begin to prepare it this month, it is not desirable to sow the seed till March; for these things cannot be planted in the open air till quite the latter end of May.

Early carrots may be sown, for succession, on a slight hotbed; and very dwarf peas also, which may be treated in the same way as French beans, also mustard and cress, and lettuces, for succession. Some roots of mint,

17

horseradish, dandelion, or chicory, may be potted and placed in a hotbed: some use them as salads.

Strawberry plants in pots placed in heat now will fruit in April: they will want liquid manure occasionally, to keep them in vigour.

Seed-beds of cauliflower, lettuce, cabbage, broccoli, radish, carrot, onions, beet, &c., may be made in the cold pit or frame: they will not come on so quickly as those sown in heat, but will be earlier than those sown outdoors.

MARCH

FLOWER-GARDEN AND SHRUBBERIES: Magnolias, delicate roses, and other scarcely hardy plants on walls, should receive some shelter from the stern bite of March frosts and winds. The later in the season tender plants can be kept in a dormant state the better, and nothing secures this object more effectually than a thin covering of dry non-conducting material, such as straw.

Grass lawns must be frequently swept and rolled; gravel walks turned, fresh-gravelled, raked, rolled, and swept, edgings cut, planted, or altered; and all planting, pruning, and digging finished as soon as possible. This is also a good season to remove weeds and daisies from the turf, and to sow grass-seeds for new lawns. Fork over flower-beds on frosty mornings. Complete pruning and training clematises, jasmines, begonias and other creepers on trellises.

This is the proper month for planting all the hardy gladioli. Drills are drawn on beds or borders about 10 cm / 4 in deep, the bulbs inserted, and covered over with the soil. Stakes about 60 cm / 2 ft high should be put in at the same time, for, if inserted afterwards, they might injure the bulbs. The distance between the bulbs should be 20–30 cm / 9–12 in.

In addition to the sowing of the annuals named in February, the ones listed opposite should be sown at once. Half-hardy annuals, which require a frame, are perhaps better left till April.

Proceed with the potting-off of all bedding-plants; keep them close for a fortnight after potting. Keep the propagating-house at a temperature of from 15–21°C / 60°–70°F.

This is also the best month for increasing dahlias by cuttings. Cut them off close to the stem, if you can find as many as you want; if not, leave one or two eyes on the old stool, and in another week these eyes will furnish two, four, or six more cuttings. Place them in light sandy soil: plunge the pots in a bottom-heat of 26°C / 80°F and a top-heat of 15°C / 60°F: in a week or ten days they will be rooted.

ANNUALS TO SOW IN MARCH

Adonis Flos	Erysimum	Saponaria
Calandrinia	Larkspurs	Sweet Peas
Calliopsis	Linum	Venus's Looking-
Campanula Lorel	Love lies Bleeding	glass
Centauria	Lupins	Veronica
Chrysanthemum	Malope	Virginian Stock
Clarkia	Œnothera	Viscaria
Collinsia	Poppies of different	
Convolvulus minor	kinds	

Shrubberies: Top-dress rhododendron beds with equal parts of cow-dung (thoroughly decayed) and leaf-mould. On poor soils this imparts a rich gloss to the foliage, and causes luxuriant growth.

☞ ROSE GARDEN: Finish planting all hardy roses, if bloom is expected this season. The excited state of the shoots from a mild winter must not make you impatient to finish pruning. The more excited they are the greater the necessity for delay, as the expenditure of the sap in the terminal buds will preserve the buds near the base of the shoots longer in a dormant state; and it is upon these buds we are dependent for next year's blossom. In pruning roses, every bit of old wood, loose bark, &c., should be carefully removed, as it is exactly amid such debris that the larvae of caterpillars, aphids, &c., are deposited.

☞ FLORISTS' FLOWERS: See that the plants have plenty of water, as they will now be throwing up their flower-stems. The material in which they are plunged may be sprinkled, to keep up a moist, genial atmosphere.

Carnations and picotees should now, if the weather is mild, be placed in their blooming-pots, and sheltered under glass during bad weather; they should be potted firmly, care being taken to keep the soil out of the axils of the leaves. Pinks in pots or open borders should be top-dressed with a mixture of the fine loamy soil and half-rotten manure.

☞ KITCHEN-GARDEN: During this month most of the principal crops must be got in. Now the whole garden is to be cropped upon a carefully-considered plan, so that no crop of the same character should follow on the same spot; for instance, where any of the Brassicae, or deteriorators, were grown the previous season, follow them with preparers, which are mostly root-crops, as potatoes, carrots, parsnips, onions, scorzoneras, salsify, &c. These, again, should be followed as

19

far as possible by surface-crops, which are mostly the shortest-lived of any, and include all saladings. We may go further, and include pot or sweet herbs, and also medicinal herbs, besides some of the shorter-lived vegetables, as spinach, kale, French beans, and early carrots.

Celery: It is too soon to sow the main crop of celery, but a little may be sown for early use. First sowings may be in seed-pans; but for the main crop shake together a small heap of stable-dung, just sufficient to give a slight heat; spread 8 cm / 3 in of soil on it, sow the seed, and cover with a frame or bell-jar. Seed sown in this month will be ready to transplant in April.

Jerusalem Artichokes should be planted. The ground for them should be rather deeply worked, for, the plants growing tall, are exposed to rough winds, which they resist better where they root pretty deeply. Almost any part of a tuber will grow and form a plant; but it is advisable to select middling-sized tubers, planting them 25–30 cm / 10–12 in deep. They should be not less than 1 m / 1 yd apart – 120 cm / 4 ft is better. No other treatment is required than to keep the ground well stirred about them, and prevent the growth of weeds. Cut them down when the leaves are decayed, but not before; otherwise the tubers will cease to grow.

Globe Artichokes will be making offsets which should be taken off for propagation.

Potatoes: About the beginning of this month is the time to get in early potatoes. To ensure a good crop, the ground should be trenched in October or November, and left in ridges; in February levelled, and some thoroughly decomposed manure forked in. In March the frosts will have left it well pulverized, and ready to receive the sets.

Carrots may be sown now, but the main crop should be deferred till the first week in April. In preparing the ground for carrots, no manure should be applied, as it induces them to fork and to become grub-eaten. A dressing of sand is advantageous.

Cabbages: It is advisable to sow some cabbage-seed of a quick-hearting sort, to follow those raised in January, or that have stood the winter. They will be of great service in July and the following months. The Early York, Large York, Nonpareil, Matchless, indeed any sort, will do. Sow on a warm sheltered spot, and protect from birds with netting. Avoid planting cabbages when the ground

is sodden after heavy rains. Mulch the roots of the young plants in a compost of soil and soot, wetted to the consistency of thick paste. This saves a great deal of trouble in watering afterwards, and in the driest weather will generally prevent flagging. Broccoli so treated will be found very free from clubbing.

Cauliflower seeds sown now will furnish plants to be set out in May and June: it may be sown in the open ground, or in a frame or bell-jar. Protect with netting.

Broccoli: Such sorts as Walcheren, Purple Cape, or any sort that heads in autumn, should be sown at this time in the same manner as cabbage or cauliflower. They will be ready to plant out in May or June, and will be very useful at a time when summer crops are over, and winter crops not ready.

French Beans may be sown towards the end of the month, choosing an early dwarf sort; but the principal sowing should be deferred till next month: those sown this month should be in a border, sheltered from cold winds but open to the sun.

Radishes may be sown thinly between the rows of the more enduring crops, such as onions.

Peas should be sown this month in succession, and coal-ashes scattered at the roots of those coming up, to prevent their destruction by slugs: sow a row of many-leaved spinach between the peas.

☛ FRUIT-GARDEN: **Apples and Pears:** Pruning should now be finished, and this is the last month for planting until the autumn; the various operations of grafting and budding are now in full progress. The grafts should be taken from the trees before the buds begin to swell.

Strawberries: British Queens, hitherto protected, should be uncovered, and the beds weeded, and the plants trimmed; the soil stirred round the roots with the fork without disturbing the dung. Runners placed in a nursery-bed last autumn should be removed to the spot where they are to remain for fruiting. Where plants have been growing in the same place for several years, weed the beds well before they begin to grow, stir the soil, and sow some guano over them in showery weather.

☛ FLOWERS UNDER GLASS: **The Conservatory:** A minimum temperature of 7°C / 45°F should be maintained, allowing for a rise from sun-heat, and give as much air as the state of the weather and the maintenance of a kindly genial atmosphere will permit.

Camellias in full flower must be liberally watered at the roots. The blossoms must on no account be rubbed, touched, or wetted: they show at once any bruise or spot of water on their clear and delicate petals.

The Greenhouse: Proceed with the shifting of all plants requiring it. Dirty putrid water is certain death to hard-wooded plants. Therefore, unless the leaf-mould is really good, add none to your compost for them. To secure plenty of roots, thorough drainage is the first desideratum; proper compost the second, firm potting the third, careful watering the fourth, and proper top-management the very last point for consideration. Keep the new soil level with the top of the old ball. All plants, however hardy, should be kept warm and moist for a few weeks after repotting, especially if they have received a large shift.

Pelargoniums will require careful training. Remove every dead leaf, thin out superfluous shoots, and keep the plants scrupulously clean. Maintain a temperature of 10°C / 50°F; spray on fine, bright mornings. If the weather is fine towards the end of the month, sprinkling may be repeated in the afternoon.

Cinerarias: Keep clean, remove decayed leaves, and throw away all but the most choice varieties as soon as they have finished flowering. Save the best sorts for seed or suckers, and sow seed at once for the earliest plants.

Calceolarias: Thin out the worst of the crowded leaves; peg down the shoots to increase the strength of the plants, and sow seed for next year.

Forcing-pit: Introduce fresh batches of azaleas, lilacs, rhododendrons, roses, &c. Remove pinks as soon as they fairly show flower, to a cooler house.

☞ FRUIT UNDER GLASS: March is a peculiarly trying month for forcing. March winds are not only cold, but dry. This renders it of the utmost importance that every space in forcing-houses should be kept damp during bright weather. The inside air is not only to be warm, but it must be kept moist.

Vineries: The above remarks are peculiarly applicable to grape vines in the early stages of their growth. The earliest grapes may now be stoning. Stoning occurs when the grapes are about three parts grown, and the grapes make no visible progress for six weeks or two months. They are, however, progressing within, forming their seeds, or stoning, as it is technically called. A temperature of 15°C / 60°F at night is enough until this work is completed.

Strawberries may now be looked over, top-dressed, raked, and plunged in a pit with a bottom-heat of 10°C / 50°F, giving sufficient air, dry and bright, to keep the top for another fortnight at 4–7°C / 40–45°F. This will secure a root-action in advance of the top; so that, when the top moves and the trusses appear, plenty of active roots are ready to support them. They will then bear a little more heat during the ripening period. Plants may also be introduced on shelves in vineries, &c.; but their own pit is the best place for them. For succession, introduce a fresh batch of plants every fortnight. Cuthill's Blackfriar is a useful early sort, but nothing beats Keen's Seedling for early and British Queen for late crops.

HOT-BED AND FRAME CULTIVATION: **Cucumbers:** Where cucumbers have not already been started, it should be done now. Let the manure be shaken and turned over three or four times: on this everything depends; the heat lasts longer, and the plants are not exposed to violent and irregular action. If the frame is not put on at once, however, it is advisable to cover the bed with litter or mats, in case of heavy rains, which would reduce the temperature of it. After the frame is on, place about a bushel of loamy soil under the centre of each light: too much soil at once would induce too much heat. If the plants have been raised in a temporary bed, they may be planted live or six days after the bed is made: they will thus be ready to start into active growth at once. If no plants are ready, sow two seeds each in 8-cm / 3-in pots, only half-filled with soil at first, and add fresh soil as the plants grow. The after-treatment is the same as that described in January.

Vegetable Marrows may be sown thickly in pots, and placed in a cucumber-frame. When up, they should be separated and planted out, two or three in a 10-cm / 4-in pot, where they may either continue till their final planting-out, or separated again, and potted singly, to, prevent their getting pot-bound. At the end of March, or early in April, plant them out on a bed of manure of sufficient heat to start them, covering them with bell-jars, In May plant them out, without any such stimulus, on ridges in the open ground. Tomatoes and Capsicums are raised in the same manner. They may be planted out under a south wall, or grown in pots, in frame, pit, or greenhouse, during the summer.

Asparagus: Slight hotbeds should still be made for forcing. Potatoes, asparagus, French beans, strawberries, and radishes, or any of these may be sown or planted on an old bed; the old lining removed and fresh but prepared linings applied to give the necessary heat. If they are forced in a pit, let the dung be well worked, laid in carefully, levelled and beaten down, and filled high enough to allow for sinking.

Salading: For a supply of potherbs, some roots planted now in a hotbed will produce young shoots or leaves. Some roots of horseradish and chicory may be planted in the same way, and blanched by excluding the light. A succession of mustard and cress may be sown every week. Radishes may still be sown in frames, or in the open air.

APRIL

▪ FLOWER-GARDEN AND SHRUBBERIES: All seeds intended to flower during the summer should be sown during this month. In places where hardy annuals are extensively grown, another sowing might be made. Place stakes to all such plants as require support, bearing in mind that 'as the twig is bent the plant inclines;' fix the sticks firmly in the ground, bring the stalks to the stake, and then tie neatly but firmly to it, without galling the plant; remove all straggling, broken, or decayed shoots, and keep all clear of weeds, raking smooth with a small rake.

▪ ROSE GARDEN: Beds for tea-scented roses should be prepared for planting towards the end of this month or in May. To grow them in perfection, a hole in the ground should be opened 60 cm / 2 ft square and 30 cm / 1 ft deep. This station should be filled with a compost consisting of two good-sized spadefuls of thoroughly-rotted dung for each plant, mixing it well with the soil.

In pruning newly-planted roses, the object is to balance the head to the vital powers of the fibrous root, so as to give a graceful form to the bush. If there only be one shoot from the bud, cut it down to two eyes; if there be a regular head formed, cut away every shoot down to the lowest eye that points outwards or downwards, and cut all weak shoots that come in the way of a better back to their base, leaving only such as are required to form the head of the tree.

As the growth proceeds, examine every bud, every curled leaf and shoot, for insect larvæ: for maggots, if not detected at once, soon destroy the vitality of the flower-bud. Do this daily, spray also, with a fine rose spray, very forcibly applied, which may destroy the greenfly, the thrip, and other enemies.

▪ FLORISTS' FLOWERS: Weak manure-water should be applied in the mornings. Seed should now be sown in shallow pans placed in some gentle heat. Dahlia roots may now be planted out in the beds, spray 3–4 in deep, and 150 cm / 5 ft asunder; tulips protected from cold winds and frosty nights by netting thrown over hoops, and by mats, in severe weather, on the beds, leaving plenty of light and air. Ranunculuses require the soil to be loosened as they come up, and watering with weak manure-water: a watering with lime-water will destroy any worms in the beds.

Carnations in pots should have the surface stirred, and a little new compost added, and be watered with lime-water, to destroy worms. Sow seeds in pots or boxes during the month, place them in a west aspect, and cover them with a sheet of glass. Pansies will now be interesting: water the fresh-potted plants sparingly, until the roots reach the edge of the pots: top-dress the beds with rotten manure; look for and destroy black slugs; plant out seedlings and put in cuttings. Hollyhocks kept in pots during the winter should be planted out, about 1.8 m / 6 ft apart, in deep rich soil.

Half-hardy annuals may now be sown in warm sunny borders. Give them the protection of hoops and mattings at night and in severe weather. The mode of sowing is to form a shallow basin in the soil, such as might be made with the convex side of a breakfast saucer; in this hollow sow the seeds, and sift half an inch of fine earth over them. Thin out the patches as the plants begin to grow.

KITCHEN-GARDEN: In the suburbs of large towns, where ground is valuable and space limited, it often happens that kitchen-gardens are severely overtasked, through a prevailing notion that high tillage and abundant manuring make up for extent of room. This is true, but it has its limits. The ground gets filled with insects – undecomposed manure is worked into the soil after each crop. The remedy for this state is either a copious manuring with unslaked lime, burning the soil, or the substitution of new soil. But prevention is always better than cure. The manure should be thoroughly decomposed or rotted. Where ground is heavily worked, as, for instance, where a spring crop of lettuces, an autumn crop of potatoes, and a winter crop of greens have been obtained from the same piece of ground, manure alone will not supply the whole of the loss. Adopt a well-defined system of rotation: such a measure will keep the ground in good heart.

Jerusalem Artichokes may still be planted where not previously done. Give 120 cm / 4 ft one way, and 90–120 cm 3–4 ft the other. This should not be delayed after the first week this month.

Globe Artichokes: The best method of propagating these is to take offsets from them in this month, and plant them, 90 cm / 3 ft apart, in a row, and the rows 150 cm / 5 ft apart. To keep them in good bearing, it is advisable to plant a fresh row every year, and remove one of the old ones. If they are protected with straw, fern, or leaves in winter, they bear rather earlier in summer. When left unprotected, they are killed to the ground, but break up strong in the spring. Before planting, the soil should be trenched 90 cm / 3 ft deep.

Parsley, Chervil, &c. should be sown for the purpose of keeping a stock of young plants to gather from, as young leaves are best.

Spinach may still be sown, in a shady spot, if possible – it will last the longer.

Potatoes for the main crop must be got in this month. As the ground is more likely to be dry at this time, they may be dibbed in whole, which yields food for the young shoot till it can find its own. In planting them, let it be in rows 60 cm / 2 ft apart; or, if space be limited, allow 90 cm / 3 ft, which admits of planting later crops between, before they are taken up.

If the ground be wet, heavy, and, indeed, under any circumstances, a good plan is to cut a drill with the spade 15–20 cm / 6–8 in deep. In this place the sets 40 cm / 15 in apart, then move the line to the next row, cut another drill in the same manner, but fill up the preceding drill with the soil taken out, covering the sets in it. On stiff soils the dibber should never be used, because it forms a basin in which water is likely to stand and rot the potato. When the potatoes have grown about 20–25 cm / 8–10 in high, a little earth should be drawn up to them – just sufficient to cover any tubers that may grow near the surface. It is advisable to pick off all the flowers, unless seed is wanted: this will throw the strength of the plant into the process of forming tubers. As to sorts, they are known to change character when transferred to different soils; but, for early crops, the Ash-leaved Kidney is deserving of culture, especially in its improved form.

Turnips: A sowing of early Dutch turnip may be made in this month. This crop is very apt to run to seed instead of swelling at the root, if sown too early; but a great deal depends on the kind of soil: it does best on a rather retentive soil; but should be in an open, unshaded piece of ground, for it never does much good if shaded or overhung by trees. A dressing of soot at the time of sowing seems to benefit turnips greatly. Broadcast sowing is preferable for this crop; but if sown in drills, let them be 40 cm / 15 in distant from each other, and the plants left not less than a foot apart in the rows; even a greater distance is better, as turnips resent anything like crowding.

Carrots may still be sown; and those who know the sweetness and delicacy of the short-horn kinds, in their young state, will take care to have a supply of them. They may be sown till the latter end of July.

Cabbages: The first week in this month is a good time for sowing the various sorts of brassicae for main crop, selecting the beginning of the month for the meridian of London, and a fortnight later north of Cheshire and Lancaster. The treatment for all sorts is nearly the same. Let the seed beds be open, tolerably dry, but not parched. Give plenty of room; sow the seed broadcast regularly over the ground; tread it well in. When the seed is up, keep the beds moist, so as to promote vigorous growth; giving a liberal dusting of lime, salt, or soot now and then. When large enough to handle, thin them, and prick out those drawn, in nursery-beds 15 cm / 6 in apart from each other.

Peas for late crops may be sown any time this month. The tall-growing sorts are best to sow now, and if stick be plentiful, these should have the preference. If on good soil, or well mulched, the yield is far above all other sorts; the Ne plus ultra yields an enormous crop: sow them 1.8 m / 6 ft apart from row to row, or 3 m / 10 ft, where crops of cabbages can be sown between the rows.

Salading: Lettuces should be sown for succession; the large drum-head, or Maltese, does well sown at this time; but Cos lettuces are generally preferred, as being most crisp. Chicory is used both as a salad in spring and also the roots as a vegetable: it should be sown late this month and the two following. Sow in shallow drills 30 cm / 1 ft apart, and thin to 20 cm / 8 in in the row: they need not be disturbed again until taken up for use. Parsley may be sown at any time; a principal sowing is usually made now. Some make sowings in shallow drills, 45 cm / 18 in apart; but broadcast is preferable, at least if the ground is in condition to be trodden. Use the small hoe as soon as up, and thin out gradually, till the plants are 25 cm / 10 in apart. Potherbs, may be sown and treated in the same way.

☛ FRUIT-GARDEN: **Apples and Pears,** in the mature state require care in selecting the shoots to be retained, preferring ripe, short-jointed, brownish shoots, shortening back these to a bud which will extend the growth of the tree, studying – first, the production of spurs; second, to keep the heart of the tree.

Vines are now pushing forth their young shoots in great numbers. At this season only those which are obviously useless, and especially those issuing from old wood, unless wanted for future years' rods, should be rubbed off with the finger and thumb close to the stem. The useless ones being disposed of, these left should be trained close to the wall, at regular distances apart, so that all may enjoy the light, heat, and air.

Strawberries, which have been under mulch all the winter, should now be uncovered; a spring dressing of half-decayed material from the cucumber-frame, mixed with soot and decayed leaves, will be useful, watering frequently towards the end of the month.

Gooseberries and Currants, pruned in January and top-dressed in March, by removing 3–5 cm / 1–2 in of soil, and replacing this with a compost of loam and decayed dung, in equal proportions, will require little attention till the fruit begins to form.

☛ FLOWERS UNDER GLASS: **The Conservatory:** While any probability of spring frosts remains, ventilation must be cautiously given, especially with newly-potted plants and tender flowers. Camellias and other plants with large coriaceous leaves, if not perfectly clean, should be washed; and a moist, genial heat maintained. Boronias, lechenaultias, chorozemas and tropreolums can now be removed to the conservatory. Place them in as airy a situation as possible, maintaining a temperature of 7–10°C / 45°–50°F at night, rising from sun-heat. The conservatory will now be enlivened by the lily of the valley, roses, sweetbriar and violets.

The Greenhouse: Azaleas will be coming forward, where there is a good stock of such plants as *A. lateritia, Gladstonesii*, Prince Albert, *praestantissima*, and others of similar habit; their bloom should be retarded by placing them on the shaded side of the house. Plants that have been forced should have the seed-vessels picked off, and shifted if the pots are tolerably full of roots.

Pelargoniums, and other soft-wooded plants, now growing rapidly, require every attention. Water using manure-water occasionally, and a little lime. Ventilate freely on warm sunny days, and spray with water of the temperature of the house. Scarlet geraniums require similar treatment to promote their growth. Cuttings struck now will fill the pots with roots by the autumn, and bloom through the winter months. Calceolarias should now have a final shift, using a light rich compost, and pegging them down to encourage roots up the stem.

Fuchsias: This is still a good time to buy in plants. Favourite flowers are:

Souvenir de Chiswick – with rosy crimson sepals and tube, and violet corolla, and beautifully recurved broad sepals.

Venus de Medici – with white tube, blush-white sepals, corolla deep violet.

Rose of Castile – blush-white sepals and tube; rosy purple corolla.

Sir Colin Campbell – crimson tube, and sepals well reflexed; corolla dark purple.

Madame Cornelissen – sepals very long; pure white corolla. The flowers of these are not only good, but the habit, a great point in double fuchsias, is also excellent.

Amazement is said to be the best double fuchsia – sepals rich crimson, reflexed; corolla rich dark purple.

Bianca – scarlet tube and sepals.

Black Prince – broad sepals, carmine-scarlet; corolla very dark purple.

Catherine Hayes – sepals scarlet; light-blue corolla; excellent habit.

Coronal – sepals vermilion, nicely curved; corolla violet and rich purple.

Crown Jewel – sepals crimson; corolla black; habit distinct; leaves long and peculiar.

Dr Livingstone – delicate white tube; petals well recurved; corolla blush; very distinct and delicate-looking.

Duchess of Lancaster – white tube and sepals; violet corolla.

Fairest of the Fair – white tube and sepals; corolla rich violet.

Forget-me-not – sepals scarlet and carmine; corolla violet, red, and purple.

Goliath – coral-red, with immense fruit, of a light green colour.

Guiding Star – blush-tinted tube; sepals white, nicely recurved; corolla velvety purple.

La Crinoline – sepals crimson; corolla bluish.

Leoline – sepals crimson; violet-blue corolla.

Le Prophete – sepals crimson; corolla violet,

Leviathan – sepals very broad, rich crimson, reflexed, and completely recurved; corolla deep purple, of an immense size; altogether, a fine bold flower.

Lord Elcho – sepals carmine-scarlet; corolla violet-blue, beautifully cupped.

Marvellous (an immense double variety) – crimson sepals and dark corona; bad habit.

Perseverance – sepals carmine, salmon-tinted; corolla rosy lilac.

Prince of Orange – sepals scarlet, wide-curved; habit excellent.

Prince Frederick William of Prussia – sepals carmine and red; corolla plum colour; good shape.

Queen of Hanover – sepals white; corolla carmine.

Star of the Night – sepals rich carmine; corolla violet-purple, a fine striking variety.

Tricolour and Tricolour flower, both striking and pretty varieties, three-coloured.

Victor Emmanuel – sepals red; corolla slate-coloured.

White Lady – one of the best white varieties – an improvement on Princess of Prussia.

Begonias: Retaining a few plants for winter decoration, compel the main stock to rest for the winter; that is, keep them warm and very dry, so that many of the leaves fade. Now is the time to shake over the dry soil, re-pot, and plunge into a bottom-heat of 23–26°C / 75°–80°F; or they will start very nicely on a shelf.

☞ FRUIT UNDER GLASS: **Vines:** It is always dangerous to give direct air in front of vineries until the fruit is ripe.

As soon as grapes begin to swell, a small temperature rise may take place, which may be continued until the first spot of colour appears. The minimum may then be from 15–18°C / 60°–65°F, with a little air constantly in the house, never omitting to close it at night. Successional houses will now require great attention – disbudding, thinning, and tying the shoots, &c. Raise the temperature through the different stages. Stop young shoots a joint beyond the bunches, excepting always the leading shoots on young vines. After a few stoppings, if the leaves become crowded, take the young wood off at the same point at every stopping, as two or three large leaves beyond the bunch are sufficient to supply its wants, and more useful than a number of small ones.

Figs: A dry, close atmosphere often causes the embryo fruit to drop. Dryness, or excessive moisture at the root, may produce the same results. Maintain a temperature of 15°C / 60°F, and spray the leaves daily.

Orchard-house: Unless this is heated, keep it constantly open when the outside temperature is above 0°C / 32°F. Success here depends upon retarding the trees as much as possible. If they start now, and we have a sharp frost in April, the chances are you will lose the crops.

Strawberries: Give plenty of air when in bloom, maintaining a drier atmosphere during that process. After they are fairly set, they will bear a temperature of 21°C / 70°F to swell off; but 15°C / 60°F to ripen, with abundance of air, is quite enough. On shelves, place each pot in a pan, or within a second pot half-filled with rotten manure. Water with manure-water, spray twice a day, and keep the plants clear of insects.

☞ HOT-BED AND FRAME CULTIVATION: **Cucumbers,** in growing condition, require more air in the daytime as the sun acquires more power; if they droop under its influence, something is wrong at the roots or collar, and fresh plants should be raised to supersede them, provided they do not recover. Peg down the bines, and pinch off shoots that are not wanted, and all shoots above the fruit; add fresh soil and fresh linings outside as required.

Asparagus should be watered with weak liquid manure, but be rather sparing of stimulants than otherwise.

Potatoes may be tried by scraping away the earth near the collar. The largest tubers are generally near the surface, and may be removed without disturbing the plants, which should be left to perfect the smaller ones: water, if required; but liquid manure is not necessary.

French Beans that are flowering should receive plenty of light and air, and be kept tolerably dry overhead, and tied up to sticks if they hang over: keep the roots moderately moist; but, if allowed to root through the pots, they will require no other stimulus.

Strawberries will require plenty of water and a liberal supply of liquid manure. While the fruit is swelling, give, if possible, more heat and more air.

Tender annuals should now be sown in heat, and half-hardy ones in cold-frames. Pot or prick off any that may be up.

Salads may still be sown in cold-frames, and a good plan is to move the frames from place to place, merely using them to protect the seeds from birds: a frame placed over rhubarb will bring it on fast: lettuces, &c., may be urged on in the same way.

MAY

☛ FLOWER-GARDEN AND SHRUBBERIES: Continue to prick off annuals raised in frames into small pots, and harden such as are established preparatory to turning them out into the open ground. Another sowing of annuals may now be made.

Large plants of some genera, as phloxes, asters, &c., generally throw up too many flowering-shoots: where such is the case, thin them out at once. Hollyhocks for late blooming may still be planted. It is better, where they are grown extensively, to plant at two or three times to insure a succession of bloom. As the soil and weather will now be in a fit state to commence bedding-out, a start should be made with the half-hardy plants first; as antirrhinums, penstemons, &c., which may be followed by calceolarias and verbenas; reserving heliotropes and the more tender kinds of geraniums for the latest planting.

Stake or peg down such plants as require it, as planting proceeds, or the wind will break many of them. Plant out in rich soil a good supply of stocks and asters for the autumn, and sow a succession of annuals for making up any vacancies which may occur, and likewise another sowing of mignonette in pots for rooms or for filling window-boxes.

Bulbous Roots and Tubers intended for removal should be taken up as their leaves decay. Even those which are usually left in the ground should be taken up every two or three years, and their offsets, which will have grown into large bunches, should be separated, if large and handsome flowers are desired. When the offsets are detached from the principal bulb, it is desirable to give it a season of rest.

Hardy Annuals may still be sown where they are to flower, watering them after sowing and in dry weather. Perennials may be increased by cuttings of the young flower-stalks.

Grass Lawns and Gravel Walks should be in high order, the grass well mown once a week if possible, and kept clean and orderly; gravel walks kept free from weeds, well swept and frequently rolled, especially after heavy rains; borders, beds, and shrubberies free from weeds, and where vacancies in the beds occur, let them be supplied.

☞ FLORISTS' FLOWERS: Hyacinths and tulips, ranunculuses and anemones, are now in full bloom. When these choice bulbs are past flowering, and the leaves begin to decay, let the roots be taken up and spread out to dry and harden, in some dry shady place for a fortnight or three weeks; the roots may afterwards be trimmed, cleaned, and deposited upon shelves or in boxes, till required for replanting in autumn.

Dahlias potted off last month, and hardened by exposure, may be planted out about the third week. If the pots are getting too small for the growing plants, it is better to re-pot them in larger pots than to plant out too early.

Carnations and Picotees in pots should have every assistance given them; sticks should be placed to support the stalks towards the end of the month, the plants watered in dry weather and kept clean, the soil occasionally stirred, and kept free from dead leaves, and a sprinkling of fine fresh soil added.

Pansies may be planted for successional beds in a north border; for this spring seedlings may be used. Plants in bloom should be shaded at noon in sunny days, and well watered in the evenings. Blooms not required for seed should be cut off as they fade, and side-shoots taken off and struck.

Ranunculuses should have the soil pressed round the collar and watered when it becomes too dry.

Phloxes, whether in pots or beds, should be watered occasionally with liquid manure.

☛ KITCHEN-GARDEN: **Asparagus:** New plantations of asparagus may still be made, but it must be well watered, unless rain occurs. Sow asparagus seed where it is to grow, and thin the plants to the proper distance. Beds that are in bearing should be kept clear of weeds, and the ground stirred occasionally, adding a sprinkling of salt, which improves the flavour.

Artichokes: Stir the earth well about them, and reduce the shoots to three, and draw the earth well about the roots. The offsets taken off may be planted in threes, 120 cm / 4 ft apart one way and five another, giving a copious watering till they have taken root.

Rhubarb roots may yet be divided and planted 120 cm / 4 ft apart: it is a good practice also to sow the seed, which may be done at this time. Sow broadcast, and leave the plants till the following spring, so as to judge of the earliest, so that thinning is unnecessary till this is ascertained. Roots for forcing may be raised thus in abundance.

Horseradish: Pinch out the tops where running to seed, and use the hoe freely all the season through; it will require little other attention the rest of the season.

Beans may still be sown: about the end of this month some will be in full bloom; pinch out the tops of such, to hasten the setting of the flowers.

Celery: Prick out that sown in March, giving 15 cm / 6 in distance from plant to plant: in order that they may get strong, let plenty of good rotten manure be worked into the soil. A little shade will benefit them in sunny weather.

French Beans: These may be sown plentifully this month; they will be found exceedingly useful, as they follow the main crops of peas. Sow in drills 8 cm / 3 in deep and 90 cm / 3 ft apart. Earth-up those that have made a pair of rough leaves, after thinning to 10 cm / 4 in. They should have no manure.

Runner Beans may also be sown; being of a climbing habit and very quick growth, they must have plenty of room. Sow in rows 2 m / 7 ft apart: drill them in 15 cm / 6 in deep.

Nasturtiums are often grown for salad. Sow in drills, the same as peas: they are ornamental as covering for fences.

Peas: To sow now, use such sorts as Knight's Dwarf and Tall Marrows, Mammoth, or British Queen, in good soils, and even in poor soils, if mulched with good sound manure, the latter sort yields immensely. Observe the same rule in sowing these as in scarlet runners, as regards distance. Dwarf sorts will not require sticks, and are very useful on this account.

Carrots that are advancing should have the small hoe employed between them; thin them to the proper distance. Fresh sowings may still be made. Horn carrot sown now will be useful in the autumn; they should be sown thicker than larger sorts.

Onions may still be sown, more particularly for salading, for which purpose thin out the earliest sowings and clear from weeds: drenching the soil with liquid manure occasionally will benefit them.

Leeks: Thin where forward enough in rows 60 cm / 2 ft from each other; give liquid manure to those that remain, and stir the ground between.

Parsnips: Thin out – 45 cm / 18 in is not too much.

Potatoes: Several good late sorts do as well planted this month as earlier. Earth-up those that are forward enough, but not too much: more earth than is just sufficient to cover the tubers is likely to prove injurious to the crop.

Turnips may do well sown now, if wet or showery weather occur: sow broad-cast, tread the seed in, and rake soot in with it. Such as are up should be hoed between and thinned out immediately: doing this early will be of great advantage to the crop – the oftener it is done the better.

Scorzoneras and Salsify may still be sown. Sow in drills 40 cm / 15 in apart, and thin to about 20 cm / 9 in when up. Hoe between them during the summer. It is as well not to give manure before sowing.

Lettuce: Sow in drills a foot or more apart: let as many as possible continue where sown. Those transplanted had better be in drills, for the greater facility of watering, an abundance of which they must have in dry weather, to insure crispness and milky flavour. The soil for lettuces cannot be too rich. Tie up cos lettuces about a fortnight before using.

Endive: The Batavian may be sown now: treat in the same way as lettuce.

Spinach may be sown; but as it is apt to run very quickly, it is advisable to sow on a north border. Give plenty of room: it is less likely to run than when crowded.

Chervil and **Parsley** sown now on a sunny border will be useful in winter. Sow either in drills or broadcast; tread the seed in before raking; thin out that which is sufficiently advanced to 20 cm / 9 in.

Radishes: Sow for succession. These must be well protected from birds. They must be well watered, to prevent their becoming hot and woody.

Cress: American, Normandy, and Australian cress, to come in in August, should be sown now in shallow drills or broadcast, treading the seed firmly in before raking: they will all require copious watering.

Cabbage: To hasten hearting, tie them in the same way as lettuces. Plant out early-sown ones, and sow again for succession.

Brussels Sprouts and **Kale** may still be sown: treat as broccoli.

Cauliflower: Plant out early-sown 45 cm / 18 in apart. Those that have stood the winter should have liquid manure, or, at least, plenty of water, unless they were previously mulched, which prevents evaporation, and also feeds the plants.

Broccoli: This being a good time for sowing late sorts, as Purple Sprouting, Miller's Dwarf, &c.: they are invaluable in the early spring time. Give them an open situation; sow broadcast, each sort separately, and rather thinly. Walcheren sown now will be very useful in the autumn: plant out early sorts.

Herbs such as balm, mint, marjoram, savory, thyme, &c., may be increased by slips, offsets, or divisions of the roots: they must be well watered. Other herbs, as basil, potted marjoram, fennel, dill, &c., may be sown on the open ground. They are not generally subject to the attacks of birds.

☞ FLOWERS UNDER GLASS: **Conservatory:** A watchful eye must now be kept on all house plants for insects. Ply the spray upon all plants not in bloom.

Roses will be coming forward from the forcing-houses.

Camellias, their season of bloom being past, are now in their full growth. An application of weak manure-water will be of great use to them if the surface soil is getting dry.

Climbers must be trained, and kept thoroughly ventilated and moist.

Azaleas as they go out of bloom should be attended to, the old flowers and seed-vessels picked off. Should they require repotting, it should be done when the new growth begins; the strong shoots of young plants stopped, except one, to form a centre for a tall pyramidal-shaped plant.

Pelargoniums trussing up for flowering require watching: tie out the shoots as far apart as possible, to admit air freely to the heart of the plant: give liquid manure two or three times a week, and check for greenfly; give all the ventilation possible.

Scarlet Geraniums should be encouraged to grow by liberal shifting; and when established, water them freely, giving liquid manure to those fully rooted.

Fuchsias, shrubby Calceolarias, Heliotropes, and Alonsoas, like the geraniums, require liberal shifting in order to grow them properly. Spray occasionally, to keep up a moist atmosphere. If they are required to be large plants, pinch out the first flower-buds and place stakes a foot higher than the plants, to tie them to as they grow. When well established, give liquid manure and ample ventilation during the day.

🖙 FRUIT UNDER GLASS: **Vinery:** The earlier crops now coming forward will be colouring; they must be kept perfectly dry, and have as much air as can be given safely, keeping the house at the temperature of 18°C / 65°F or thereabouts. Hamburgs, and the more hardy grapes, will require to be kept near 18°C / 65°F as a night temperature as they approach the time of flowering; but the Canon-Hall and the common Muscat, the Damascus and West's St Peter's, will require an additional few degrees as they get into bloom; and this heat should be maintained till the berries are wholly set.

Thinning, stopping, and tying in should now be done daily; water freely, and some sorts with more delicate foliage shade for a few hours about noon. When the grapes in the early house are cut, great care should be taken to preserve the foliage in a healthy condition for the next three months, by frequent spray, to keep down the red spider, which the dry air of the house during the ripening of the fruit will have encouraged. If the foliage is unhealthy, or the vines weakly, and new wood is required to furnish healthy leaves, the growth should be stopped when three or four joints are formed. Abundance of air and light are indispensable auxiliaries.

Figs will now be ripening, and in this stage watering should be discontinued, as it injures the flavour of the fruit. When in tubs, however, and a second crop is coming on, manure-water may be given in moderation.

Orchard-house: Ventilation must still be strictly attended to. Open all ventilators during the day, except in fierce north and east winds. Summer-pruning of trees to be so treated to commence early this month.

🖙 HOTBED AND FRAME CULTIVATION: Hotbeds may be made for starting cucumbers. Give plenty of air to growing plants, particularly in sunny weather. Attend well to pinching back undergrowth and pegging down the stems: they will root at every joint by so doing, and continue bearing much longer. Water must be given more freely as the weather gets warmer; but see that the plants are not chilled

Frame potatoes, carrots, cauliflowers, &c., will be fit for the table this month, and the frame may be used for any of the above, taking out the old soil and replacing it with fresh, and applying new linings. Such are also very useful for growing capsicums and tomatoes; they should be grown in pots. They may be used for other tender annuals, which always do best when plunged in heat, and grown in a frame or shallow pit.

Frames are also excellent for hardening off all sorts of bedding-stock for the flower garden; the windows can be pulled quite off, and the plants are thus inured gradually to the open air.

JUNE

🖙 FLOWER-GARDEN AND SHRUBBERIES: As soon as the beds, borders, &c., of the flower-garden are finished, the baskets and vases filled, and the general spring planting-out brought to a close, the remaining stock of bedding-plants should be looked over. A portion will be required for stock; and as a considerable number of plants will in all probability be required to make good failures, or to replace beds now occupied with short-blooming plants – these had better be kept in pots.

The newly-planted beds require constant watching. All failures should be instantly made good, and the tying and staking of everything requiring support attended to. Where an early display of flowers is not wanted, the buds may be pinched off. Cuttings of *Iberis saxatilis* root readily under a bell-jar at this season: when placed in a shady situation, they form a beautiful edging, and may be cut like box for a week or two, to encourage the plants to cover the ground. Pansies, anemones, double wallflowers, and other spring plants, should be removed as they go out of bloom, to make room for autumn-flowering ones, the beds being made up with fresh compost, in planting the later. Creepers against walls or trellises should be gone over and tied or nailed in.

Watch the different annuals as they come into flower, and mark those varieties whose seed should be saved.

🖙 ROSE GARDEN: Standard and pillar roses should likewise be looked over to see that they are properly secured to their stakes. Weak-growing shoots should be tied up and regulated, and all fading flowers and seed-vessels removed, cutting back the perpetual or autumn-flower kinds, as soon as all the flowers of the branch are expanded, to the most prominent vertical eye, stirring the ground and saturating it with manure-water.

Towards the end of the month many shoots will be firm enough for budding, and some sorts work best on the flowering shoots, provided the buds are taken before the flowering is over.

☛ FLORISTS' FLOWERS: **Dahlias** already planted out should be watered in the evenings with soft water overhead, the soil being previously stirred, and others planted out for later bloom, taking care to mulch round the roots. As the shoots advance, train and tie up carefully; search for earwigs and slugs in the mornings. **Ranunculuses** will be making rapid growth. Always water in the evening.

Carnations, Picotees, and Pinks as they advance, should be tied to their stakes, reducing the number of the shoots according to the strength of the plant. Care should be taken that the flower-pods of pinks do not burst; and those having ligatures round them will require easing and re-tying.

Auriculas and Polyanthuses should be removed into a northern aspect, all decayed petals taken away from the seed-pods, and as the capsules turn brown, they should be gathered. Water as they require it, and keep free from weeds.

Pansies: struck from cuttings in April and May will produce fine blooms if planted in shady situations, or potted, and shaded in very bright weather. Cuttings may still be taken from promising plants.

☛ KITCHEN-GARDEN: Peas, beans, cauliflowers, carrots, potatoes, and many other vegetables, come in all at once, that could not be produced earlier in the open ground. This month being generally a dry one, the watering-pot must not remain idle. Most kinds of salads are worthless if stinted of water, but let it be applied copiously, for mere surface-watering only attracts the roots to the surface, to be burnt up by the sun.

Asparagus: Water newly-planted beds, and keep clear of weeds. Beds in bearing will be benefited by an application of liquid manure.

Beans: The last sowing of these should be made for the season. Mulching will increase the quantity and quality of the crop.

Runner Beans do well sown any time before midsummer. Water the drills or holes at the time of sowing. Those sown last month should be earthed and staked

before they begin to run. This plant is often used to form or cover an arbour or fence, for which it is well adapted, except on account of its ephemeral character.

Nasturtiums may still be sown, being very quick at this time. Those already up should have their supports about 120 cm / 4 ft high.

Peas: After the second week this month, it is not advisable to sow strong-growers – such sorts as Auvergne or Champion of Paris. The time from sowing to bearing is less, and there is more certainty of a crop.

Celery will probably be in condition for final planting towards the end of this month: the main crop had better be deferred till next month. Celery requires a rich, highly-manured soil and abundance of water.

Carrots: Thin without delay, but not too closely, as some are apt to run, even under the best culture. From 20–30 cm / 9–12 in is a good average. A succession may be sown any time before midsummer.

Onions should receive a final thinning, allowing 20 cm / 8 in for the main crop. Use the small hoe as often as possible, and keep them clean. Onions for salading may still be sown. A shady border on the north side of a wall will suit them.

Leeks: Plant in deep drills, to admit of earthing-up: give an abundance of water in dry weather. Soot dredged over them will stimulate them, and prevent the attacks of insects in a great measure.

Potatoes: Earth up before they get too tall, but leave the top of the ridges nearly flat, so that the tubers are not buried too deeply. Potatoes that have been retarded may be planted this month: they will yield new potatoes in the autumn.

Turnips: Sow a good breadth of these – they will come in well and be very useful in the autumn. Sow immediately after rain, or, if the ground is light, immediately after digging. They grow very quickly; but some slight protection from birds will be necessary the short time they are germinating.

Scorzoneras, &c: Thin to about 25 cm / 10–12 in, and stir the ground well between them.

French Beans: Sow a few rows of these for succession. The larger-growing sorts are considered the best to sow now. Thin to 10 cm / 4 in, and earth up, but give no manure.

Lettuce: Sow on a north border, but plant in an open situation. It is necessary to sow often to insure a succession. Water the ground thoroughly, or not at all.

Endive may be sown this month, as it is less likely to run now than formerly. The seed grows very quickly, and birds do not seem to care about it; it may therefore be merely sown broadcast, trodden and raked.

Vegetable Marrows and Pumpkins should be got out early this month. If good strong plants, they may be merely planted on a sunny border; but they delight in a loose bed of light but well-rotted dung that they can root into easily. Give plenty of water if the weather holds dry.

Capsicums and Tomatoes the beginning of this month – Plant these against a south wall if possible – otherwise against a sloping bank: the full sun is necessary to induce them to bear well.

Cress: Sow American and Normandy for succession.

Broccoli: Defer not later than the middle of this month the final sowing of late sorts. Walcheren sown now will very likely come in during the winter. Plant out those that are ready, and never allow them to draw up in the seed-bed; but prick them out temporarily: they will pay for it.

Brussels Sprouts, Kale, and Savoys: Get these planted for good as early as possible; plant in drills 60 cm / 2 ft apart, and water freely. Puddling the roots in clay and soot mixed with water may prevent clubbing. Watering once a day will be necessary in dry weather.

Cabbage and Cauliflower should also be planted out when strong enough. The latter will prove very useful in August and September.

FRUIT-GARDEN: The trees will have been mulched last month to prevent evaporation, and should now be watered copiously, pouring the water into the roots.

In disbudding pears, plums and cherries, the fore-right shoots, and those not wanted for laying on, should remain for the present, as stopping them at this time would only cause a fresh breaking into wood, either of the eyes at the base of the stopped shoot, or some portion of the spurs; as they, however, look unsightly on well-regulated trees, it will be better to tie them slightly to the main branches for the present. The precise time at which shoots should be shortened must be regulated according to the vigour of the tree, and should be deferred till all danger of the remaining eyes again breaking into wood is over. Cherry-trees now progressing towards maturity should be gone carefully over, the shoots stopped and laid in, and the trees netted, to save the fruit and protect it from birds.

Place straw, or some similar material, between strawberries now in bloom, to preserve the fruit clear in heavy rains, and to keep the ground moist.

Figs – stop all except the leading shoots, when they have made three or four joints, and lay on leaders and shoots required for filling up. Watering the roots with soapsuds is found greatly to benefit the fruit.

Vines will require going over. Thin out what wood is not wanted for bearing, and stop the bearing shoots at one joint above the shoot: nail in the leading shoots close to the wall. Where the long-rod system of pruning is adopted, a shoot must be selected and carried up from the bottom of each stem, to furnish bearing wood for next year.

■ FLOWERS UNDER GLASS: **The Conservatory:** Avoid crowding; remove all decayed or decaying blossom, and guard against insects. Regulate the luxurious growth of creepers and border-plants, watering copiously, occasionally using liquid manure. Air should be admitted night and day, except in cold gloomy weather, and shading from the burning sun attended to for an hour or two daily.

■ FRUIT UNDER GLASS: Houses where the grapes are ripe should be kept dry, and succession crops encouraged by a little heat, according to their several stages. Stop all lateral shoots in the succession-house after thinning the crop, that nothing may interfere with the swelling of the fruit. As the season advances, air must be given in abundance. To prevent the atmosphere from becoming too dry during hot weather, keep the floors and interior walls damp by sprinkling several times a day. This will also assist to keep in check the ravages of the red spider.

Cucumbers at this season of the year do best with a considerable amount of shade: this should be attended to, and the necessary bottom-heat and moisture kept up. In planting out at this season, use a rather poor, in preference to a rich soil, which in cold wet seasons produces canker.

Orchard-houses: In hot and dry weather trees will require watering abundantly every evening; in all weathers spray morning and evening, at 7 a.m. and 6 p.m. Thin the fruit, pinching in all shoots to the third leaf.

Remove plum trees into the open air to ripen. On the 10th, and again on the 25th, lift up the pots in order to break off the roots which have protruded through the drainage-holes, and attend to summer-pinching of bush trees.

■ HOT-BED AND FRAME CULTIVATION: Making hot-beds is seldom deferred till this time of the year; yet it may be done advantageously. Cucumbers in an advanced stage will want clearing of dead leaves, and the soil stirred about them, and probably fresh earth added.

Plants intended for open-air culture, if sown last month, will be ready for ridging out. A south border, or between rows of tall peas or scarlet runners, ranging north and south, will suit them. Open a trench 120 cm / 4 ft wide, and fill with prepared stable dung, to the thickness of 90 cm / 3 ft; cover this with 30 cm / 1 ft of soil; place the plants 150 cm / 5 ft apart, two or three together, and cover with bell-jars.

JULY

☛ FLOWER-GARDEN AND SHRUBBERIES: Hollyhocks planted on the lawn, whether singly or in groups, should be staked in time: in fact, they should be staked when planted, and the leaves and plants kept in a healthy state by watering and spray in hot and dry weather. Tie up oenotheras neatly. Speciosas, planted pretty thickly over the beds, will produce a fine mass of white flowers, if trained so that they have plenty of light and air, and watered abundantly in dry weather.

The first week or so in July will be chiefly occupied by the usual routine of pegging-down plants intended to be kept dwarf, tying others up, and keeping the surface of the beds free from weeds until it is covered by the growing plants. Pinks should now be propagated; cuttings may likewise be put in of tea and China roses, selecting wood of the present year when it becomes a little firm at the base. Roots, bulbs, anemones, tulips, crocuses, scillas, fritillarias, &c., which have been out of the ground for some time to dry, may now be replanted. Plants in flower, will require regular supplies of water.

☛ ROSE GARDEN: Autumn-flowering roses now require a liberal supply of liquid manure; guano sown on the ground, and thoroughly soaked with rain-water, will serve the purpose. Remove faded flowers and seed-capsules every morning; plants which have flowered in pots keep growing freely, as the future bloom depends on their vigorous growth at this season. Climbing roses should now be pushing out strong shoots from the roots and main stem; if not required for future training, these should be taken off entirely, or have their tops pinched off a foot or so from the stem. Budding should be in full operation, watering the roots and plants freely in dry weather, both before and after budding.

☛ FLORISTS' FLOWERS: Take up tulips whenever the weather will permit. When lifted, do not separate the offsets from the parent bulb, nor remove the roots or skin: these had better remain till a later period. When lifted, ridge up the soil of the beds for exposure to the air. In taking up seedlings, great care must be used, as their bulbs will often strike down from 10 cm / 4 in. Tie carefully, but not too tightly, the spindling shoots of carnations and picotees; keep the pots free from weeds, and in dry weather do not let them suffer from drought.

By the end of the month, seedling ranunculuses should be taken from the pans or boxes in which they may have been grown; but as many are so minute, and so like the colour of the soil, that without great precaution, they may be overlooked, the best way is to put soil and roots together in a fine wire sieve, and by holding it under a tap, the soil will be washed away and the roots left;

they must then be placed in the sun for an hour, and afterwards removed to an airy shady place to dry gradually. The large roots of named varieties must be taken up at once, for should they start again, which they are very apt to do previous to removal, death is inevitable. Attend diligently to dahlias; tie as they require it, and give a good supply of water.

Baskets will require an occasional regulating; those having plants in them which require to be tied up, should be examined.

▰ KITCHEN-GARDEN: It may be observed, that where rows of vegetables have previously grown, the ground is usually dry and hard. It is not, therefore, advisable to crop immediately over the same spot. It is best not to plant winter crops on ground that has been newly-dug or trenched. All brassicae are far more liable to club on loose or newly-trenched ground. Keep the weeds down at this season, as their growth is very rapid in showery weather.

Asparagus: Cease cutting early this month, unless some part of the bed can be spared for late use, in which case it must have a rest the following season.

Artichokes will now be in bearing. Cut when the heads are about three parts open. These root deeply, and scarcely require water.

Beans: Pull up early crops as soon as they have done bearing. Make a groove each side of those advancing, and give enough to soak the ground to a considerable depth.

Runner Beans: These beans may be kept dwarf by picking off the runners; but it is much better to provide supports: the produce is tenfold greater.

French Beans: A late sowing of these may be made now: dwarf kinds, as the Newington Wonder, are best. Sow on unmanured soil; thin out sufficiently above ground to 10 cm / 4 in apart, and draw plenty of earth up to the stems.

Peas: If any are sown this month, let it be sorts that bear equally, or the shortening days will prevent their bearing at all. Dwarf early sorts are best. Clear away any that have ceased to be productive, and stake those that are just above ground. Copious waterings will greatly benefit those coming into flower, but may be discontinued when they begin to pod, excepting for tall sorts, which continue bearing and flowering at the same time.

Celery: The main crop should be got out directly. If this is planted where peas had previously grown, make the trenches between, not on the rows where the ground has been heavily drawn.

Beet: See that this crop is properly thinned, and keep the ground well hoed between.

Carrots may be sown any time this month; they will be useful in winter and spring. Sow on an open spot, and do not dig the ground deep; look over the main crop, and pull up any runners: they will be of no use if left.

Onions may be sown now for salad in the autumn. Towards the end of this month some of the main crop will be showing signs of maturity, when they may be pulled up and laid on their sides, and thick-necked ones may be pinched.

Leeks: Plant out the main crop on well-manured ground in deep drills or shallow trenches. Leeks are strong feeders, and should be well watered.

Potatoes: Pick off the flowers, if possible: if allowed to seed, they diminish the produce, the tubers growing less in proportion to the quantity of seed allowed to ripen. Some advise cutting off the haulm as soon as any disease appears.

Turnips: At the beginning of the month, make a principal sowing for autumn and early winter use, and make another sowing towards the end of the month.

Lettuce sown now do well on a shady border. An open well-manured spot is best for them, if kept well watered.

Endive: Two sowings should be made this month; one at the beginning, another towards the end. Sow as lettuce, and plant out when large enough to handle.

Tomatoes should be carefully trained, and stopped as they grow. Unless the ground is very dry, they do not require watering.

Vegetable Marrows will be in active growth; and, planted on a manure-heap, they will grow freely enough without watering; but if on the common soil, they should be freely watered in the morning.

Spinach: It is not advisable to sow this month; but the ground should be prepared for sowing next month.

Broccoli, Brussels Sprouts, and Savoy: The principal crops of these should be got out. Plant them in drills 60 cm / 2 ft apart, and 45 cm / 18 in in the rows.

Cabbage: Sow for kale early in the month, and for early cabbaging about the end of it: strew lime in soot over the young plants, to drive away the fly. This should be done in the morning, while the dew is on them. Plant out for autumn.

Cauliflower sown now may be useful late in the autumn.

Mint, and such-like herbs, should be cut for drying just as they begin to flower; savory, sage, and others, may be now propagated by cuttings or divisions; parsley and chervil may be sown for winter use.

☞ FRUIT-GARDEN: **Plums, Cherries and Figs**, on walls, should be carefully looked over, and all shoots that are not really useful should be removed. It is important to do this in time, because, if neglected till the fruit begins to ripen, the real advantage of doing it is lost. Figs, especially, are apt to make strong superfluous wood, the leaves of which throw a dense shade over the fruit and impede the ripening. Spray freely over wall-trees about two or three times a week, to wash off dust and insects.

Dwarf fruit-trees should receive the same amount of attention. The summer training and pruning is of the greatest importance.

Vines out of doors should be closely stopped and trained in. All the heat of the sun is necessary to the well-doing of this fruit.

Gooseberries, Currants, Raspberries, and other bush-fruit will require some protection from birds. Nothing is better for the purpose than netting, spread over and round the tree, completely covering it in.

Strawberries: This is by far the best month of the year for making new plantations. There are various methods of doing it; perhaps the best is as follows: The earliest runners are laid in 8-cm / 3-in pots, fixed in their place by means of small pegs; in three weeks they have rooted into the soil with which the pots are filled. During this time they require an occasional watering, but may be planted out permanently as soon as rooted, placing them 45 cm / 18 in apart in rows 90 cm / 3 ft apart. They should then receive good culture till the autumn, when they may be stored in frames. Strawberries are sometimes grown on permanent beds 120 cm / 4 ft wide. Another method is to have them in narrow beds, 60 cm / 2 ft wide, with 60-cm / 2-ft alleys between. When they have ceased bearing, the runners are allowed to trail over the alleys, and when they are well covered, the old beds are dug in. Next year the same process is repeated: thus a succession of young plants is kept in bearing with very little trouble.

In hot summers the earth about the roots of fruit-trees, &c., often becomes so parched, that the fruit is not properly nourished in the process of swelling or stoning. The following mode, especially in the case of vine borders, cannot be too strongly recommended – Perforated pipes are laid about 30 cm / 12 in below the surface of the soil – in the case of strawberry-beds, about 15 cm / 6 in; from these a tube is carried to a convenient place for filling with water or liquid manure, with which they are charged twice a day.

FLOWERS UNDER GLASS: **Conservatory:** Exotic bulbs have nearly finished flowering, and require a state of rest; those whose stems are still green should have water, in order to mature the bulbs. When done flowering, keep them in dry earth or sand, and in a warm situation, to ripen. Cinerarias and calceolarias require as cool an atmosphere as the house admits of; those which have flowered may be cut down and planted out in a light loamy border; seeds of both for flowering in spring should be sown. Cuttings of geraniums and most greenhouse shrubs may now be struck, and forwarded by plunging in a gentle hotbed, taking as cuttings only strong and healthy shoots 8–15 cm / 3–6 in long, according to the size of the plants. These cuttings should be planted in pans, boxes, or pots of rich light compost, 8 cm / 3 in apart, moderately watered, and placed in a frame shaded from the midday sun till they are rooted.

Fuchsias, geraniums, achimenes, and salvias, requiring larger pots, should be shifted, removing the entire ball, and placing them in the centre of the new pot, properly drained and half-filled with fresh compost. Having first trimmed the roots when the pots are filled up with compost, let them be well watered, and put away in an airy but shaded situation, to settle. All pots and tubs, especially orange and lemon plants, require stirring on the surface of the soil, and to be top-dressed and watered. Oranges, camellias, azaleas, and other hard-wooded plants, can now be budded or grafted: in the beginning of the month, myrtles, oleanders, and jasmines may be propagated by layers.

Hard-wooded plants will about the middle of the month be so far advanced in their new growth that any requiring re-potting should at once have a shift. After turning them out, loosen the outside roots before placing them in their new pots, to enable them to take up the fresh soil more readily. Keep them close for a few days and damp them once or twice daily overhead.

Such plants as are intended to flower in the winter, as justicias, *Eranthemum pulcellum*, euphorbias, jasmines, &c., should be looked to. Many of these things require to be kept in small pots, and should be watered with liquid manure, to grow them on without getting into too large pots.

Balsams, thunbergias, and other annuals intended to decorate the conservatory and show-house for the next two months, should be finally potted, using soil of a light and rich description. Ipomoeas, thunbergias, and other creepers, should be neatly trained, keeping them fresh and healthy by frequent watering, and by picking off all decaying leaves; and, where the plants are flagging, water them with very weak liquid manure.

Brugmansias, and similar plants of vigorous habit, should be frequently assisted with manure-water: as they are often troubled with red spider, the spray must be used frequently, taking care, however, not to injure the fine foliage. Succulent plants, as cactuses, euphorbias, cereuses, sedums, and others of similar habit, require a full exposure to the sun, in order to obtain a fine bloom.

Achimenes, gloxinias, &c., out of bloom should be removed to a pit to ripen their bulbs.

Greenhouse: Greenhouse plants, after they have done blooming, should have a comparatively cool temperature.

Camellias, whenever the young wood appears getting ripe, may be removed to the open air: they thrive best in the shade; they must be placed on a dry bottom to prevent worms from getting into the pots.

Chinese azaleas should also be turned out. Unlike camellias, they require full exposure to sun and air, and should be placed in an open situation, that their wood may become thoroughly ripened. It will, however, perhaps be necessary to place them for a week or two in a partially-shaded situation, to harden their foliage sufficiently to bear the full sun.

Orange and lemon trees will now be in bloom, and should be supplied with water at least three times a week in dry weather, and occasionally supplied with liquid manure after stirring the surface of the soil and top-dressing. Orange trees when too full of bloom should have the flowers thinned out.

FRUIT UNDER GLASS: **Vinery:** Ripe grapes, if required to be kept, must be shaded during hot sun, to prevent shrivelling. The Cannon Hall, Muscat, Sweetwater, and Frontignans, having tender leaves, are most liable to burn, either from bad glass or imperfect ventilation. They must be well watched, as the injury done to the foliage not only affects the present crop but the succeeding one. Any heat given now should be given during the day.

As the houses are cleared of their fruit and the wood is ripened, air must be given in abundance by night as well as day, and the necessary stopping of lateral growths and thinning of the fruit in the last house proceeded with. Watch for mildew. Vines in pots, intended to fruit next season, should now be well supplied with manure-water.

Figs swelling off their second crop should be assisted with liquid manure, more especially if growing in pots or tubs. As the fruit ripens, care must be taken to preserve it from damp, which the frequent spraying to keep down insects induces.

Strawberries: Proceed to pot strawberries for forcing: as soon as the pots in which the runners were layered becomed filled with roots, pot them in 15- or 18- cm / 6- or 7-in pots, using rich loam of medium texture, and well-rotted dung, with plenty of drainers. When potted, place them in an open situation exposed to the sun, on boards, or a prepared bottom, to prevent worms from getting to the roots.

Orchard-house: Ventilation is now the greatest care. Spray night and morning, and water copiously when dry. If any trees are growing too rapidly, tilt up the pots, and cut off all the roots on that side which are making their way into the soil. A week later, serve the other side in the same way. Pinch in all lateral shoots to within two buds of their base. Remove all trees into the open air, to ripen their fruit in a sheltered sunny spot.

HOT-BED AND FRAME CULTIVATION: The purposes of hotbeds are limited at this time of the year, at least in most places. Cucumbers are usually grown in houses and pits that are otherwise unoccupied at present; and as their culture is more cleanly in this way, hotbeds may be dispensed with; those, however, already in operation will require attention. We sometimes have sudden and heavy showers, which would drench the plants and beds if they were uncovered, probably to their destruction. Plenty of fresh air is necessary; and the sudden changes produced by clouds obscuring the sun for a time, and then bursting forth hot and fierce, must be provided against: it is in such cases that a little shade may be advantageous.

Cucumbers in bearing should be watered. If the soil is not sufficiently moist, take care to water plentifully, as at this time of the year there is less danger of overwatering. Pickling cucumbers may be planted in the open ground at the beginning of this month. The soil should be well dug, and made pretty firm again, and well mulched after the plants are put in. Choose a warm sheltered spot for them.

Capsicums &c., in fruiting condition, should remain in the pots, and be plunged in the bed; the roots will ramble through the pots.

AUGUST

FLOWER-GARDEN AND SHRUBBERIES: The flower-garden will now be in its greatest beauty, and every means must be taken to keep turf, gravel, and edgings of all kinds in neat order; dead flowers should be picked off daily, and stray growth reduced within proper limits. Trailing and climbing plants should frequently be gone over to keep them neat and secure after high winds: for the same purpose examine hollyhocks, dahlias, and other tall-growing plants. After removing the dead flowers from roses, encourage the production of autumn blooms in perpetuals, by watering with liquid manure and mulching the surface of the ground. Continue the propagation of plants for next season: no time must be lost with the more delicate pelargoniums.

Many of our most beautiful flowering-plants may be propagated this month; among them may be classed crassulas, lantanas, hydrangeas, mesembryanthemums, &c., all of which should be struck early, to flower freely the following season. Petunias, verbenas, heliotropes, salvias, and lobelias may be taken in hand next, reserving calceolarias till the last, as they strike better during the cold weather of autumn. Verbenas and calceolarias may be struck or in a cold frame. Geraniums will strike freely on a south border inserted in sandy soil. Ten-weeks stocks should be sown before the middle of the month, and intermediate stocks to be kept in pots throughout the winter for spring-flowering; pot a quantity of Bromptons for the same purpose.

Roll lawns well, and meet the rapid growth by frequent mowing. Gravel-walks will likewise require frequent rolling and surface-weeding, especially in shady places.

Plant out all recently-struck pinks, double wallflowers, and pansies, keeping a few of the latter in pots for protection during the winter.

Seeds sown in the beginning of August, and potted off into store pots when large enough, make good plants for spring purposes. The process of stopping retards their bloom, and strengthens the flowers: where earlier bloom is required, a modified treatment is to be adopted. When the flowering season is over, remove the plants to a shaded place, preserving all the leaves, and watering slightly, guarding them from insects until August, when cuttings may be taken from the old roots. The roots may also be separated and potted out; these old ones are the best for early flowering; they may be divided even up to October.

Geraniums may be propagated by thinning out the beds here and there, and inserting the cuttings in small beds on a border, putting a little silver sand in the holes made to receive them. Intermediate stocks should be sown early in the month, and ten-weeks stocks before the middle. All double-flowering perennials that have done flowering may be propagated by slips, and parting the roots towards the end of the month. Let every root be trimmed by cutting off the straggling parts; pick off all dead leaves, then replant them in some shady border, and give some water.

In shrubberies prune off all exuberant branches, keeping up a dwarf and full foliage, and watering where required.

Autumnal bulbs, such as cochicums, narcissuses and amaryllis, may still be planted in borders, beds, or pots, in light sandy loam.

🡆 FLORISTS' FLOWERS: Carnations and picotees should now be layered, but without shortening the grass. Where seed is required, pick off all decaying petals, to prevent damp injuring the pods. Make pansy-beds.

Clean and prepare tulip-beds, and arrange the plants in their drawers, discarding stained varieties, and adding new ones in their place.

Dahlias require constant watering and attention in tying out lateral shoots, removing superfluous ones, and relaxing the ties. Stir the soil, but not deeply, and give special attention to seedlings, selecting those worth preserving, and throwing away worthless varieties. Attend to the training and thinning of the shoots of dahlias.

Hollyhocks require the same attention as to staking and selecting.

Pinks: First-struck pipings may now be planted out, potting a quantity in order to fill up vacancies which may be caused from the ravages of the wireworm.

🡆 ROSE GARDEN: Perpetual-flowering roses in dry weather require copious supplies of water. If mildew appears, spray the plants with soft water in the evening, and dust the affected parts with flour of sulphur. Towards the end of the month any roses budded last month may have their bandages removed, the place examined to see that nothing has interfered with the bud, and the bandage restored. Cuttings may be struck in light sandy soil over a gentle hotbed. When rooted, pot off and replace the cuttings in the frames for a few days till the roots begin to move, when they may be removed and hardened off.

The Ayrshire, Boursault, Sempervirens, and other climbing roses, frequently send out very luxuriant shoots near the bottom of the stem. These, if not wanted to cover some weak part of the plant, should be removed.

☞ KITCHEN-GARDEN: Attention will be drawn towards the multitudes of garden pests, which exhibit their effects at this time of the year more than any other. Caterpillars should be looked for and destroyed. A free use of lime, scattered over the plants on dewy mornings, will, in a great measure, save the crops. The wireworm and other insects may be trapped by means of potatoes cut in half, and the cut sides laid downwards. It is a good plan to trench all the vacant ground at this time of the year; grubs and wireworm are then buried deep enough to destroy them. The effects of the club become apparent on hot, sunny days: cabbages, &c., hang down and turn blue, and are infested with aphids. This disease is one of the most vexatious with which the gardener has to deal. How far it may be prevented by the use of lime and wood ashes, &c., is a matter of doubt. The causes of it may be traced, first, to an injudicious application of manure in small gardens that are already too manured; and secondly, an exhausted state of the soil, arising from the too unvaried use to which it is put. Plants that are subject to this disease are strong feeders, and exhaust the soil very much; it is, however, reasonable to suppose they leave food suitable for other plants. Instances are not rare of ground being left to weeds for several years, where, although cabbages clubbed badly before, they did not after the vacation.

Artichokes: Cut these down as the heads are gathered, and fork the ground between – they will come up again before winter.

Asparagus: Unless seed is wanted, it is advisable to cut off most of the bearing heads, which would exhaust and weaken the roots in ripening seed: it is, however, as well to sow every year, and some seed may be left for this purpose.

Beans: Pull up the haum of any that have done bearing: lay the stalks together, and they will soon rot, or dry them, and they will burn. Some may be cut in lengths, and dried for earwig traps, to place among flowering plants.

Runner Beans should be stopped after reaching the top of the sticks. Give plenty of water at the roots if necessary, but none overhead.

French Beans: A row or two should be left for seed. It is not advisable to leave any to ripen on bearing plants, as they cease to yield while ripening seed.

Cabbages: Sow early this month for a full crop of summer cabbage. Sow thinly on an open spot, and scatter lime on the ground to protect from birds and insects. Get out a supply of early kale; they will most likely harvest in November.

Carrots: Early sowings may be taken up and stowed away for use; but if the ground is not needed, it is quite as well to let them remain till required for use. A little seed may be sown early this month to stand the winter; plants will be useful in the spring, when the winter store is exhausted.

Cauliflowers: seed sown at the beginning, middle and end of the month, will give a succession. Sow as cabbages. It will be necessary to give them the protection of frames during the winter; but the sowing may be in the open ground.

Celery: This may be got out in any quantity. If young plants are used, and kept growing, they will stand the winter well, but must not be earthed-up till November; those put out in June may now be earthed-up for blanching. As celery grows quickly at this time, three weeks will blanch it; but it should be quite moist at the roots before being banked up.

Endive: Sow early this month for the last time this season; prick out the plants as soon as large enough: a good watering now and then, after planting, is all the attention they require. When endive is ready for blanching, use inverted flowerpots with the hole stopped.

Leeks may still be transplanted; but the sooner the better. Plant in deep drills 60 cm / 2 ft or so apart, and water freely; draw earth up to those in full growth. Liquid manure given occasionally will benefit them.

Lettuce: The first week in this month sow cabbage-lettuce for winter use, and from that time onwards, both Cos and cabbage-lettuce may be sown to stand the winter for spring use; sow rather thin on an open spot.

Onions will most likely be arriving at maturity, and had better be pulled up as soon as this is the case, and laid on their sides. Green thick-necked ones should be turned down at the collar, and used first. It is necessary to ripen onions thoroughly before storing them away. Garlic, shallots, &c., will most likely be fit to take up this month, and may be treated in the same way as onions. Sow Tripoli, globe, or Welsh hardy, to stand the winter, for planting out in spring, or for salading: a warm sunny border is the most suitable place for sowing them.

Parsnips: Stir the ground well between, so that the rain may penetrate quickly.

Peas: Pull up as soon as all are gathered: it is not advisable to leave them a moment longer. The haulm may be dried in the sun, and will be useful in winter for covering and protecting many things from frost.

Potatoes: Early crops will be ready for taking up; but they will take no harm if left in the ground till wanted. If the disease appears, remove the haulm instantly from late crops; small and good are better than large and bad.

Radishes may be sown any time this month. The Black Spanish should be sown early for winter use.

Spinach: About the second week in this month, sow the main crop of winter spinach – where a good supply is wanted, it would be best to sow every week this month. The earliest sown will grow quickly, but the later will stand the winter best, and prove valuable in the spring: sow in drills a foot apart, or sow, thinly, broadcast, treading it in either case.

Tomatoes: Attend to these as directed last month. To have them bear well in our short seasons, it is necessary to pinch out all superfluous growth, exposing the flowers, and training as close to the wall as possible.

Turnips: Continue to use the hoe unsparingly among advancing crops: this is most important in the culture of the turnip.

Herbs: The gathering and drying of herbs should not be left later than this month. The propagation of herbs, if not done before, should now be finished.

☛ FRUIT-GARDEN: Wasps and flies must be dealt with. An old-fashioned plan is to hang bottles, containing sugar and beer-dregs, about the trees, in order to entrap them: this, however, is unsightly. The best thing to he done is to cover the fruit with suitable netting.

Tack in all useful wood. This should not be omitted this month, and the trees will scarcely require it after: remove every shoot that is not really wanted and every scrap of wood that is not useful.

Standard trees, where a regular thinning is not adopted, should be shaken occasionally, to bring down any fruit that may be blighted.

Towards the latter end of this month raspberries have generally ceased bearing, and the old canes may be cut down. All borders about fruit-trees should receive a forking about this time. If currant-trees are netted, the fruit will keep good till late in the year. Blackcurrants will not keep, and had better be gathered as soon as ripe.

Strawberry-beds may be planted; but it is advisable to get the planting done as soon as possible, if a crop of fruit is expected the following year. It is a good plan to lay the runners in pots, but generally it will be found that strong runners have already rooted, and may be removed with a trowel. Plenty of water is necessary at this time to newly-planted things.

July and August is generally the time for budding fruit-trees.

☛ FLOWERS UNDER GLASS: **Conservatory:** Those plants that remain should now have plenty of room and a free circulation of air. Camellias and acacias now require copious watering, care being taken that they are not started into second growth. Train and prune all climbing plants in graceful festoons. All plants intended for early forcing should now be placed so that the wood may be thoroughly ripened: on this chiefly depends their future bloom. Strong-growing plants, such as diosmas, the epacridœ, chorozemas, which have been in shade to prolong their flowering, should now be placed in a bright sunny place. Late-flowering azaleas require shifting and training, so that the foliage draws out properly before winter. On the slightest indication of thrips, spray as advised on page 244. Camellias require shifting, if not done last month. *Daphne indica*, both red and white, as well as *Magnolia fuscata*, are very suitable companions to the Camellia, requiring exactly similar treatment and temperature. Pelargoniums which have gone out of flower should be exposed in the open air to ripen their wood, preparatory to being cut down in September.

The principal plants that decorate the conservatory at this season will be fuchsias, scarlet geraniums, with achimenes. Brugmansias may be liberally supplied with liquid manure to maintain them in vigorous health.

Continue to plants yet growing the requisite amount of heat and moisture to carry on the present year's growth, but avoid unnecessary stimulants at this season, which might induce a fresh growth, and to many be injurious to the bloom of next season. Plants suspended on blocks and baskets must be daily examined to see that the growing material is kept sufficiently moist, while, at the same time, stagnant damp must be avoided.

Vigorous-growing plants, whether out in the open border or in pots, must be liberally supplied with water. Amaryllids which have perfected their growth may be placed in a dry place to winter. There is one section of this tribe, however, with elongated bulbs, which will not bear to be kept entirely without water, even when in a state of rest. These latter, with *Pancratium speciosum* and *fragrans, &c.*, should be placed on the back shelves of a vinery, or in any house of medium temperature and supplied only with water sufficient to keep their foliage from dying off.

Complete the potting of chrysanthemums, and plunge them in sawdust to save watering. Stake neatly, and stop mildew by dusting a little flour of sulphur over the infected leaves. Water with liquid manure freely.

Achimenes, as they go out of bloom, may be placed in a frame to ripen their tubers, exposing them fully to the sun, but keeping them rather dry. Pot off seedling cinerarias, Chinese primroses, and calceolaria.

FRUIT UNDER GLASS: **Vinery:** Whenever the leaves in the early house show indications of ripening, shades should be removed and the vines should be fully exposed: beyond stopping any late laterals, vines should not be touched until the leaves fall. Young vines, planted during the past or present season, should be stopped when once they reach the top of the house. Where the rods are intended to carry fruit next season, and the vines are growing freely, six or eight joints beyond where it is intended to cut them back should be left, as a too close stopping might cause the principal eyes to break, and thus endanger next season's show of fruit. Lateral shoots may be kept stopped back pretty close, as the object will now be more to ripen the existing wood than to encourage fresh growth; besides looking over ripe grapes to remove decayed berries.

Fires, especially to houses containing Muscat grapes, should be made each evening, and during wet, dull days, that abundant ventilation may be kept on. Vines in pots, intended to fruit next season, must be closely watched to get the wood perfectly ripened. As they have now completed their growth, liquid manure may be given pretty freely. The plants must be kept close to the glass, and thus exposed to the full influence of light. Lessen water and allow a lower night temperature.

Cucumbers, as the nights get colder, may have a slight covering, and the bottom-heat, if declining, should be renewed. Keep down mildew with sulphur.

☞ HOT-BED AND FRAME CULTIVATION: This is a good time to strike the winter stock of bedding-plants, for raising cinerarias, &c. Frames without hotbeds are very useful. Mignonette, nemophila, and other annuals sown now in pots, and kept in cold frames, will flower in the winter. Horn-carrots sown now in the manner described in January will be useful in the winter; that is, without making a new hot-bed for them, but renewing the soil on an old one. Cauliflowers are often sown in a frame to save them from birds; but it is necessary to uncover them as soon as the seed is up.

Cucumbers that have been carefully stopped, trained, and pegged down, will continue in bearing. If mildew appears, sprinkle the leaves and dust with sulphur; but if very bad, it is better to start with new plants. If started on new beds now, they will continue to bear until Christmas; but they need good 120 cm / 4 ft beds so that linings may be applied as the weather grows colder. Give fruiting plants gentle showers.

SEPTEMBER

☞ FLOWER-GARDEN AND SHRUBBERIES: All trimmings of verbenas, ageratums, geraniums, calceolarias, &c., &c., that are cut off to maintain sharp lines, clearly-defined edgings, &c., must be inserted as cuttings, Where enough cannot be thus secured, the thickest parts of lines or beds must be thinned for this purpose.

Dahlias will require careful tying, disbudding, and thinning off the shoots; a good soaking of manure-water in dry weather will also be most serviceable to them. The blooms of hollyhocks may be much prolonged by similar treatment. All offsets of the best varieties ought to be inserted as cuttings.

Roses – perpetuals may still be cut back with the hope of a third bloom; and late-budded plants will require watering, and training to stakes.

Pot off layers of carnations as fast as rooted, water sparingly, and place in a cold frame for a few days until they make a fresh start.

Plant out in beds early-rooted pansy cuttings, insert a succession of cuttings, and prick out seedlings. Here also let seedling polyanthuses, offsets of these and auriculas, be planted on rich shady beds. Stocks sown in pans in August, will now be fit either to pot off and place in frames until established, or to prick out on shady beds in this department. The first sowing of hardy annuals to stand the winter in the open air should also be made towards the end of the month. Prepare beds for, and plant out, pinks for next year's blooming; hunt for and destroy earwigs on dahlias, hollyhocks, &c.

🖝 KITCHEN-GARDEN: To secure a supply of vegetables in the winter and early spring; the growth of those already planted must be encouraged by hoeing and stirring the earth round the roots, and where slugs abound, their ravages counteracted by sowing soot, salt or lime on the soil.

Celery: The earthing-up of this useful vegetable now demands special attention. The sowings made in July and August will be ready for transplanting.

Cauliflowers may still be sown in some situations, and those sown last month pricked out under bell-jars, or in frames as they advance: if the season is mild, they may be planted out under a south wall. Those plants advancing and heading should have the large leaves broken and turned over them, to give shelter from sun and rain, and the earth drawn round the stem. The plants sown in May will now be ready for planting out in rows 75 cm / 2½ ft asunder; give them a copious watering.

Cabbages: Prepare a piece of ground by deep trenching and heavy manuring, for spring cabbages, savoys, and winter greens, and keep it forked over regularly until the plants are sufficiently advanced for planting out. When ready, plant in rows 60 cm / 2 ft apart, watering well to settle the earth at their roots.

Broccoli also require a good soil richly manured. Plant them out from the beds in rows where they are to grow, 60 cm / 2 ft apart each way: water till the plants have rooted. This crop may follow peas with advantage, or be set between the rows of late sorts. Broccoli seeds may be sown to stand the winter, and come up for a late spring crop.

Brussels Sprouts and Winter Greens: Plant out for autumn use.

Endive seeds sown now will come in to supply plants for winter use. Water the beds in dry weather, and tie up to blanch plants advancing to maturity.

Small Salading: Sow cress, mustard and cress, radishes, &c., every seven days, choosing a shady border and sowing in very shallow drills: water daily.

Lettuces: Sow cos and cabbage lettuces in a bed of rich mellow ground; in the first, second, and fourth week, prick out on nursery-beds the plants last sown, and plant out the strongest in the open ground. Dig neatly and rake evenly, and put in the plants 30 cm / 1 ft apart each way: continue to water till rooted.

Spinach, for winter use, sown late in July or early in August, should now be planted out. The prickly-seeded or triangular-leaved spinach is the hardiest for winter use.

Onions may be sown of the Strasburg and Welsh sorts, early this month; the former to transplant in the spring, the latter for use in salads. The general crop will be ready for harvesting.

Carrots should be sown in an open situation, and on light soil, sowing them as soon as the bed will work after digging.

Turnips may still be sown for autumn and winter use, the Early Stone being a good sort: sow immediately after digging. Hoe the crops sown in May and June in dry weather, and thin out till the plants are 18–20 cm / 7–8 in apart.

☞ FRUIT-GARDEN: The chief work to be done in the fruit-garden and orchard is harvesting the fruit and preparation for planting. Let it be understood with regard to the latter, that while something of the future success depends on soil, subsoil, and situation, perfect drainage is the main point. Soil and subsoil may both be corrected by properly-prepared stations, if the drainage be sufficient.

Early Apples and Pears should be gathered a day or two before they are ripe. As they are gathered, lay the pears singly, and the apples in tiers, not more than two deep; and separate carefully all bruised fruit.

Gooseberries: Mat over where necessary, to retard ripening.

Strawberries: Alpines and other late sorts are sow in full bearing. This is also the season for saving seed, if seedlings are desired for planting. Selecting a few of the finest bearers. Take the fruit and rub it on a piece of glass or slate, so that the pulp may dry up, when the seed may be rubbed off and preserved till the season for sowing in the spring. Runners, which are the only means by which plants are obtained true to the sort, should also be encouraged to grow, but not more than are required for new beds.

☞ FLOWERS UNDER GLASS: **Conservatory:** The house can hardly be kept too cool at this season. During this month the climbers on the roof must be gradually thinned and the shading partially withdrawn, to allow the wood of both permanent and temporary occupants of the house to ripen well. To most plants, except balsams and fuchsias in small pots, liquid manure must now be given but sparingly, if at all.

The object now is not rapid growth, but abundance of flowers and matured wood; therefore, even pure water must be given as sparingly as is consistent with good health.

Greenhouse: This house must at once be got ready for its winter occupants. Many of these, such as ericas, epacrises, azaleas, camellias, have probably been in cold pits, or sheltered situations out of doors, for the last four months. In ordinary seasons they will be safe enough there until the end of September. Greenhouses that have no climbers on the roof should all be fumigated with burnt sulphur several days before any plants are brought into them. This is certain death to all animal life, if the outer air is cut off.

Pelargoniums – The grand secret of profuse bloom is early strong autumnal growth. 'I would have given ten times the value of this entire work to have known this fifteen years ago,' writes a very successful gardener. 'I have worked my way to this fact by many failures and dear-bought experience.' The moment pelargoniums begin to fade, they should be placed out of doors in the full sun to ripen their growth. When the wood becomes slightly browned, cut them down to within two, three, or four eyes of the old wood. Leave them in the same position, or place them in a house or pit to break. When the young shoots have advanced from 3–5 cm / 1½–2 in, shake them entirely out of the pots, slightly pruning the roots; pot them in any light soil in as small pots as the roots can be got into; return them to a close house or pit, and the reduction, re-potting, and re-starting are finished. All plants intended to flower next May or June should now be ready for removal to their blooming-pots. Harden-off, cut down, and start afresh, plants for late summer and autumn blooming as soon as they are ripe enough,

Cinerarias – Pot-off suckers from old shoots; prick-off, pot, and shift seedling plants, and push forward the first batch for flowering from November to February. Calceolarias require the same general treatment. Shift chrysanthemums, liberally water at top or late blooms, and stake. Likewise primroses, pansies, &c., shift into larger pots, in order to maintain them in health.

Provide plenty of linums, *Salvia splendens*, oxalis, &c., for winter or spring; likewise hyacinths, narcissus, tulips, &c. &c.; pot the first batch, as early rooting is the only certain foundation for good flowering.

Stephanotis, passion-flowers, jasmines, &c., on the roof, must be carefully trained, cleaned, and regulated. Gloxinias and gesnerias will also make a splendid display here during the month.

☛ FRUIT UNDER GLASS: **Orchard-houses** cannot have too much air. Fruit on the north side of an orchard-house, with a thorough draught through the house, will be a month or six weeks later than the same varieties on a south or west wall.

Vines: Care must be taken, in preserving the foliage of grape-vines, not to allow too many leaves on the lateral shoots. It is the large leaves at the base of the fruiting-branches, near to the main stem, that are of most consequence. The buds at their base will yield next year's crop, and the fuller, rounder, and more plump they become, the larger that crop will be. The great point is to maintain these leaves in health without inducing new growth or causing the buds to break. A comparatively dry atmosphere and cool temperature are the chief things necessary for this.

Ripe grapes must be frequently looked over, and every specked berry be at once removed. If mildew makes its appearance in the late houses, sprinkle the infested parts with dry sulphur. Prevention, however, is much better than cure. Leave air on all vineries, night and day, except where the air is admitted by the roof-windows in wet weather, and use fire in rainy weather to maintain the requisite temperature. 15 C / 60°F is high enough for all ripe grapes; but late Muscats, now ripening, should enjoy a minimum of 21°C / 70°F, rising to 29–32°C / 85°–90°F with sun heat. See that grapes intended to keep till January, February, or March, are well thinned: the Muscat of Alexandria and West's St Peter's are the best adapted for this purpose.

Figs require plenty of water when in full growth: in fact, in this state they may be treated almost like aquatics. The second crop of fruit will now be ripening, and those who wish for a third crop in November and December should have stopped the shoots in the middle of August; but where a very early crop is required, the shoots must not be stopped after this period. Great care must be exercised in ripening the wood, and seeing that the embryo fruit-buds are formed in the axils of the leaves. Water must be gradually withheld, and a dryish atmosphere maintained for this purpose.

OCTOBER

☛ FLOWER-GARDEN AND SHRUBBERIES: Prepare pots and space for potting or boxing the chief stock of geraniums, calceolarias, jasmines, &c. If frost should come, get everything you intend to save under cover directly, and proceed to store them away at leisure. The great business of propagating for next year should now be completed.

🖝 FLORISTS' FLOWERS: Place auriculas, polyanthuses, pinks, carnations, &c., if not already done, in their winter quarters. Gather hollyhock and dahlia seeds if ripe. Pot up pansies for stores and flowering in pots. Plant out seedlings and put in cuttings. Prepare beds of good, light, fibrous, sandy loam for tulips.

🖝 KITCHEN-GARDEN: Towards the end of the month the asparagus-beds may be cleared of their haum, but not till it is yellow and the seed ripe.

Beans: Small crops of Masagan beans may be planted, with a chance of their standing the winter, and coming in May or June. A crop of early peas may be sown at the same time, either on a warm south border or under a fence; the early Hotspur pea being the best for the purpose.

Carrots, Potatoes, and Parsnips are now at maturity. Dig them up and store for the winter, so as to protect them from frost. A little carrot-seed may also be sown on a warm border, with a chance of young carrots in spring.

Cabbages: Transplant cabbages at the end of the month. Kale should now be planted out for spring use, and all the late-planted broccoli cabbages, &c., hoed, to loosen the soil and destroy weeds.

Cauliflowers sown in August will require pricking out, not less than 10 cm / 4 in apart, where some kind of protection can be given: those formerly pricked out and hardened off require planting out under bell-jars till rooted, and then supporting them on props 5–8 cm / 2–3 in thick for air.

Celery: Earth-up as often as it becomes necessary, not only for blanching, but to preserve the plants from frost.

Lettuces for a spring supply may be pricked out under a frame: the hardier kinds will frequently stand the winter on a warm border. Lettuce and endive formerly planted out now require tying up.

🖝 FRUIT-GARDEN: The planting of fruit-trees should be proceeded. The preparations consist in draining, where planting in the open ground is intended, and in digging and manuring the border where the wall-trees are to be planted. The most important point in planting is to keep the collar of the stem at the surface of the soil, removing all diseased or bruised fibres, spreading the roots out carefully, and putting fine soil over them; keeping the young tree firmly in its place by stakes, without lifting or treading upon the roots: the autumn rains will settle the earth about the roots better than any other means. Root-pruning should now be performed either by lifting the trees altogether, or by digging a trench and removing or shortening old roots of over-luxuriant or perpendicular growth.

Apples and Pears are now ripening fast. Gather on fine days, taking care that pears especially are tenderly handled.

Plums: In wet seasons gather the late sorts, with their stalks attached. Quinces, medlars, and all sorts of nuts, are now fit to gather.

Raspberries of the autumn-bearing kind should be bearing a good supply of fruit. If the weather be fine, the canes which have fruited should be cut out, and the young ones left three or four to a stool. Manure, and dig between them.

Strawberries: Remove all runners from the plants, and manure and dig between the rows.

☛ FLOWERS UNDER GLASS: The chief duty of the month is to see that all tender and all hardy plants intended to be bloomed in winter are placed under requisite shelter.

Plants that have stood for months in the free air are most impatient of confinement. Unless the wind is very cutting, or the thermometer is under 4°C / 40°F, the houses should stand open night and day for several weeks after the plants are admitted; otherwise the sudden change of temperature will either cause flower-buds to drop or excite to premature wood growth, perhaps both.

The Conservatory: The temperature should never, unless in the severest weather, be lower than 7°C / 45°F. From 7°C / 45°F as a night temperature to 12°C / 55°F as a day, is a safe range for the next four months, 10°C / 50°F being a safe day medium and 12°C / 55°F the maximum by artificial means. If the sun is genial enough to raise the temperature to 15°C / 60°F a few hours in winter, and air is admitted, it will do no harm. The proper balancing of air at rest and air in motion, and the right proportion of moisture to be suspended in it, constitute the true secret of successful conservatory management. Little or no spraying will be necessary, except over chrysanthemum and camellia leaves for the first week or fortnight after their introduction from out of doors. Chrysanthemums will require a liberal supply of clear manure-water every day in bright weather, and must never be allowed to droop from want of it. Chinese primroses will require the next largest supply of water; then early-flowering epacrises, camellias, &c.

Greenhouse Plants require lower temperatures than the conservatory.

Forcing-pit: Introduce the first batch of rhododendrons, kalmias, Ghent and Indian azaleas, &c.; also some tea and hybrid perpetual roses, and early-flowering and sweet-scented geraniums, white and Anne Boleyn pinks, perpetual carnations, and lily of the valley; also *Salvia gesneraflora*, late gesnerias, and *Euphorbia polygonifolia*. Towards the end of the month, some hyacinths, tulips, &c., potted late in September, should now be pushed forward. Procure, and pot forthwith, hardy bulbs.

Cold Pit and Frames: Give all the air possible, unless it actually freezes; guard against damp and over-crowding. Provide covers against frost; keep the glass clean.

🖙 FRUIT UNDER GLASS: **Vinery:** In all forcing, either of flowers or fruit, let cleanliness be your first care. Let every bit of loose bark that will rub off with your hand be removed; severe barking – scraping it off with knives, &c., is not desirable; for although vines have endogenous stems – that is, increase from the inside, and not from the out, and their bark is consequently not essential to their healthy existence – still it is useful in retaining moisture about their stems; and certainly nature never intended that vines should present the appearance of so many peeled sticks. The varieties best for early forcing are the Dutch White-water, Royal Muscadine, Joslin's St Albans, and Black Hambro.

Prune other vines as soon as the fruit is cut, if the leaves are thoroughly matured, the wood almost as hard as bone, and they are required to start afresh in January. If these conditions are not complied with, defer pruning for another month. Carefully look over grapes twice a week, removing every dead berry and leaf that may have fallen on a bunch.

If late grapes, such as Muscats and West's St Peter's, are not ripe, they must be ripened off with a brisk fire as speedily as possible. When bunches of grapes have to be cut at once, either to make room or to prune the vines, 20–30 cm / 9–12 in of the branch should be cut with them, and the bunches be suspended in a cool dry room: they will often keep better in such positions than on the vine. Grapes may be so kept for three months; Muscats keep best, Hambro and West's St Peter's next, and Frontignacs worst of all. Grapes cut for this purpose must never be laid down. Cut them carefully, leaving all the leaves on the branch; hand a couple of bunches, one at a time, to an assistant, and proceed to hang them up. The slightest bruise by laying them on their side, or allowing two bunches to be carried in one hand, would prevent their keeping.

Figs: These may possibly be ripening their third crop; if so, a brisk temperature of 18–21°C / 65–70°F must be kept up. If the second crop is gathered, and a third is not wanted, reduce the supply of water and the temperature.

Orchard-house: This house, unless used to ripen fruit that has been retarded behind a north wall, must now stand open night and day, or the trees be removed outside, and the house be devoted for three months to storing bedding plants, &c. In all cases secure a season of perfect repose for the trees.

Strawberries: These ought to have completed their growth for the season: the sooner they go to rest the better. To be kept as cool as possible, without being frozen, is all the winter treatment they require.

NOVEMBER

☛ FLOWER-GARDEN AND SHRUBBERIES: Plants to be taken up and potted should be attended to immediately, or at least protected during the nights, for fear of sudden frosts. Pelargoniums, calceolarias, and similar plants, are greatly benefited by being placed in a gentle bottom-heat until the fresh roots break. Now is an excellent time for propagating cuttings of calceolarias and most herbaceous and shrubby plants, if placed in a cold frame. Chinese, Bourbon, and hybrid perpetual roses will now root freely under the same treatment.

When the beds are cleared, trench them up; manure and add new soil where necessary, and plant the bulbs for spring flowering. Hardy annuals sown last month, if large enough, may be transplanted at once to their permanent beds, with pansies, alyssums, phloxes, primulas, and other herbaceous plants.

Now is the best time to collect leaves from lawns and drives, and to stack them in some out-of-the-way place for use. Lawns should be swept when leaves are numerous, as well as to remove worm-casts, &c. An occasional rolling will keep the surface in good order.

The stock of cuttings should be looked over, and additional heat applied, when the roots are not fully formed. To preserve verbenas, petunias, &c. &c., properly through the winter, they must be kept dry to prevent mildew, to which they are very liable in frames during wet weather.

The herbaceous ground will now require a thorough cleaning, cutting down the stalks of plants done blooming, and seeing to the support of the few things still in flower, as the Michaelmas daises, and rake and hoe the borders neatly.

During this month the flower-beds should be enriched with manure or fresh loam, and the soil turned up before frost sets in. All flowering plants standing in pots or frames should be fully exposed to the sun on every favourable occasion, so as to harden their tissues; and all growing plants, like the verbenas, stopped back to secure a bushy habit by-and-by. Most of the verbenas may be kept in a cold pit, dusting a little slaked lime over the soil in the pots or boxes; applying the same treatment to the shrubby calceolarias.

☛ ROSE GARDEN: Planting and transplanting are now the chief employment; if very dry during the month, give a good watering to each plant before the soil is fully filled in. Stocks should also be collected and planted for budding on next season. Prune the old roots close to the stem, cutting all strong shoots close off.

☛ FLORISTS' FLOWERS: At this season of the year the amateur cannot do better than get together those soils, &c., which are indispensable for the proper growth of his favourite flowers. Turf, pared 5 cm / 2 in thick from a loamy pasture, stacked together to decompose, will be the foundation of composts. A large heap of manure should also be secured, not forgetting as large a quantity of fallen leaves as possible. A cartload of sharp river-sand is an indispensable adjunct, and the florist should look out for willow-dust and decayed and rotten sticks. A quantity of excellent food for plants may be scraped out from hedge-bottoms.

Auriculas are in their winter quarters; they require abundant air, and occasional inspection to see that no worms are in the pots; the indications being castings on the surface: if such appear, water them with lime-water.

Carnations and Picotees, layered in previous months, should be potted off, and placed in their winter quarters, protection from dampness being the chief consideration: in fine weather let them be fully exposed. Pinks planted last month must be protected from the wind.

Dahlias should frost appear, no time should be lost in taking them up. Store them away carefully labelled, stalks downwards, secured from damp. Seedlings that have bloomed late, and weak plants, are benefited by being potted and kept dry through the winter.

Hollyhocks: Cut down and propagate from the old stools. Take eye from the flowering stems, but without forcing.

Pansies should be potted off as reserves for filling up vacancies, and for new beds in the early spring.

Polyanthuses in beds will be benefited if the surface of the soil is stirred, and mulched.

Tulips, not yet planted, should be got in without delay, taking care, however, that the soil is not wet: hoop them over, and protect against rainy weather.

☛ KITCHEN-GARDEN: In the kitchen-garden the crops will make little progress for the next four months. Now will be apparent the amount of forethought displayed in summer and autumn cropping. If a fair amount of Brussels sprouts, savoys, and other winter vegetables have been provided, and supposing herbs, salading, and minor crops have been attended to, then, if any ground is unoccupied, lay it up in ridges, having first trenched it or dug it deeply. In digging heavy ground, lay the soil in solid spits as they are cut out with the spade: the spits should not be broken, but laid roughly together, with plenty of openings for the air and frost to act on them. Ground managed in this way is easier to crop in the springtime than that which has lain in ridges. Ground ridged this month, therefore, should be levelled again in February, and another surface exposed and pulverized.

Asparagus, if not already done, should be cut down, and the beds receive a dressing of very rotten dung. If it is intended to make new beds, no better time can be chosen than the present for trenching the ground.

Artichokes: A good mulching of leaves will be of considerable benefit to these in protecting the crowns from the frost. Let the ends of the leaves be exposed, and be killed.

Beans: On light ground and sunny borders, these may be put in without fear of failure. Without such advantages, autumn-sowing of them is not recommended.

Runner Beans: Pull up these, as they will produce nothing more this season; the haulm may be pulled off the sticks; or, if all pulled up together, the leaves will soon drop off and the haulm dry, when all may be chopped up together for firewood, or tied in fagots.

Peas, like beans, may be sown, and with the same proviso as to the nature of the ground. Early sorts are of course best for sowing now.

Celery: It is advisable to give the final earthing-up during this month: it grows much slower now, and must be allowed time to blanch. If dusted with lime to destroy slugs, before earthing, so much the better.

Beet: Get this crop housed or pitted at once; it will not stand frost. Cut off the leaves not too close to the roots, which should lay a couple of days to heal or callow; then stow them where they will not mould or damp till pitted.

Carrots: Treat in a similar manner to beet. It is advisable to get them housed before there is any danger of very severe frost. Young crops to stand the winter should be carefully thinned and hoed between.

Onions: The autumn-sown should be treated in a similar manner.

Leeks ought to be earthed up, if not done before, when they can be taken up as wanted: they will continue to grow in mild weather.

Parsnips are as well left in the ground till wanted.

Potatoes, if any are still left in the ground, should be taken up without delay, and stored.

Turnips should be hoed and kept clean.

Scorzoneras, &c., are best left in the ground till wanted.

Lettuce, if tied up for blanching, should be kept dry, if possible, or they will soon rot. Some may yet be planted out to stand the winter.

Endive: Continue to blanch in succession. If this is done with flower-pots, these, as they are removed, can be placed on others.

Spinach: If this has been properly thinned and kept clean, it will continue to grow, the leaves alone being picked for use. If the plants stand 20–30 cm / 9–12 in apart, it will be all the better.

Brocoli: Such as are coming in now should be watched. Remove dead leaves, and use the hoe between them.

Brussels Sprouts, Kale, and Savoys are best kept free from dead leaves, which in damp weather become unpleasant.

Cabbage may still be planted out for the next summer's crop; but the earlier it is done now the better. Use the hoe freely amongst those planted last month.

Cauliflowers: Stir the soil about those in bell-jars, and keep the windows off unless there is fear of frost.

▸ FRUIT-GARDEN: Let the bulk of kitchen and dessert apples be often looked over to remove decaying fruit. In doing this, be careful not to bruise the others. Clear off the remaining leaves from wall trees; and, now that the greater part of the fruit-tree leaves have fallen, the whole should be cleared off the ground preparatory to pruning and turning up the borders for winter. Figs against walls should have any odd remaining fruit taken off. Thin out superfluous shoots, and pinch out the points of the wood selected for bearing, when the branches should be tied together and protected.

Towards the end of the month is the best time to commence pruning dwarf apples and pears. Shoots to form the skeleton of the tree should next be selected. How far these require shortening will depend on their strength and the shape of the tree. The remaining shoots must be cut back so as to fill up the figure. Before tying or nailing, examine the trees, and if infested with scale or other insects, dress them with soft soap dissolved in hot water, to which add sulphur and quick-lime; mix the ingredients well together, which should be of a consistency to adhere well; dress the branches with this, but not during frost.

Plums: All late sorts should be gathered before the frost sets in, and either wrapped in paper or hung by the stalk. Pruning should follow.

Currants and Gooseberries: Plant and prune both while the weather is favourable. For the production of large gooseberries, short pruning is necessary. Where quantity is required, and the trees are young, shorten the young shoots one-half or two-thirds. If they are of full growth, only take the points off the young shoots, and when the branches are thinned out, cut back to a bud on the upper side of the shoots. When the trees are pruned, lime the ground, and, if necessary, add manure and dig it slightly.

Strawberries: Continue as last month.

☞ FLOWERS UNDER GLASS: Plants under glass, though in the best possible health, would rather sleep just now than grow; and if a dry atmosphere and rather a low temperature is maintained, houses may be kept shut up close for a fortnight or three weeks together; this, however, supposes that the external atmosphere is ungenial; but such is not always the case. Embrace every opportunity of admitting the external air to conservatories and greenhouses when it is of a temperature of 7°C / 45°F.

As the quantity of external air admitted may now be safely reduced to its minimum, so may also be the quantity of water.

In watering thirsty roots, see that the flowers and succulent leaves are kept dry. This is a point of considerable importance at almost any season – at this, it is a question of life or death to many plants. The water given to plants should always be a few degrees higher than the house in which they grow. Never water a plant until it is dry, and then water thoroughly. Regulate the quantity given by the state of growth and drinking capabilities of each plant. A chrysanthemum coming into flower will require three times as much as a camellia in the same state.

Greenhouses must be kept cool, dry, and clean. They may also have more air than the conservatory, and a temperature of 4°C / 40°F will suffice.

Camellias: Where these have a house devoted to them, they require careful management. The buds will just be swelling, and a sudden change of temperature, a scarcity or excess of water, or a cutting draught of cold air, will often cause the tender buds to drop. Maintain a genial growing atmosphere of 7°C / 45°F.

Pelargoniums: The same temperature will suit these during the month. If worms make their appearance in the pots, water three or four times in succession with clear lime-water. Remove every dead leaf; thin out and train the shoots; shift late-flowering plants into their blooming-pots; keep pansies at the warmest end of the house, and give fire-heat enough to drive out damp.

FRUIT UNDER GLASS: One of the chief duties here is fruit-preservation. Houses of ripe fruit must be examined daily, and every specked berry or decayed leaf removed. Brisk fires must also be lighted in the morning, to enable you to give air both at front and back, to agitate the atmosphere and expel damp.

An increase of temperature in the absence of a current of air is most injurious to ripe grapes, and causes them to decay almost sooner than anything; unless during very cold weather, a current of air should always be maintained through vineries containing ripe grapes. If the houses are not waterproof, or plants must be placed in them, the best plan will be to cut and store the grapes as recommended in October.

Another great point in preserving late grapes, is to keep the rain off the borders in which the roots are growing. This is sometimes effected by thatching with straw, and sometimes by the use of boarding or tarpauling.

After taking care of the grapes that we have, let us look after those that are to come. The vinery started last month will now be breaking, and a genial temperature of 10–12°C / 50°–55°F must be maintained. This should not be exceeded during this month: the absence of the sun renders rapid growth dangerous. What is gained in rapidity will be lost in solidity and strength. It the sun should shine, however, it will do much good. See that the heat of the outside borders is kept regular, avoiding all extremes. If maintained by the aid of dung and leaves, frequent examinations and turnings will be necessary to keep it right. Where it is used, it must be partially sweetened before it is introduced, as too much rank ammonia would prove destructive to the tender foliage of the vines.

Vines in pots may be started in a bottom-heat of 11°C / 53°F in hotbeds, unless means are found for giving them bottom-heat over flues, in the houses in which they are to be fruited. After they have fairly started, they can be carefully moved to their fruiting quarters; in many places the first vinery will now be started.

Orchard-houses: If these are either open or unroofed, see that the hungry birds do not destroy your next year's crop. The windows should be placed on these houses, it is a dangerous practice to allow standard trees to be much frozen.

Fig-trees grown under glass should never be frozen. The embryo fruit will most likely be destroyed, and a whole month's or six weeks' forcing lost in consequence. This is a good time to examine the wood thoroughly for scale, &c.

Cold Frames: Plants in these are often treated as if they were more tender than they really are. The object is not so much to stimulate them into growth, as to protect them from such injury from frost and storms as they would be exposed to in the open air. Endive, lettuce, cauliflower, parsley, carrots, radishes, onions, and many more light crops, are not so tender but that they will stand out of doors; but then they keep so much better and fresher under the protection of frames, that it is well worth while to have a few windows devoted to them. They also begin to grow rather earlier in the spring, and continue growing later in the autumn, than they would do if quite exposed; but it should be strictly observed not to keep them in any way close, so as to breed mould. Water should be given rather carefully. Avoid giving enough to chill the roots; a medium state, rather approaching dryness, is better than the least overwetting, especially in frosty weather. Seeds of radishes, lettuce, and small salading may be sown any time during the month, or any time in the winter. They will germinate slowly, but may come in very useful in the spring. In frosty weather the protection of a mat will, in addition to the windows, be sufficient for most of these things.

Garden-frames are very useful for protecting other plants than those above named. Many plants generally accounted hardy when planted in the borders, will, when in pots, require the protection of a frame, or, if planted in a bed of soil placed within the frame, they will flower earlier and stronger.

DECEMBER

☛ FLOWER-GARDEN AND SHRUBBERIES: The pruning of deciduous trees and shrubs should also be proceeded with, unless during severe frost. Most evergreens are best pruned in April. We prune mainly for three leading purposes: to improve the shape, curtail size, and to induce a profusion of bloom or fruitfulness. One of the chief points in the management of shrubberies is so to prune them and cut down the plants as always to preserve a dense thick bottom.

The beds in the flower-garden, now disrobed of their summer beauty, will either be furnished with shrubs, herbaceous plants, annuals, or bulbs, or simply roughed up for the winter. Previous to either being done, it is hoped that they received a liberal top-dressing of manure. If every bit of weed, short grass, and other refuse that comes off the garden annually, is conveyed to a heap, occasionally turned over and saturated with manure water, a most valuable dressing for the beds will be provided. Roses should have something richer: in fact, nothing is too good for them. Roses may still be planted, although the sooner this work is finished the better for next season's bloom. Plant as many on their own roots as possible: they are more durable, more beautiful in this form than any others. All newly-planted roses should be mulched over with 8–10 cm / 3–4 in of light dungy litter on the surface.

☛ FLORISTS' FLOWERS: Dahlia roots stowed away in cellars, &c., must be carefully and frequently examined to see how they are keeping, and any scarce sorts placed in heat towards the end of the month, to insure a large stock before May. Below is a list of some first-rate fancy and show varieties.

Carefully dry dahlia seed preparatory to sowing in pans next month.

Pinks and carnations in beds will require pressing firmly into the earth after severe frost. Examine the beds for slugs in mild weather, and see that the plants are not destroyed by rats and mice.

The same precautions are necessary with pansies in beds. It is best to keep a stock of autumn-struck cuttings of these in pots, to fill up blanks and insure against accidental deaths. The list opposite will be found good.

DAHLIAS

FANCY CLASS

Blondin – yellow-flaked; bright red, large, and good crimson, 120 cm / 4 ft.

Beauty of Etruria – dark buff, spotted, and striped, 120 cm / 4 ft.

Confidence – crimson-striped, 90 cm / 3 ft.

Eclat – purple-tipped, white, 90 cm / 3 ft.

Gem – rosy crimson; small tip, bright yellow, 90 cm / 3 ft.

Miss Jones – maroon, tipped white, 90 cm / 3 ft.

Norah Creina – orange, tipped white, 120 cm / 4 ft.

Pauline – tipped white, 90 cm / 3 ft.

Striata – superb lilac, striped deep purple, 120 cm / 4 ft.

Spotted Gem – buff, striped, and spotted orange 120 cm / 4 ft

Summertide – chocolate tipped white, 120 cm / 4 ft.

SHOW VARIETIES

Andrew Dodds – darkest flower out, 90 cm / 3 ft.

Beauty of Hilperton – purple, large, and fine, 120 cm / 4 ft.

Criterion – rose-lilac: large and fine, 120 cm / 4 ft.

Etonia – buff; fine shape, 120 cm / 4 ft.

Heroine – soft peach, with bronze tip, 120 cm / 4 ft.

Joy – blush-white, tipped with cherry, 90 cm / 3 ft.

Madge Wildfire – bright light scarlet; fine, 120 cm / 4 ft.

Madame Perault – bright pink-carmine, 90 cm / 3 ft.

Mrs Barnes – blush-white; constant, 90 cm / 3 ft.

Mrs Crawford – deep scarlet, 90 cm / 3 ft.

Mrs H. Oakes – primrose-yellow; fine shape, 5 m / 5 ft.

Norfolk Hero – chestnut-brown, 90 cm / 3 ft.

PANSIES

Dr Fleming – shaded purple: large and fine.
General Havelock – deep golden yellow.
Vesta – primrose; self.
Lord Palmerston – rich velvety purple.
Caroline – white ground, heavy purple belting; fine.
Isa Craig – medium belting; clear and fine.
Mrs Hopkins – white ground, purple belting; dense blotch.
British Sailor – gold ground, heavy maroon belting.
Chancellor – gold, with crimson maroon belting.
Richard Headley – yellow ground, shaded bronze, belting fine.
President – rich gold, dark maroon belting.
Wallace – dark belting on a yellow ground; fine.

FANCY CLASS

Anna – yellow, shaded maroon; black blotch.
Belle Esquimoise – white ground, immense dark blotch.
Butterfly – white and blue upper petals, under bronze; striking and beautiful.
Duchesse de Brabant – yellow and bronze; fine.
Etoile du Nord – yellow-bordered, purple-lilac blotches; extra fine.
Iris – light purple, lucid yellow; fine.
Miss E. Bining – white; dark blotches; fine.
Noemi Demay – gold, with immense blotches: fine.
Octave Demay – rich yellow, large blotch; fine.
Princess Alice – creamy white, with dark blotch.
Talma – yellow maroon top: immense blotches.
Zuuave – light yellow blush: purple belt.

Tulips: If planted early last month, some of them may be peeping through the soil: if so, they must be protected by having a slight pyramid of sandy peat-earth or leaf-mould placed over them. During very frosty weather the beds or rows must be covered with mats, &c., as nothing injures these bulbs more than severe frosts on their crowns just as they are coming through the ground. The soil for these bulbs should be trenched from 60–76 cm / 24–30 in deep, mixed with a liberal dressing of well-rotted manure. It is also a good plan to place a layer of manure about 15 cm / 6 in from the surface, so that it may be readily and speedily available for the roots. The bulbs should be planted 15 cm / 6 in square and

TULIPS

SINGLE TULIPS

Bride of Haarlem – white striped, crimson.

Canary-bird – pure yellow.

Couronne Pourpre – dark wall-flower.

Cramoise Royale – white, with rosy-violet crimson.

Dorothea Blanche – white, striped with cerise.

Due de Brabant – yellow, striped and feathered crimson.

Duchesse de Parme – bronze-crimson, bordered yellow.

Globe de Regant – white, striped with violet.

Grootmaester von Maltha – white-striped rose.

La Belle Alliance – brilliant scarlet.

Pax alba – pure white; fine.

Pottebakker – white.

—red, striped yellow.

—yellow.

Royal Standard – white, striped bright red.

Silver Standard – white, striped with scarlet.

Vermilion – brilliant vermilion-scarlet.

Violet Hative – purplish violet.

White and Red bordered – white feathered.

White Swan – pure white; very fine.

DOUBLE TULIPS

Blue Flag – purplish violet.

Blanc Borde Pourpre – violet, purple-bordered; white.

Conqueror – pure, white, feathered with violet crimson.

Duke of York – bronze-crimson; margined lines.

Gloria Solis – crimson, striped golden yellow.

La Candeur – pure white.

Mariage de ma Fille – crimson, and white striped.

Over-winner – violet and white striped.

Paeony Gold – golden yellow; feathered crimson.

Purple Crown – velvety crimson.

Tournesol – scarlet and yellow.

Yellow Rose – golden yellow.

PARROT TULIPS

Coffee colour.

Constantinople red.

Margraff – striped, red and yellow.

Monster Rouge – crimson.

Perfecta – scarlet and gold.

Fern – brilliant scarlet.

…and Monstrosa, which is monstrously beautiful.

10 cm / 4 in deep, and any period from the middle of October to the middle of December will do for planting them.

Show, or late-flowering tulips, are divided into three classes – bizarres, which have yellow grounds, feathered or striped with crimson, purple, or white; byblomens, white ground, flaked or striped with black, lilac, or purple; and roses that have white grounds, feathered or striped with crimson, pink, or scarlet. Soon after tulips have finished flowering, their leaves will ripen and die off. They should be immediately taken up with all the soil that will adhere to the bulb, slightly dried, and put away in drawers or paper bags, each sort by itself. During the summer they should be frequently looked over to see that they are not decaying. On the 1st October rub off all the offsets, plant these by themselves, and prepare for planting the entire stock as already directed.

☛ KITCHEN-GARDEN: The experienced gardener knows the importance of winter operations. Respecting crops, individually, little can be done; but collectively, some attention should be given to the various stores of seeds and vegetables; the latter should be looked over occasionally, turned, sorted, and cleaned; kept moist without being damp, cool without frost, and where there is a free circulation of air. As to seeds, it is well to have them ready for sowing; that is, thoroughly dried and rubbed out, every particle of husk and light seed blown out, and carefully papered and labelled. Also see to the tools or implements, and ascertain that they are in good condition; replace or repair any that are broken. Another thing to attend to, is proper composts and manures. These may be collected on a spare or vacant piece of ground in the kitchen-garden, where there will be plenty of room to turn them over and mix, and where all kinds of woody refuse can be collected and charred and mixed with them. In frosty weather, when the ground is hard, these should be wheeled on to vacant ground. Again, much time is saved in the spring and summer by making a general pruning and trimming of trees.

Rhubarb: Place a bell-jar over a bunch of crowns; see that enough is covered: then, having previously prepared and shaken out the dung, and got it into a condition to maintain a moderate heat, cover the pots to a thickness of about 90 cm / 3 ft from the ground: too great a body of dung is apt to heat too violently and spoil the crowns; and none but the earliest sorts should be forced.

Celery: Cover with litter in frosty weather.

Parsnips and other crops that remain in the ground ought also to be covered with litter or leaves.

Endive: Blanch with pots, and cover with litter; and a good supply may be kept up the whole winter without having recourse to frames, the litter helping to blanch it before the pots are put on; but a dusting of lime should be given occasionally to destroy slugs, which are very fond of endive.

Broccoli, &c: It will now be seen what advantage there is in giving the various sorts of brassicas plenty of space. Those planted among other crops are shanky, and more exposed to the frost, while those planted open, are short, firm, and stocky, and far more likely to stand severe frost.

This is the best time to make any general alterations. Where old bushes are to be grubbed up, and the ground prepared for cropping, or where young bushes are to be planted, also where drainage is necessary, now is a good time to do it before the winter rains make a swamp of the garden. Carefully remove any accumulation of rubbish which is likely to harbour vermin.

FRUIT-GARDEN: **Standard Apples and Pears** should receive their final autumn pruning and thinning out, chiefly of the interior branches, so as to admit of a free current of air; badly-placed shoots should be removed. Trees planted against a wall for horizontal training, do best when the shoots are tied down.

FLOWERS UNDER GLASS: Climbers on roofs and pillars may also have their final pruning, cleaning, and tying; every dead leaf and every particle of dirt removed. The interest of this house is often much increased at this season by introducing some pots of Christmas roses, hyacinths, narcissuses, &c., from the forcing-pit. The edges of the beds, shelves, and vases may also be decorated with variegated and plain holly; and pillars from which fuchsias or other climbers have been removed, be wreathed in the same manner.

These, with occasional spraying, will keep fresh for six weeks, and very much increase the interest of the house. The chrysanthemums will continue flowering during the month, and camellias be coming on to supply their place. *Rhododendron arboreum*, grown for several years under glass, will also flower in the conservatory at this season without any forcing.

Next to rhododendrons, and even superior to them in usefulness, are camellias. This is the month when these are especially useful. By inducing early growth and early maturity, they will flower from habit in December as well as, if not better than, in any other month. The same may be said of Indian azaleas, of winter heaths and epacrises.

Where a temperature of 7°C / 45°F is maintained, grow the various sorts of *Epiphyllum truncatum*. There are now several varieties of this charming winter-flowering plant grown as dwarfs in suspended baskets, or as tall plants, umbrella fashion. It will flower for six weeks or two months in a warm conservatory. Potted in a rough mixture of peat, leaf-mould, loam, rubble, old plaster, and charcoal, and kept in a temperature of 15°C / 60°F, its progress is rapid.

During the summer and autumn months, the plants should be fully exposed to the sun in an airy house. Place them in a temperature of 12°C / 55°F towards the middle of October, and now every leaf will terminate in one, two, or three beautiful flowers.

Poinsettia should now be in flower. Few plants are more easily propagated or grown. They can be had in flower from October to March.

Greenhouses: Preserve a minimum temperature of 4°C / 40°F; give as much air as possible; see that the stock is kept perfectly clean; put on a fire on dull mornings to expel damp; remove plants to the conservatory as they come in flower and keep everything in a quiet semi-dormant state until the new year awakens them.

Pelargoniums: Early varieties for cut flowers may be forced into bloom. The latest flowering specimens may receive their final shift, and all will require careful training, a genial temperature of 7°C / 45°F, and great skill in watering and ventilating. Fancy varieties often show a disposition to bloom prematurely. These early flowers must be perseveringly removed, to throw the strength into the shoots, for a perfect inflorescence at the proper season.

Cinerarias: The earliest of these will now be in flower, and few plants are more effective for decorative purposes.

Cold pits and Frames: Water and cover with care; give all the air possible in mild weather. During severe weather these may remain hermetically sealed for a week at a temperature of 1–4°C / 35°–40°F. After such a long nap, unwrap cautiously, and shade for a few days from the sun's rays.

Forcing pit: Keep up a growing temperature of 12–15°C / 55°–60°F. Introduce fresh batches of shrubs, roses, bulbs, and everything that will flower early, to supply the place of those draughted off for other service.

FRUIT UNDER GLASS: The vines are now showing branches. Bring artificial heat to your aid, and keep a night temperature of 15°C / 60°F and a day one of 21°C / 70°F; admit every possible ray of light: keep the leaves within 20 cm / 9 in of the glass, and create a midsummer climate in December. Examine frequently the state of the borders, and keep the roots as warm as the tops. Stop the shoots a joint beyond the branches. Where a succession of grapes is wanted, start another vinery; proceed as directed in November.

Continue to look over and preserve late grapes, and maintain for these a cool and equable temperature of 4–10°C / 40°–50°F. If a gentle current of air can be kept up through the houses by night and by day, the fruit will keep all the better. Old vines may also be taken up where the borders are bad, the roots carefully preserved, a new border made and skilfully planted, and half a crop

taken the first season. Young vines may be planted in a dormant state or first started in pots, and then put in the border in June or July. The great point in planting at any season is carefully to surround the roots, sprinkle leaf-mould over them, and keep them within 15 cm / 6 in of the surface. A mulching of dung or some litter will be necessary to prevent them being dried up; and if the vine is in full growth when planted, the top must be shaded a few days until the roots have laid hold of the soil; then let the top run as far as it chooses. Leave laterals and all on. The more growth for the next four months the better, because the larger the top the greater the number of healthy roots.

Figs: Lee's Perpetual fig is the best sort grown; the white Ischia and Marsella are perhaps a little better flavoured; but they are small.

Strawberries: The first batch of strawberries should now be introduced. Cuthill's Black Prince the best for the early season, and if they can have a little bottom heat, so much the better. Plants in smaller pots do best for early work, the cramping inducing fruitfulness.

▰ HOT-BED AND FRAME CULTIVATION: Little can be added to what has been already said. Let the weather be the principal guide as to giving air, &c.; be careful that the frames are ventilated without causing draught, which might injure the plants considerably. See that the heat is maintained, and cover with mats at night; but do not shorten the days more than they are. The mats should be taken off as soon as it is light in the morning, and not put on till it is getting dark at night, so that the plants may have all the daylight they can get.

3

GARDEN TYPES

From gardens adapted to city living and small spaces, to restoring old gardens and creating an orchard or vegetable garden, this chapter gives suggestions for planting schemes and advice on how to make the most of your available space.

ALLOTMENTS

A VISIT to your local library or a telephone call to the local authority or council is the first step to finding an allotment. The extent of each allotment will usually measure about 9 x 6 m / 30 x 20 ft.

Dwarf trees and bush fruit should be considered admissible; but no high trees should be allowed as they may do harm to a neighbouring allotment. Special permission is required to erect a shed or greenhouse. Ordinary garden-frames can be used.

The following rotation of crops is very simple, and has been strongly recommended. Make three equal divisions, and crop as follows:

First division

• Plant, first week in March, rows of potatoes, 60 cm / 2 ft between each row; sets to be 30 cm / 1 ft apart in planting. Sorts: York Regents, Flukes, and Fortyfold, or a portion of each. An alley of 30 cm / 1 ft between this and the next division.

☛ NOTE Winter and spring broccoli, and winter cabbage and spinach: take this division directly the potatoes are off.

Second division

• Plant, middle of March, 2 rows of Windsor beans.
• Early in March, 4 rows of hollow-crowned parsnips.
• End of February, 4 rows of Altringham carrots, and 6 rows of onions, globe or James's keeping.
• End of March, 1 row of Windsor beans.
• Early in May, 4 rows of turnips, and 2 rows of mangold wurzel.
• First week in May, 1 row of scarlet runners, with a 30-cm / 1-ft alley between each.

☛ NOTE Root crop: this division is to be trenched for the main crop of potatoes next year directly the roots are off.

Third division

• Plant, last week in February, 2 rows of ash-leaved kidney potatoes and 3 rows of matchless cabbage, or York cabbage.
• Early in March, 1 row of marrowfat peas and 3 rows of ash-leaved kidneys (Cape broccoli after).

- Last week in February, 6 rows of ash-leaved kidneys (celery after); 1 row of early long-pod beans, and 1 row of early peas (celery after).
- End of March, 1 row of cauliflowers (stone turnips after).
- Plant, as early as possible, 2 rows of lettuce (autumn cabbage after), with a 30-cm / 1-ft alley between each.

☞ NOTE Mixed or early crop: this division is to be occupied with flying crops, such as turnips and lettuces, &c., in the autumn, and to be sown with the usual root crops next spring.

CITY GARDENS

IT SHOULD be observed that turf grows well under the influence of smoke, that trellis-work will hide any unsightly object, and the large quick-growing Russian ivy will soon cover a wall; a light verandah, also, at the drawing-room windows may be made available for creepers. The common nasturtium will do well, and so will the different varieties *tropaeolum*, also *canariensis*; but care must be taken that they do not suffer from drought, for drought in a smoky atmosphere is far more injurious to plants than it is where the air is clear and pure.

The list on page 78 will be found to contain most of the trees, shrubs, herbaceous plants and annuals at present introduced into this country, which are not so susceptible of the injurious influences of a vitiated atmosphere as many others, and which are consequently suitable for our cities and large towns. Of trees, the plane, which sheds its bark annually, and the poplar in its different varieties, are decidedly the best where the air is most charged with soot.

It must be remembered that deep digging and plentiful manuring are not less essential in the sooty atmosphere of our crowded towns. Every year the collected surface-soot should be buried by trenching about 18 inches [45 cm] deep, and a good dressing of manure be worked in to renovate the soil.

CONSERVATORIES

THIS structure may well be termed a winter garden, for such is its most useful purpose. In houses of smaller dimensions it is the storehouse for display-ing the flowers as they are forced into bloom in the greenhouse or frames, as well as for growing certain climbing and creeping plants festooned and trained under its roof and over its walls.

PLANTS FOR CITY GARDENS

Acer pseudoplatanus
— *A. rubrum*
Achillea millefolium
Acuba japonica
Aesculus
    hippocastanum
Ageratum
Alyssum
Ampelopsis hederacea
Amygdalus communis
Antirrhinum
Aristotelia macqui
Artemisia abrotanum
Aster – varieties
Betula alba
Bignonia radicans
Calceolarias
Carnations
Chronanthes virgineum
Chrysanthemums –
    varieties
Clematis flamula
— *C. montana*
— *C. vitalba*
Cornus mascula
— *C. sanguinea*
Crataegus oxyeantha
    and varieties
Crocus
Cytisus laburnum
— *C. alpinus*
— *C. scoparis*
Dahlia
Daisies
Daphne mezereum
Dracocephalum
Enonymus europaeus
Epilobium
    angustifolium
    (willow-herb)
Fagus sylvatica
Foxglove

Fraxinus – sorts
Genista purgans
German stocks
Gladiolus
Hardy phloxes
Heartsease
Hedera helix
    and varieties
Helleborus niger
    (Christmas rose)
Hollyhocks
Hypericum calycinum
Hypericum elatum
— *H. androsaemum*
Ilex aquifolium
    and varieties
Iris germanica
Jasminum officinale
Juglans regia
Lavender
Lily of the Valley
Lycium barbarum
Magnolia grandiflora
— *M. conspicua*
Mahonia aquifolium
Mespilus germanica
Mignonette
Mimulus
Morus nigra
Negundo fraxinifolium
Philadelphus
    grandiflorus
Phillyrea – sorts
Phlomis fruticosa
Pinks
Polyanthus
Populus fastigiata
— *P. nigra*
Pyrus aucuparia
Rhamnus alaternus
Rhododendron

ponticum
Rhus typhinum
— *R. cotinus*
Robinia pseudoacacia
Rockets
Rubus – varieties
Salix – sorts
Sambucus nigra
Santolina
    chamaecyparissus
Scarlet geraniums
Snowdrop
Sophoria japonica
Spartium junceum
Staphylea trifolia
— *S. pinnata.*
Sunflower
Sweetwilliams
Symphoricarpos
    racemosus
Syringa – varieties
Taxus baccata
— *T. fastigiata*
Thuja occidentalis
— *T. orientalis*
Tulipa
Ulmus – sorts
Verbenas – varieties
Viburnum opulus
Vinca major
Virginian stock
Wallflowers
Wistaria sinensis

Dwarf Roses:
    Maiden's Blush
    Provence
    Rose de Meaux
and most of the
common hardy
annuals

There are some few points which should influence the choice of a site for every kind of plant-structure, the first and foremost being that it is not over-shadowed on the south, east, or west, or exposed trees or houses in any direction. A lean-to house, which, however, is the very worst form, may have any aspect between south and south-south-east; south, inclining a point or two to east, being the best, as it receives the early sun as it gradually rises, without being exposed to its full meridian glare. The span-roofed house would probably be well placed which ranged from north-west to south-south-east also: it would thus receive all the morning sun on one side, while the other would receive the meridian sun slightly oblique, and all the afternoon sun, varying according to the angle of incidence of the roof. This would also be the most favourable aspect for a ridge-and-furrow roof, whether it were supported against a back wall or had a rectangular roof with vertical lights on each side.

As regards its architectural style, the conservatory should, at least, be in harmony with that of the house: in this, as in all other matters, congruity is to be studied.

COTTAGE GARDENS

Taking a medium course, let us describe one of about thirty yards (about 27 metres) each way. Here, as in other cases, economy recommends simplicity of design. Supposing the frontage to be laid out as a flower-garden; let the walks present a curve rather than sharp angles; let the beds be circular or oval rather than pointed; and let the space for flowers be as open as possible. Nothing is more beautiful than a smooth green plat of grass, on which one or two of the smaller ornamental trees may be planted – such trees as the silver birch, copper beech, or some sort of conifer, a pine, cypress – some of the araucarias, now easily procurable, or a deodara. Let the edgings be of box, if obtainable – nothing is so handsome; otherwise thrift, white alyssum, or some of the ornamental grasses.

Ornamental tiles are both cheap and elegant. The path should be of gravel, if possible, if paved, let it be with pebbles, or of coarse sand. Let the main parts of the ground be devoted to kitchen crops. If drainage is necessary, ascertain where the water can be carried to. Open a trench along the whole breadth of the plat, either into the intended outlet or into a well sunk in the ground, and into this trench lead the several earthenware pipes from the higher part of the ground from one end of the garden to the outlet, gradually sloping towards the lower trench. This done, let one main walk pass through the centre, of about 150 cm / 5 ft wide, or more if it is to be made a drying-ground. At the end of this main walk an arbour may be formed of *Clematis Vitalba*, of the white jasmine, or yellow winter-flowering jasmine. On each side of the arbour flowers or herbs may be grown. On the sunny sides of the house let a vine be planted. The main part of the ground should be devoted to kitchen crops, following out a system of rotation-cropping, and using also a little caution in the application of manures: green, unprepared, or rank-smelling dung, breeds no end of insects, which become ruinous to crops. The following is a list of vegetables and fruit trees suitable for a cottage garden:

VEGETABLES SUITABLE FOR COTTAGE GARDENS

Beans: Mazagan – early, Sword Longpod – main crop.

Broccoli: Early Cape, Purple Sprouting, Walcheren, or Cauliflower.

Cabbage: Enfield Market – main crop, Early York, East Ham, Colewort.

Carrot: Early Horn, Intermediate.

Celery: Coles's Crystal – white, Coles's Crystal – red.

Cucumber: Southgate – for outdoors.

Endive: Green Curled.

Kale: Green Curled, Brown, or Ragged Jack.

Lettuce: Hammersmith – for winter, Black-seeded Brown Cos – all year.

Onion: Brown Spanish, Silver Globe.

Parsley: Best Curled.

Peas: *Early:* Emperor, Ringwood, Tom Thumb and Bishop's Long Pod – dwarf. *Medium:* Auvergne, Blue Imperial, Scimitar. *Late:* Knight's Dwarf Marrow, Knight's Tall Marrow.

Potatoes: Improved Ash-leaved Kidney, Kirk's Kidney.

Radishes: Scarlet Short-Top, Turnip, red and white.

Savoy: Brussels Sprouts.

Spinach: Round – for summer, Flanders – for winter.

Turnip: Early Dutch, Late Stone.

Vegetable marrow: Custard.

FRUIT TREES SUITABLE FOR COTTAGE GARDENS

Apples: *Early:* White Juneating, Red Juneating, Red Quarrenden, Keswick Codlin, Manks Codlin. *Medium:* Hawthornden, Kerry Pippin. *Late:* Blenheim Orange, Fearn's Pippin, Lemon Pippin, Cockle Pippin, Ribston Pippin, King of Pippins, London Pippin, Scarlet Nonpareil, Old Nonpareil.

Cherries: *Early:* May Duke, Archduke. *Medium:* Bigarreau, Kentish, Morello. *Late:* Duke.

Currants: Large Grape – red, Grape – white, Black Naples.

Gooseberries: *Green:* Cock's late Green, Greengage, Favourite. *Red:* Champagne, Warrington, Lancashire Hero. *Yellow:* Amber, Golden Drop, Early Yellow.

Pears: *Early:* Ambrosia, or early Beurre, Beurre Gifford, Jargonel. *Medium:* Beurre Diel, Duchess of Orleans, Marie Louise, Williams's Bon-Chrétien. *Late:* Napoleon, Passe Colmar, Crassane d'Hiver and Catillac – baking.

Plums: *Early:* Goliath, Victoria, Greengage, Rivers's Prolific. *Late:* Purple-gage, Magnum Bonum, Coe's Golden Drop, Damson.

Raspberries: Falstaff.

Strawberries: Keen's Seedling, Sir Harry, Oscar.

Vines (for outdoors): Royal Muscadine, White Sweetwater, Black Cluster.

CUT-FLOWER GARDENS

A FLORIST'S flower-garden is usually planted in formal and rather stiff-looking beds, the flowers in right lines, those of dwarf habit occupying the outsides of the beds, with the taller sorts in the centre. The garden itself should be very near to the dwelling of any one who has charge of it, for no plants require greater attention to grow them properly; they need all the air that can possibly be given to them, while a slight frost coming suddenly on after a warm April day – above all, heavy storms of rain, a hailstorm, or even a boisterous wind – will be destructive to many of them.

Heat is nearly as injurious. They should only meet the morning and evening sun: a shade for an hour before and after noon, during the flowering season, will much prolong their bloom.

A useful bed or stage for the reception of potted flowers may be prepared by laying down about 15 cm / 6 in of coal ashes upon the natural soil, over which a platform should be made by a flooring of square tiles, closely fitting into each other. Over this are to be laid seven rows of bricks, equidistant from each other; and on these, at regulated distances, the pots may be ranged after the operation of potting has been performed in May.

A mixture of flower forms and sizes creates interest. Ensure that you also provide striking foliage. By careful scheduling, the garden can be full of blooms all year. To guarantee abundant blooms, frequent watering, fertilizing and cutting are required. Harvesting should occur first thing in the morning, plunging the stems directly into cold water. Daffodils should be kept apart for a day, as they initially exude a toxic chemical that adversely affects other flowers.

GREENHOUSES

THE greenhouse, however small, then comes in very useful for keeping a supply both for the garden in summer and the window and rooms during winter. A stock of geraniums, verbenas, petunias, lobelias, are struck in the months of July and August, and stored away for planting out the following season. After this is accomplished, a small collection of fuchsias will make the house lively; and as these are very easily cultivated, and may be stowed under the stage of the house during the winter, till the house is emptied in May, nothing is better for the purpose (see box below).

If it is desired merely to maintain a succession of plants in bloom during the year, it is advisable to select plants for the time in which they flower. Thus

---

FUCHSIAS IDEAL FOR GREENHOUSES

The following sorts would give satisfaction:

Dark		
Elegans	Crinoline	Duchess of Lancaster
Catherine Hayes	Big Ben	Fair Oriana
Autocrat	Sir Colin Campbell	Clio
Little Bo-Peep		England's Glory
Orlando	**Light**	Madame Sontag
Excellent	Queen of Hanover	Princess of Prussia
Tristram Shandy	Schiller	Madame Cornelison
	Fairest of the Fair	Mrs Story

The last three have white corollae, with red sepals, and make a pretty variety.

---

half a dozen azaleas, which flower in May; pelargoniums flowering in June; fuchsias in the three following months; then a few chrysanthemums, followed by *Primula sinensis* and heaths. A few dozen of bulbs will present a succession of flowers till May. By this simple process, which is easily managed, a continuous show of flowers can be obtained.

☙ Good plants for a small collection are:

Abutilon striatum. A. venosum
Acacia lophantha, A. armata, A. Rotundifolia, A. Virgata
*Azaleas – Indica alba,*Variegata
Camellias – Old white, Chandlerii, Imbricata, Genista racemosa
Clianthus magnificus
Coronilla pentaphylla
Corraea bicolour
Daphne japonica
Deutzia gracilis
Diosma ambigua, Speciosa, Ericoides
Epacris odorata alba, Hyacinthiflora, Impressa and several other varieties
Erica Bowieana
Helichrysum proliferum
Linum trigynum
Metrosideros floribunda
Myrtus communis tenerifolia
Pimelea Hendersonii, Decussata
Plumbago capensis
Solanum crispum, Capsicastrum
Veronica Lindleyana

☙ A selection from such as these will give satisfaction. A few geraniums might be added; such as:

Alba multiflora
Crimson King
Multiflorum
Viola
also *Primula sinensis* and Cinerarias

Calceolarias of the herbaceous kinds are well worth cultivating, and where grown in a small way, had best be sown in July, covering the seed-pots or pans with a piece of glass, and placing them in the shade. A few bulbous-rooted plants would be found very useful – *Lilium album, punctatum* and *rubrum; Oxalis tubiflora variabilis, Rosea-flava, Ixia aurantica, Lachenalia tricolor; Cyclamen coum, Persicum* and *Europaeum* are all very attractive in their season, giving them a season of dry rest soon after the bloom is over.

A few useful large varieties of chrysanthemums for autumn-flowering might be named:

Plutis
Racine
Alfred Salter
Madame Lebois
Mrs Holborn
Prince Albert
Madame Cameron
Annie Salter, &c.

Useful climbers for a small greenhouse are:

Passiflora caerulea
Ecremocarpus scaber
Hibbertia volubilis
Solanum jasminoides

Maurandia Barclayana might be trained up the back or pillars. It is necessary to make a proper bed or border of earth for these to grow in.

Plant culture is not the only use to which a small greenhouse may be put: the practice is not uncommon to grow fruit in them. For this purpose, small fruit-trees are grown in pots; the roots being confined, they are not liable to run to wood; but keep within bounds for the more certain production of flowers and fruit. Any one who can cultivate flowering-plants may grow fruit-trees in pots; the only points being to keep them well supplied with water while in a growing state, and to ripen the wood well in the autumn.

A long list of fruit-trees suitable for the purpose might be named; but the list below may serve as a guide.

FRUIT TREES FOR GREENHOUSES

APPLES Braddick's Nonpareil, Cellini, Golden Pippin, Orange Pippin, Newtown Pippin.

CHERRIES Bigarreau, Elton, Mayduke, Morello.

PEARS Beaurré, Hardy, Marie-Louise, Bon Chrétien, Winter Nelis.

PLUMS Victoria, Greengage, Purple-gage, Topaz.

HANGING BASKETS

A VERY important feature in window-gardening is the introduction of suspended baskets, usually made of wire, for the purpose of displaying to advantage the beautiful habit of trailing plants. These should be potted in ordinary flowerpots, and surrounded with moss in the basket, the latter being made to hook on to a staple in the ceiling, so that it may be taken away when the plant requires water. When the baskets are of wood, they should be lined with zinc; for wood, as it decays, is sure to breed fungus. One of the most suitable plants for the purpose is *Saxifraga sarmentosa*, which does well under ordinary treatment; it is of variegated foliage and highly ornamental. Another is *Disandra prostrata*, with bright yellow flowers, and pretty foliage like ground ivy. Both these will trail 45 cm / 18 in or more from the basket in very graceful festoons.

In planting a basket, if it is to be filled with ordinary soft-wooded flowering plants, that is geraniums, verbenas, petunias, &c., the soil ought to be two-thirds loam to one of very rotten dung or leaf-mould, and a little sand; if planted with ferns or hard-wooded plants, as *Myoporum parviflorum, Monochaeton ensiferum, Pultenaeas* and the like, the soil should be one half turfy loam and one half peat, using rather more sand than for the freer-growing plants.

If the baskets are made of wire and lined with moss, they are sufficiently drained; if of wood, there should be one or more holes in each to let out surplus moisture. In filling the baskets, put some rough lumpy soil at the bottom, with some broken pieces of potsherd mixed with it.

The best plants for suspending in baskets are fuchsias of a pendulous habit, as Nil desperandum, the Duchess of Lancaster, a splendid white variety, and the Princess of Prussia, a neat-growing plant, very showy, the corolla of the flower being white, and the calyx and tube red.

Next to fuchsias, are ivy-leaved geraniums, petunias, and verbenas, which are of rich and varied colours. *Saxifraga sarmentosa*, of variegated foliage and pretty trailing habit; *Disandra prostrata*, with pretty yellow musk-like flowers. The common moneywort (*Lysimachia nummularia*) does well and is effective; also the trailing snapdragon (*Linaria cymbalaria*), which will soon cover a basket and look very pretty.

Among hard-wooded plants, suitable for suspended baskets may be reckoned *Myoporum parviflorum*, bearing small white flowers in autumn, winter, and spring; *Pultenaea subumbellata*, a neat spreading plant, flowering in spring. There are also one or two acacias, as *A. rotundifolia* and *A. ovata*, which are of a pendulous habit. *Monochaeton ensiferum* is a beautiful winter-flowering plant, but will require tying down at first, and training neatly over the basket. In planting the hard-wooded plants, it should be remembered that though it may be that the softer plants are more easy to cultivate, and thus safer to begin with, these are more permanent, and do not so soon outgrow their room. One of the best ferns for baskets is the common polypody, or *Polypodium vulgare*: this may be planted in nearly all moss, with a small portion of soil. Another excellent fern, and, indeed, one of the handsomest, is *Asplenium flaccidum*. Let this fern be placed in the centre of the basket; it will require nothing more, but will show over the sides and look exceedingly beautiful, being of a bright lively green, and one of the best and handsomest ferns in cultivation. *Pteris serrulata* and *P. rotundifolia* are also good ferns for baskets, and easily grown.

There are also several sorts of British ferns which may be grown in this way, particularly the true British Maidenhair (*Adiantum capillus veneris*), which, spreading at the roots, will soon cover the surface of the basket. Next to this we should place *Asplenium lanceolatum*, then *A. marinum*. Other kinds might do in the same way, but we would not recommend those who are not well skilled in fern-culture to grow more than three or four at first.

HEDGES

HEDGES, if properly managed, undoubtedly constitute the cheapest and most lasting, as well as the most ornamental, of all he artificial divisions of land. The different kinds of thorn certainly embrace all the constituents of a good hedge; they are of easy culture, quick growth, and capable of being trained in any direction; they branch out and thicken under pruning, and are not over particular as to soil; but there are many other plants far more ornamental which will fulfil all these conditions equally well. Few things have a better appearance than a well-kept holly hedge, although they are not advised if children use the garden. The best variety for the purpose is *Ilex aquifolium*, the common holly. In forming a holly hedge, the ground should be prepared by trenching, and, if the soil be poor and sandy, it will be well to let it have a dressing of manure. The best plants are those of three years' growth, which have had one shift from the seed-bed. They should be taken up carefully with as much soil on the roots as possible, and planted soon after midsummer, if possible, during the rains of July. A broad trench should be dug, copiously watered, and the plants placed in it singly, with their roots well spread out. The next season, if they be well rooted, the young plants may be moderately pruned with the knife, after which they will branch out and form themselves into a good hedge.

The box and the privet should be kept out of the way of cattle. They bear clipping almost better than anything else, and are very neat and compact. The privet mixes well with the thorn, where greater strength is required than can be had by using privet alone.

Those persons who have travelled in Holland and Belgium have no doubt noticed the neat manner in which small enclosures are separated from one another. The hedges are trained along stakes and rods placed for the purpose, and to these, the plants of which they are composed are tied. In this way every slender branch is laid in, and, as they are made to cross each other frequently, a regular network is formed. It has often occurred to us that in this way many of our ornamental shrubs might be trained to form hedges; the *Pyrus japonica*, for instance, which is close, quick-growing, and bears a most beautiful flower.

The cotoneaster, again, may be employed for the same purpose and in the same way. Cuttings of cotoneaster taken in August and put into the shade, will be rooted well enough for planting out next spring. This hedge will require, at first, a good deal of attention in training and entwining the branches; but when established, it may be clipped and kept in shape.

The different veronicas also make firm hedges, and are very handsome when in flower. Strong bushes may be planted 90 cm / 3 ft apart and trained to stretched wires, which, in this case, are better than stakes. We have seen in Guernsey the purple hydrangea forming a hedge to a grass field, and nothing could be more beautiful. Both this and the veronica, however, are not sufficiently hardy to admit of their being used except in the extreme south. Such, however, is not the case with the aucuba, which is so hardy that we imagine it might be used in most parts of England.

HERB GARDENS

THE *olitory*, or herb garden, is a part of horticulture somewhat neglected, and yet all the sweet herbs are pretty, and a strip of ground halfway between the kitchen and the flower-garden would keep them more immediately under our attention. This would probably recover, for our soups and salads, some of the neglected tarragons, French sorrel, purslain, chervil, dill and clary. Laid out after a simple geometric design, the herb-garden might be rather ornamental than otherwise. Most of the herbs are propagated by slips in the autumn. Basil, burnet, and other herbs require to be sown early in spring, on slight hotbeds of about 60 cm / 2 ft in depth; but many cultivators leave them later, and sow in the open ground. Thyme, marjoram, savory and hyssop, chervil, and coriander, may be sown in dry mild weather, to be transplanted afterwards. Sow in shallow drills about 1 cm / ½ inch deep and 20 cm / 8 in apart, and cover evenly with the soil. Mint may be propagated by separating the roots, and planting them in drills drawn with a hoe 15 cm / 6 in asunder, covering them with 2.5 cm / 1 in of earth, and raking smooth. They will quickly take root, and grow freely for use in the summer. This method may be applied to the several sorts of spearmint, peppermint, and orange mint.

The whole family of borage, burnet, clary, marigolds, dill, fennel, sorrel, and angelica, may be sown about the middle of March, when the weather is open. Sow them moderately thin in drills or beds (each sort separate), in good light soil; if in drills, 15 cm / 6 in apart; some of the plants may remain where planted, after a thinning for early use; others may be planted out in the summer.

LAWNS

D URING spring, and the early summer months, all garden turf and lawns will require very great attention. If they are to look well for the rest of the year (and we must remember that the general appearance of the whole garden depends much upon the state of the turf), it is at such times that the broom and the roll must be kept in constant use. If the grass, from the nature of the soil, is inclined to grow rank and coarse, it will be much improved by a good dressing of sand all over it; if, on the other hand, it has a tendency to scald and burn up, it will receive great benefit from a sprinkling of good guano or bone-dust just before a shower of rain.

Before regular mowing commences, it will be well to go over all grass, carefully removing rank and unsightly weeds, daisies, dandelions, the little buttercup, &c. Wherever the turf is mossy, it is a very good plan to rake it well with a sharp five-toothed rake; but it must be borne in mind, that under-draining is the only effectual cure for moss. Daisies should never be allowed to flower: a good daisy-rake, with a little trouble, will remove all flowers as they come out; but the only plan to clear a lawn effectually of these disagreeable weeds is to take them out with the daisy-fork wherever they are found. This clever little tool, which consists of a wooden shaft of any length, shod with a cleft iron prong, having a half-round of iron at the back to act as a fulcrum, may be used by anyone; and in process of time the most hopeless pieces of grass may be cleared by it.

ORCHARDS

THE grafting of most of our fruit trees upon stocks being calculated to produce short, stunted growth, has considerably modified the practice of hardy-fruit culture; and unless the demand for fruit is very great, we would not generally recommend the formation of orchards. Should an orchard be deemed necessary, the spot selected should be entirely sheltered from the north and north-east, and it should have a gentle inclination, and full exposure to the south. The best soil is a good loam, 120 cm / 4 ft in depth, resting upon chalk, thoroughly drained by tiles inserted 15 cm / 6 in beneath the chalk-level, the tiles being covered over to that depth with broken stones. The permanent trees, which, if it is intended to lay the orchard down in grass, must be standards and half-standards, with 120–170 cm / 4–5 ft of clear stem, should be planted in rows, 9–12 m / 30–40 ft apart, and in what is termed the quincunx style, thus:

The north or coldest side of the orchard should be planted with walnuts, cherries, medlars, chestnuts, &c., to provide shelter for the others. These might be succeeded by the hardiest plums and apples, to be followed by the tender pears on the south or warmest side. If a gradation of height were also followed, the shelter provided would be more efficient, and the general effect more pleasing. Filberts and mulberries may also be introduced. The rows should run east and west.

All young trees should be carefully staked and protected from the wind, and, if a dry spring should succeed the autumn of their planting, they will require to be watered, or, what is better, to have manure laid round their roots and be watered through it.

APPLES

Nineteen Orchard Apples

K = kitchen purposes; D = dessert

Bedfordshire Foundling: K. Very large, pale green when ripe; flesh yellowish, acid. November to April. A handsome kitchen apple, but rather fitful in productiveness.
Bess Pool: K., D. Large, conical, handsome, yellow suffused with red next the sun; flesh white, sugary, vinous. Good from November to May. Rarely fails to give a good crop, and fit for any purpose.
Blenheim Orange: K., D. Very large, ovate, yellowish, red next the sun; flesh yellow, sugary. November to June.

Court of Wick: D. Medium size, very handsome, greenish-yellow, orange, and russety; juicy, high-flavoured.

Dumelow Seedling: K. Large, round, yellow and light red; flesh yellow, first-rate. November to March. Also known as Wellington and Normanton Wonder.

Devonshire Quarrenden: D. This is the famous 'sack apple' of the western counties. Medium size, deep crimson; flesh greenish-white, juicy, subacid. August.

Dutch Codlin: K. Very large, conical, and ribbed, greenish-yellow, with light tinge of orange; flesh white and firm. A first-rate kitchen apple, always bears, and will keep till Christmas.

Fearn's Pippin: D., K. Full medium size, round, and handsome, greenish-yellow, russety, and bright red; flesh greenish-white, sweet, and rich-flavoured. November to March.

French Crab: K., D. Large, dark green, brownish next the sun; flesh green, firm, subacid. Bears immensely, and will keep any reasonable length of time.

Gooseberry Pippin: K. Large, roundish, bright green; flesh greenish, tender, gooseberry flavour, which it retains till May or June, and it may be kept to the following August.

Hawthornden: K. Large, ovate, yellowish-green, reddish blush next the sun; flesh white, juicy, almost good enough for dessert. The new Hawthornden is more robust, and produces a finer fruit, but is scarcely so prolific as the old. If but one apple-tree could be planted in the garden, we would have the Old Hawthornden in preference to any other. September to February.

Hanwell Souring: K. Medium size, greenish-yellow, red blush; flesh firm, crisp, acid. No orchard should be without it. November to April.

Kerry Pippin: D. Small, pale yellow streaked with red; flesh yellow, firm, juicy, and sweet. First-rate in every respect. September to November.

Nonpareil, Old: D. Small, greenish-yellow, one of the hardiest; pale russet and brownish-red; flesh tender, juicy, rich. January to May.

Norfolk Bearer: K. Large, green, yellowish, and crimson; flesh tender, brisk flavour. A prodigious bearer. December to February.

Northern Greening: K. Medium, dull green, brownish-red; flesh greenish, subacid. First-rate. November to May.

Sturmer Pippin: D. Medium, yellowish-green and brownish-red; flesh yellow, firm, sugary, and rich. January to June.

Winter Pearmain: K., D. Large, conical, handsome greenish-yellow and deep red; flesh juicy, sweet, and brisk-flavoured. October to April.

Yorkshire Greening: K. Large, roundish, irregular, dark green striped with dull red; pleasantly acid. October to February.

For very exposed situations on the east coast and north of the island the following varieties are recommended:

DESSERT: Devonshire Quarrenden, Early Julien, Kerry Pippin, Nonesuch, Summer Strawberry, Franklin's Golden Pippin.

KITCHEN: Carlisle Codlin, Hawthornden, Keswick Codlin, London Pippin, Manx Codlin, French Crab, Tower of Glammis, Yorkshire Greening, Winter Colman.

PEARS

Bergamotte Esperen: Medium, late, melting. Forms a handsome prolific pyramid or bush; but in wet or cold climates it requires a wall. March to May.

Beurré d'Aremberg: Medium, delicious, melting; forms a handsome prolific pyramid. December and January.

Beurré d'Amanlis: Very large, melting; one of the best autumn pears, not particular as to soil. End of September.

Beurré Rance: Large, late, melting, insipid from a wall; but on the quince, in the open grounds, its flavour is quite exquisite. Requires double working, and forms a better bush than a pyramid. March to May.

Beurré Easter: Large, melting, perfumed, insipid from a wall; best on the quince, and forms a beautiful bush. January to May.

Bon Chrétien (Williams's): Large, perfumed, melting; should be gathered before it is ripe. September.

Broom Park (Knight's): Medium size, melting pear; partakes of the flavour of the melon and pineapple; on the quince must be double-worked; a prolific bush. January.

Chaumontel: Large, well-known, melting. December. This is the pear which grows so fine in Jersey and Guernsey.

Duchesse d'Angoulême: Very large and handsome, insipid from a wall; forms a fine pyramid. November.

Forelle or **Trout Pear:** Medium; a very handsome speckled pear, melting and good. Forms a prolific bush, or a pyramid of moderate growth. December.

Josephine de Malines: Medium size, delicious melting pear, aromatic. On the hawthorn it forms a spreading, fruitful tree; succeeds well on the quince, but does not form a handsome pyramid; as a bush or espalier it is very prolific. February to May.

Louise Bonne of Jersey: Large. It is worthy of the orchard-house. October.

Peach or **Poire Pêche:** Medium, early, melting, slight aroma, very juicy; a prolific bush. September.

Seckle: Small, highly-flavoured, melting; bears profusely as a pyramid on the pear. October.

Winter Nelis: Small, roundish, buttery and melting, rich and aromatic; an abundant bearer, and a beautiful bush. November to February.

The following pears are also suited to orchards and well worth growing:

Aston Town, Autumn Bergamot, Beurré de Capiaumont, Bishop's Thumb, Grosse Calebasse, Hacon's Incomparable, Napoleon, Swan's Egg, Lusette de Bavay.

There are several sorts of baking and stewing pears, but the best are:

Catillac, Vicar of Winkfield, Summer Compote, and Uvedale's St Germain for a wall.

The following pears are best adapted for a cold climate:

Alexandre Lambré, Gansel's late Bergamot, Beurré d'Amanlis, Williams's Bon Chrétien, Calebasse d'Ete, Colmar d'Ete, Citron des Carmes, Hessle, Jargonelle, Louise Bonne of Jersey, and Thompson's Pear.

CHERRIES AND PLUMS

As we have spoken of cherries and plums as orchard fruit, it may be well to give a small list of each for the guidance of those who are intending to plant an orchard. The earliest cherries are the Black Tartarian, the Early Purple Guigne, and the Early May. These are succeeded by the May Duke, the Bigarreau, the Elton, and Black Eagle; the Late Duke is the latest of sweet cherries. For cooking purposes, there is the Kentish; and for brandy, the Morello; for drying, the Belle de Choisy, the Flemish, and the Kentish. Waterloo is a good cherry, ripening in July, so are Werder's Black Heart, Adams's Crown, and Archduke.

Of plums the varieties are infinite. Among the best may be classed:

Cloth of Gold, Coe's Golden Drop, Denniston's Superb, Denyer's Victoria, Rivers's Early Favourite, Old Greengage, Goliath, Guthrie's Late Red and Guthrie's Late Green, Jefferson's Yellow, Kirke's Dark Purple, Magnum Bonum, Mitchelson's Large Black, Early Black Orleans, Purple Orleans, Oullen's Goldengage, Reine Claude de Bavy, Rivers's Early Prolific, Sharp's Emperor, Violette Hâtive, Walshington, Winesour, and Woolston's Blackgage.

For filberts, see page 137.

RESTORING OLD GARDENS

IT NOT infrequently happens in gardens once famed for the luxuriance of their plants on bog or peat borders, that a period of decay arrives. This is evidence that renovation is required, and should be forthwith attended to. A top-dressing of the soil, with a mixture of well-rotted manure from the cow-yard, may do some good; but if evidences of decay are very striking, it will be far better to take up all the plants and dig in a good change of soil. Those rhododendrons which have run too far from home, and bear leaves only at the extremities of long sticky branches, must be cut down. The season of the year best suited for pruning rhododendrons is immediately after the flowering season, that they may have all their growing period of the year before them to make fresh shoots. In cases, however, where plants come up very easily, having no hold in the ground, and with a hard ball of earth about the roots, which appears disinclined to blend with the surrounding soil, it is frequently of great advantage to loosen this ball and open the roots a little before the plants are placed in their fresh bed.

OLD APPLE-TREES

Open a deep and wide trench all round them, remove the soil, and fill in with fresh rich loam with a good top-dressing of well-rotted manure that can be washed into it with every shower. It will do no harm to cut through a few of the roots, especially at some distance from the stem. After this, in early spring, scrub the bark of the stem and larger branches with a strong brine.

OLD BOX EDGING

In old gardens, the box edgings often look coarse and bushy, and full of gaps; for this there is no remedy but to take all up, and replant. The plan is this: Fork up the old box, and pull it into small pieces, with not more than one or two stems each, selecting the youngest and freshest pieces for immediate planting. These should be cut with a sharp spade or garden-shears, so as to be even at the top and also at the roots. Annual clipping should never be omitted, and the best time for it is towards the end of June; for the box, after this, will soon recover its freshness at this season.

OLD EVERGREENS AND HEDGES

Few things afford stronger indications of the necessity of renovation and reform in a garden than the state of the evergreens and hedges. Portugal laurels and many other evergreens may be cut in; but with the common laurel it is a saving of time to cut it down at once; so also with the arbutus and sweet bay. Thorn, privet, and holly hedges, which from years of neglect are found to be occupying too much space, must be cut in. The two former may often be cut down with advantage to within 10–20 cm / 4–9 in of the ground, and the latter cut close on all sides to the single stems.

OLD GARDENS

In a long course of years, from the sameness of cropping and over-working, most gardens show signs of decay. When the rich top-soil has been removed, spread a good dressing of quicklime over the lower surface and fork it in: if the lime is 2.5 cm / 1 in in thickness it will not be too much. Rather than do this imperfectly, it will be better that only a small portion should be done at once, commencing with those portions on which peas, cauliflowers, cabbages, onions, and carrots are to be grown, leaving the parts appropriated to asparagus, kale, and rhubarb for after-consideration.

Above all, the fruit-tree borders, if they cannot be entirely renovated, should only have one half of the old soil removed and replaced by fresh loam, having previously made a good rubble bottom 30 cm / 1 ft deep, over which 60 cm / 2 ft of the above com. post should be placed for the trees. Many kinds of fruit-trees may safely be lifted, if done carefully, and the roots laid in any spare piece of ground while the borders are being renewed – more particularly pears and plums.

OLD SHRUBBERIES

In old gardens, it is no unfamiliar thing to find the lawn and borders skirted by long, unbroken belts of shrubs, the lower part of most of the deciduous shrubs lean and naked, long since denuded of their smaller twigs. When a shrubbery has acquired all or any of these characteristics, renovation, in whole or part, has become indispensable.

Shrubberies must be cultivated with much care. Evergreens should be selected for their close habit of growth, and this habit increased by high dressing, judicious pruning, and pegging down. This compact habit, however, can only be maintained in beauty for a number of years by planting the shrubs so far apart that they may not touch each other; the ground between being kept clear by frequent raking and hoeing. There are some exceptions to this rule of planting. Rhododendrons do well planted in masses, and where the shoots are pegged down, they soon present a broad mass of green on the margin of the clump or shrubbery.

In planting or renovating lawn and shrubberies, due attention should be paid to their different seasonal effects. There are a few shrubs which herald in the spring; such as *Chimonanthus fragrans* and *Cornus mascula*, Mezereon, *Ribes sanguineum*, *Corchorus japonicus*.

Supposing this state of things has gone on until entire renovation has become necessary; that the border is exhausted by continually growing the same things for years, and a radical remedy is required, there is only one which is effectual. Remove the plants to a place of safety, and after that exchange the soil to the depth of 60 cm / 2 ft before planting again.

SMALL FLOWER-GARDENS

ARRANGING flowers in small gardens being a matter of taste, we can only give general directions for his guidance. In planting beds with half-hardy plants, which is generally done at the end of May, the plants should be ready to start into flower. Much time is lost by using small and late-struck plants. The best effect is produced by massing, every bed being planted with one distinct class; viz., one with verbenas, another with geraniums – and these, again, arranged according to their various colours, either in groups or ribbons, with due regard to height. (See box below.)

FLOWERS FOR SMALL GARDENS

VERBENAS are very much of the same habit and height; but a very fine effect is produced by planting beds entirely with them, they combining all colours but yellow.

GERANIUMS are much the same, but vary in height. Thus, Little David is very dwarf; Tom Thumb, rather taller; Punch Queen (perpetual), taller still. The Zonale, or horseshoe-leaved, are mostly of tall habit; cerise and pink-flowering sorts are generally dwarf.

CALCEOLARIAS embrace all shades of yellow and orange: some are very dwarf, as aurea floribunda; others are taller, but rarely exceed 45 cm / 18 in in one season.

BLUE LOBELIAS are all of very dwarf habit, and are very effective for frontage, being continuous bloomers.

CUPHEAS grow about 20–25 cm / 8–10 in high.

PETUNIAS are much the same in habit as verbenas, being dwarf and trailing; this tribe embraces many colours.

HELIOTROPES are mostly of lilac colour, but some are darker: they are mostly dwarf and spreading; but they are chiefly valued for their perfume.

LANTANAS are much the same in habit, growing about 40 cm / 15 in high.

AGERATUMS grow still taller, and some are variegated: all these, and many others of a like nature, may be raised from cuttings in heat, in February and March, and hardened off in frames before planting; or they may be struck from cuttings in July and August, and wintered in a greenhouse, pit, or even in a window, it being merely necessary to guard against frost and damp.

VEGETABLE GARDENS

Fresh vegetables are one of the most delightful rewards for your gardening efforts. They are no more difficult to grow than other plants, but there are some important things to remember when you begin:

1. Choose a sunny site that is not shaded by trees.
2. Don't be too ambitious at first. Grow a few of the easier vegetable crops.
3. Rotate your crops so as not to encourage specific pests and diseases, or deplete the soil of particular nutrients.
4. Avoid using pesticides unless absolutely necessary.

Prepare the ground well over autumn and winter so that you are ready to start sowing in spring. Lettuces, radishes, spring onions, French and runner beans, onions, potatoes, cabbage, courgettes and leeks are excellent starter crops.

WALKS

A GOOD walk may be formed of concrete, consisting of six parts of coarse gravel and one of lime, 10 cm / 4 in deep, with 2.5 cm / 1 in of fine sifted gravel sprinkled over and well rolled into the top; and 15 cm / 6 in deep, including gravel, will be a good average for walks formed of stones, &c., in the ordinary way. Perfect dryness is even of more importance upon walks than roads, as they should be clean and comparatively impenetrable in all weathers

and at all seasons. Although some recommend walks to be sunk below, and others raised above, the general level, as shown in the diagram, yet they generally look best on a level with the surface: they must be sunk 1 cm / ½ in at the edge. 1 cm / ½ in is a sufficient convexity for a 3-m / 10-ft walk. The wider the walk the smaller is the permissible rise in the centre. There are few persons who do not think a handsome seat or temple, a beautiful fountain, or a statue, a pleasing termination to a walk. The size and importance of the terminal objects must, however, always correspond in magnitude and importance with the length and width of the walk. Generally a walk should not terminate at any particular object: it is unsatisfactory to be compelled to return by the same route as we advance.

Other walks should diverge from it, to give a choice of routes. The proper line of divergence is of consequence; Repton says, where two walks separate from each other, it is always desirable to have them diverge in different directions, as at *a*, rather than give the idea of re-curvity, as at *b*. When two walks join each other, it is generally better that they should meet at right angles, rather than leave the sharp point, as in the acute angle at *c*.

Walks should always avoid skirting the boundary of the garden, although they may occasionally approach it; and, as a general rule, one should never be *vis-à-vis*, for any great distance, to another; and then these walks should be of different widths, according to their relative importance; each walk should also maintain the same width throughout, unless it passes through rock-work, when it should be distinguished by irregularity of width, abrupt bends, and capricious undulations. Grass walks are not so common as they were. On well-drained lawns the whole surface becomes a walk at pleasure. Where there is much traffic on grass walks, their bottom should be formed with stone, as if for gravel; but it will be more satisfactory to make good gravel walks for the general traffic.

WALLS

THE best practitioners consider that for small gardens, 2.5-m / 8-ft walls are most suitable, provided the trees on them are planted so far apart as to admit of their horizontal extension. For gardens of larger size, 3-m / 10-ft walls will not be too great.

The position of the walls being determined, the foundations should be excavated. Their depth must depend upon the subsoil, and the workmen should dig until they reach a solid bed. The trench completed, it should he filled up to within 15 cm / 6 in of the surface, with concrete, consisting of six or seven parts of coarse gravel, stones, or brick rubbish, to one part of freshly-slaked lime, reduced to a thin paste, which may be thrown over a thin layer of the gravel; but the better foundation is formed by mixing the material thoroughly in a heap, and turning it out of the wheel-barrow into the trench, from a raised bank, raking each layer level as it is thrown in.

The thickness of the wall must depend on its height, and the foundation should be thicker by 8–10 cm / 3–4 in than the wall itself, this thickness rising 13–15 cm / 5–6 in above the surface-level. Walls of these proportions are capable of supporting a lean-to greenhouse of corresponding height, if they are properly bonded, and hot lime or good cement is used. There is this practical difficulty in the more weak wall, that the bricks shrink unequally in drying. This inequality might be remedied by using the shorter ones as 'stretchers', as bricks laid longitudinally on the wall are called, using the regular-sized bricks for 'headers.' But the bonding or tying, which is the object of laying headers and stretchers, would not be attained. It is, therefore, to be provided for by using half-bricks, and throwing out the short ones.

No material for kitchen-garden walls can equal good red brick of medium hardness of texture. The joints should be formed as narrow as possible, of the best lime and sharp sand, and can either be left white, or the lime can be coloured a few shades lighter than the bricks. The bricks are better without any colouring whatever.

WINDOW GARDENING

WHERE a window happens to be in a recess, a wooden trough, lined with lead or zinc, may be used for holding earth, in which climbing plants may be planted and trained about the recess. For this purpose the Passion flower is very suitable; if allowed, after crossing the top, to hang down before the window in festoons, displaying its naturally graceful pendulous habit, it will form a pleasant screen for a sunny window. A grape-vine may be grown in the same way. But it is advisable to attempt nothing in this way which cannot be carried out perfectly; for instance, climbing plants must be very closely watched and carefully trained, or they become so entangled as to be anything but ornamental: they are apt, also, to harbour spiders and other insects, to drop their dead leaves and flowers, and, in common with other plants, they must be watered, which is always inconvenient in a room, for the pots must be well drained of superfluous moisture, otherwise the earth soddens in them. If the plants are in ordinary pots, which are certainly best, let them be plunged in ornamental pots or vases, and fill up the vacancy between the roots, being kept cool, will retain the moisture longer, and less watering will be necessary. When the pots are placed in the pans or saucers, fill the vacancy with a mixture of silver-sand and finely-broken – not powdered – charcoal: this will absorb the water that runs through the pot, and yield it back again to the plant, besides preventing stagnation. The time to water a plant is just when the soil begins to present an appearance of dryness, which is best seen when the surface is pretty firm, although it is advisable to stir it sometimes; but if, after stirring, the plant wants water, give it from a fine rose. This will settle the soil again, so that it is easily ascertained when the plants want water afterwards. If any plants are infested with aphids or green. fly, use a small brush, without injuring the plant. Various sorts of herbaceous plants may be cultivated outside, on the window-ledges: being hardy, they will stand all weathers, but are best protected from severe frost and a scorching sun.

Among these we may mention sedums or stonecrop, houseleeks, London Pride, with other saxifrages, campanulas, and a few phloxes.

Fast-growing plants, as fuchsias, geraniums, genistas, &c., grown under glass cases or in windows, should not be frequently turned, since they always make a face towards the light, and the process might weaken them: it would be better to train them out fanlike, by means of thin painted sticks. Lycopodiums may be allowed to trail over the surface of the soil. *Pteris arguta* makes a good centre plant; also *Adiantum pedatum*, one of the most graceful of ferns, but it dies down every winter.

The *Aspleniums* offer an extensive and numerous family to choose from, particularly *A. viviparum, bulbiferum, paniculatum*, and others, producing young ferns on the old leaves, and roots in the air. The *Scolopendriums* are also suitable, and show well their broad shining leaves or fronds. In a dry warm room many ferns that are considered very tender may be grown successfully; but they will require more water, which should be warm when given, and less ventilation; for the dry air of a warm room, ill suited to most plants, is very injurious to ferns; and some of them naturally come from warm, humid climates; they must therefore be carefully treated in this respect.

Caladiums are almost too tender for window-culture, but several kinds of begonias will not only stand the air of a room, but thrive in it.

There are also plants hardier still – *Farfugium grande*, for instance, which produces a grand effect: it is closely allied to the Tussilago, or Coltsfoot family, and is very easily cultivated. Then, again, there is *Cineraria maritima*, with its white silvery foliage; also *Centaurea gymnocarpa* and *C. ragusina*, of similar habit; *Acacia lapantha, Fuchsia spectabilis*, and other plants of ornamental foliage, all of which have peculiar characteristics, and many of them admirably adapted to window decoration. I have known a plant of *Ficus elastica* kept for a dozen years in a window, maintaining a lively foliage and vigorous habit the whole time. This, and similar plants with shiny leaves, have this recommendation, that when the leaves get dusty they are easily cleansed with a damp sponge.

The various species of cacti are also very suitable as permanent window-plants: the varieties of creeping cereus may be grown in suspended baskets, and last for many years without requiring any change in the soil – they naturally droop and hang down, which gives them an interesting appearance. The smaller kinds of aloes may be grown in the same way: many of these are curiously and prettily marked, and those who fancy this sort of plant consider them quite as ornamental as flowers. They are all succulent, and may be given plenty of water in hot weather, and little or none in winter, taking care that the soil is well drained.

The most necessary condition to successful window culture is to have proper appliances – that is, for instance, provided only one single window is available, then it should be fitted with a ledge or shelf, both inside and out, so that the plants can be close to the glass when inside, where they can have the full light; and also that they can be exposed to the open air on every occasion when the weather will permit. If a window is fitted in this way, half a dozen plants can be grown creditably, with very little trouble. They can be placed outside for the purpose of watering them, even in winter; and in wet weather they can be inside, with the window closed.

4

A-Z of TRADITIONAL GARDEN PLANTS

From Acacia to Zinnia, this A-Z guide offers suggestions for traditional and unusual plant varieties for the modern garden.

ACACIA

Elegant-growing plants, nearly all are evergreen. During winter and early spring they flower freely in greenhouses, but they are not hardy enough to endure our climate unprotected except in the summer, when they may be planted with their pots in south-facing areas with good effect. All may be grown readily from seed, which is best imported, and from cuttings in pots of very fine mould, set in a hot-bed. One of the most beautiful varieties is *A. dealbata*, fragrant and yellow with feathery silver leaves.

🞕 CULTURE: All kinds require a sandy loam, well drained.

ACANTHUS or BEAR'S BREECHES

Perennials attractive for the glossy beauty of their foliage: natives of Southern Europe. The most common varieties are *A. mollis* and *A. spinosus*. From the former of these the original idea of the capital of the Corinthian order of architecture is said to have been derived.

🞕 CULTURE: All the sorts grow readily from seed grown in spring, or they may be increased by dividing the roots in February or April. They require a sandy soil and free space.

ACHIMENES

A genus of truly splendid plants, suitable either for the sitting-room or greenhouse, and especially adapted for hanging-baskets; they combine great individual beauty with a variety of rich, and brilliant colours.

🞕 CULTURE: Use a compost of peat, loam, and leaf-soil; or leaf-mould, loam, and silver-sand, and secure good drainage. Plant five to seven tubers in a 13–15-cm / 5–6-in pot, with their growing ends inclining towards the centre, and their root ends towards the circumference of the pot, and cover them with about 2.5 cm / 1 in of the compost. While growing, they should be well supplied with liquid manure; start them when convenient in heat, and when about 4 cm / 1½ in high they may be removed to the greenhouse. To keep up a succession, commence starting them in heat in January; and as one lot is taken out another should be put in, till May: do not neglect tying up the stems, or they will fall down and get injured. Water well, keep humidity high and dry out dormant winter rhizomes till they sprout again in spring.

AGAPANTHUS

An African lily blooming in August, combining graceful foliage with large handsome umbels of blossom. When mixed with gladioli, either ramosus or gandavensis, the effect is unique. Protect the bed or patch during winter.

☛ CULTURE: A 23-cm / 9-in pot will be ample for a strong plant, but a large pot or tub is required for several plants; and this is the most effective and more usual way of growing the agapanthus. Use a well-draining loam, and during the summer months give abundance of water, and liquid manure twice a week. In winter protect from severe frost, and water sparingly.

AGERATUM

Useful half-hardy annuals. The shades are blue, white, and red. The seed should be sown in a light soil in April or May.

ALYSSUM

Free-flowering, useful, pretty little plants for beds, edgings, or rockeries. The annual species bloom nearly the whole summer; the perennials are amongst our earliest and most attractive spring flowers. The varieties are:

A. argenteum – yellow, with silvery foliage, hardy perennial, 30 cm / 1 ft.
A. atlanticum – fine light yellow, very ornamental, hardy perennial, 20 cm / ¾ ft.
A. saxatile – yellow, extremely showy, hardy perennial, 30 cm / 1 ft.
A. saxatile compactum – golden-yellow, very compact, free-flowering and beautiful, hardy perennial, 15 cm / ½ ft.
Alyssum, sweet (*Koenigia maritima*) – white, very sweet, hardy annual, 15 cm / ½ ft.

AMARANTHUS

Half-hardy annuals, very graceful, with highly ornamental foliage. *A. ruber*, with dark carmine foliage, is a most strikingly beautiful plant and *A. caudatus*, or love-lies-bleeding, has drooping, dark-carmine spikes. Other varieties are bicolor, leaves crimson and green, and tricolor, red, yellow, and green.

☛ CULTURE: Sow in heat in early spring and plant out in May and June in very rich soil.

AMARYLLIS

Flowers of rare beauty, whose large, drooping, bell-shaped, lily-like blossoms range in colours from the richest crimson to pure white, and striped with crimson or scarlet. They are easily cultivated.

Interesting varieties include:

Bella-Donna purpurea (Bella-Donna Lily) – white flushed with rosy purple.

Bella-Donna blanda.

Johnsonii – scarlet, with pure white stripes, very showy.

Johnsonii striata – striped.

Prince of Orange – bright orange, large and handsome.

☞ CULTURE: Place the bulbs in front of a wall facing south, at least 15 cm / 6 in under the surface, giving them a little winter protection: should the growing season be dry, water freely till the plant blooms, but when at rest the bulbs should be kept as dry and warm as possible.

ANEMONES or WIND-FLOWERS

Anemone blossoms are of the most dazzling hues of scarlet, purple and blue, self-coloured and striped. The foliage is elegantly cut, and the growth is neat and compact.

The flowers of the double anemone have outer guard petals, resembling a semi-double hollyhock. If planted from October to December, they will bloom in succession during the early spring months, while those planted in February and March will bloom from April to June.

The single anemone, with its beautiful poppy-like blossoms, may be had from February to December.

☞ CULTURE: The anemone delights in a light, rich, loamy soil, but generally succeeds in any which is well drained. Sea-sand, or a little salt mixed with the soil, is a good preventive of mildew.

ANTIRRHINUM or SNAPDRAGON

The antirrhinum is a hardy perennial, and one of our most showy and useful border plants. They succeed in any good garden soil, and are very effective in beds. *A. nanum* and varieties are valuable for rockeries and old walls.

APPLES

Some apple trees prefer clay soils, while others do better in sandy loam. Apple planting, therefore, requires some observation as to the sorts most successfully grown in the locality. The following are among the most useful varieties:

Dessert apples

Early Harvest – ripens end of July.

Margaret – early in August.

Calville rouge d'Eté – middle of August.

Devonshire Quarrenden – middle of August.

Barowski – end of August.

Early Julian – in August and September.

Summer Pippin – beginning of September, but of short duration.

Monstrous Pippin – September and October.

Oslin, a high-flavoured apple – ripens in September.

Reinette blanche – in October and November.

Scarlet Crofton – ripens with us in October.

Early Nonpareil – in October, and keeps till March.

Court of Wick – in use from October, and keeps till March.

Calville de St Saveur – ripens in November.

Belle Fleur de Brabant – in November.

Downton Pippin – ripens in November, and keeps till January.

Golden Pippin – grows vigorously on a warm soil and in sheltered situations, ripening in November, and keeping till March.

Reinette Dorée (Golden Reinette) – ripens in November, and keeps till April. Ribston Pippin – in November, and keeps till March.

Ross Nonpareil – in December; keeps till February.

Cornish Gillyflower – in December; keeps till February.

Queen of the Reinettes – in December; keeps till February.

Reinette du Canada – in January and February.

Roi d'Angleterre – in January, and keeps till March.

Wyken Pippin – in January; keeps till March.

Lamb Abbey Pearmain – in December; keeps till June.

Cooking apples

Keswick Codling – fit for use in July and August.

Golden Winter Pearmain – in use from October till January, as a kitchen as well as dessert apple.

Beauty of Kent – in use from October till February.

Bedfordshire Foundling – in use from January till March.

Winter Pearmain – in use from November till April.

Winter Majetin – in use from January to June.

Norfolk Beefing, – keeps till June.

Gooseberry Apple – ripe in January, and keeps till June or July.

The modern system of dwarfing fruit-trees, by which space is so much economized, is produced by a special course of pruning, commencing a year from grafting, when the apple-tree should be pruned back, leaving about eight buds on the shoots. In the second year the head will exhibit eight or ten shoots, and a selection must now be made of five or six, which shall give a cup-like form to the head, removing all shoots crossing each other, or which interfere with that form; thus leaving the head hollow in the centre, with a shapely head externally, shortening back the shoots retained to two-thirds or less, according as the buds are placed, and leaving all of nearly the same size. In the course of the summer's growth the tree will be assisted by pinching off the leading shoots where there is a tendency to overthrow the balancing of the head. At the third year's pruning the same process of thinning and cutting back will be required, after which the tree can hardly go wrong. The shoots retained should be short-jointed and well-ripened; and in shortening, cut back to a healthy, sound-looking, and well-placed bud.

Large standard trees in their prime only require pruning once in two or three years.

AQUATIC PLANTS

For ornamenting ponds, the sides of running streams, and other artificial pieces of water.

Aquatic plants with showy flowers

MAY: Red. – *Equisetum fluviatile, Hydrocolite vulgaris.* White – *Nasturtium officinale, Ranunculus aquatilis.* Yellow – *Ranunculus aquatilis.* Blue – *Veronica Beccabunga.*

JUNE: Red – *Equisetum palustre, Butomus umbellatus.* White – *Hydrocharis morsusranae, Phellandrium aquaticum.* Blue – *Myriophyllum spicatum, M. verticillatum, Pontederia cordata, Veronica anagallis.* Green – *Potamogeton densum.* Brown – *Potamogeton lucens, P. pectinatum.*

JULY: Red – *Hippuris vulgaris, Polygonum amphibium.* White – *Alisma damasonium, A. natans, A. plantago, Calla palustris, Nymphrea alba, N. odorata, Poa fluitans, Stratiotes aloides.* Yellow – *Iris pseudacorus, Villarsia nymphaeoides, Nuphar advena, N. lutea, Utricularia minor.* Purple – *Utricularia vulgaris, Trapa natans, Sagittaria sagittifolia.* Green – *Ceratophyllum demersum, Cicuta virosa.*

AUGUST: Red – *Hydropeltis purpurea, Polygonum hydropiper.* White – *Cerastium aquaticum, Poa aquatica.* Yellow – *Potamogeton natans.* Blue – *Alisma ranunculoides, Lobelia Dortmanna.* Brown – *Potamogeton perfoliatum, Scirpus fluitans, S. lacustris, S. triqueter.*

HEIGHT FROM 0–20 CM / 0–¾ FT: White – *Pinguicula lusitanica.* Blue – *Pinguicula vulgaris.* Brown – *Carex dioica.*

HEIGHT FROM 20–45 CM / ¾–1½ FT: White – *Oenanthe peucedanifolia.* Yellow – *Carex flava, Ranunculus flamula, R. repens.* Green – *Carex disticha, C. pulicaris, C. precox, C. stricta, C. muricata, C. elongata.* Brown – *Carex crespitosa, C. digitata, Scirenus nigricans.*

Marsh plants with showy flowers

For the borders of ponds, the margins of streams, and ornamental pieces of water. Time for flowering: May and June.

HEIGHT FROM 45–75 CM / 1½–2½ FT: White – *Oenanthe fistulosa.* Purple – *Comarum palustre.* Brown – *Carex paludosa, C. riparia, Juncus conglomeratus.*

HEIGHT FROM 75–105 CM / 2½–3½ FT: Green – *Carex pseudocyperus, C. vulpina, Cyperu longus, Juncus compressus.*

HEIGHT FROM 105 CM / 3½ FT UPWARDS: Red – *Scrophularia aquatica.* White – *Oenanthe crocata.* Yellow – *Senecio paludosus.*

Marsh plants, &c., which flower in July and August

HEIGHT FROM 0–20 CM / 0–¾ FT: Red – *Teucrium scordium.* White – *Littorella lacustris, Samolus Valerandi, Schoenus albus.* Yellow – *Hyperocum elodes.* Blue – *Schoenus mariscus.* Variegated – *Scutellaria minor.* Brown – *Schoenus compressus, Scirpus acicularis, S. caespitosus.*

HEIGHT FROM 20–45 CM / ¾–1½ FT: Red – *Menyanthes trifoliata.* White – *Galium palustre. G. uliginosum, Pedicularis palustris.* Yellow – *Hottonca palustris, Rumex maritimus.* Purple – *Pedicularis sylvatica, Triglochin maritimum. T. palustre.* Brown – *Juncus squarrosus. Schoenus nigricans, Scirpus palustris, S. sylvaticus.*

HEIGHT FROM 46–76 CM / 1½–2½ FT: Yellow – *Acorus calamus, Myosotis palustris, Rumex palustris.* Blue – *Phormium tenax.* Purple – *Aster tripolium.* Brown – *Scirpus maritimus, Rumex crispus, Juncus sylvaticus.*

HEIGHT FROM 75–105 CM / 2½–3½ FT: White – *Rumex obtusifolilis.* Yellow – *Cineraria palustris, Senecio aquaticus.* Green – *Juncus effusus.* Brown – *Scirpus holoschcenus.*

HEIGHT FROM 105 CM / 3½ FT UPWARDS: Red – *Malva sylvestris.* White – *Dipsacus pilesus, Selinum palustre.* Yellow – *Sonchus palustris.* Variegated – *Angelica sylvestris.* Brown – *Rumex aquaticus, Cyperus longus, Juncus acutus, J. maritimus.*

The situation best adapted for hardy aquatics will be found to be in accordance with their height. Many that are not hardy may be introduced for summer decoration in pots sunk either wholly or half deep in water. These can be removed in winter to warm-water tanks under cover of glass.

ARDISIA

Small shrubs, several of which will flourish and fruit in a moderately warm greenhouse. All require loam and peat; and they may be increased by cuttings, which root very freely in sand. *A. crenulata* is a very favourite variety. Its bright red berries, which last so long, render it invaluable in a conservatory.

ARTICHOKES, GLOBE

These are best propagated by offsets taken in March. The plants bear best the second or third year after planting; so that it is advisable to plant one or more rows every year, and remove the same quantity of old roots. It is better to trench the ground first, and fork the manure well into the surface-spit, which gives the plants a better chance of immediately profiting by it. The offsets may be dissevered with a knife, or slipped off and cut smooth afterwards. Some plant in threes, about a metre or a yard apart, and 120 cm / 4 ft from row to row; or they may be planted singly, 60 cm / 2 ft apart in the row, and 120 cm / 4 ft from row to row. They should be well watered, and the ground kept loose between.

ARUM

This splendid plant, with its snow-white flower, its yellow tongue and arrow-shaped leaves, is not hardy with us but it admits of an easy cultivation even where there is no greenhouse. The arum grows from offsets, which are very freely produced. The plants should be repotted every October, in rich, light mould, with a few drainers, the offsets having been carefully removed, and all the old soil well shaken from their roots. From this time till June, or earlier, if the plants have flowered and are off blooming, they should have abundance of water; but after this they must be kept quite dry, and may be put away in an outhouse till the following October, when the same treatment should be renewed. The arum, in a growing state, requires so much moisture that it is best to keep the pot always standing in a deep saucer full of water. Under this culture, offsets may be brought into flower in their third year.

ASPARAGUS

☞ PREPARATION OF THE LAND: The ground should be well drained to a depth of 120 cm / 4 ft, and heavily manured, the surface being covered to a depth of at least 8 cm / 3 in, with rich, well-decayed farm or stable-yard manure. If the soil is of a clayey or strong nature, sharp sand, or finely-sifted ashes, may be added with advantage. Trench to a depth of 75 cm / 2 ft 6 in, well intermixing the manure as the work proceeds. The bottom of the trench should be loosened a spade's depth still lower, if the subsoil is such as will retain moisture, or otherwise benefit the plants; but if it is gravel, it had better be left undisturbed.

☞ TIME AND MANNER OF SOWING: As early in April as the ground can be found in fair working condition, sow in drills about an inch deep, scattering the seed very thinly and covering it evenly with the finest of the soil. The seed may be sown in drills 40 cm / 15 in apart, thinning out the plants so that they may stand 10 cm / 4 in apart in the rows, to furnish plants for transplanting after one or two seasons' growth; or it may be sown at once where the crop is intended to stand. In either case the plants should be thinned out to 30 cm / 1 ft. We recommend sowing in consecutive lines. The asparagus is very impatient of stagnant moisture about its crowns during the winter, and, on strong soils, trenches should be made 8 cm / 3 in deep and wide, and filled with sharp sand previous to sowing. The plants will probably not make as much progress in the first season as if they had been sown in the soil, but the roots will soon extend beyond the sand, and later this will prevent water lodging about the crowns and rotting them.

☞ TRANSPLANTING AND AFTER-MANAGEMENT: The plants, if sown with the intention of transplanting, after one or two seasons in the seed-lines, should be encouraged by an occasional soaking of manure-water during the growing season; and a liberal dressing of rich manure should be spread between the rows in winter. Transplant in April, when the ground is in good working order. If the ground has been properly prepared, set a line and take out a trench sufficiently wide and deep to allow of spreading the roots, and cover the crowns about 5 cm / 2 in. On strong, heavy, imperfectly-drained soils, place sand about the roots and over the crowns, as recommended under the head of Sowing. The roots should be carefully taken up, avoiding all cutting or injury; and any that are decaying should be rejected. During the growing season keep the ground free from weeds, and the surface free and open by frequent hoeings; a soaking of manure-water may be given with advantage when the weather is droughty. Clear off the haulm in autumn, when it will part from the crowns by a slight pull, and apply a dressing of well-decayed manure, which may be lightly forked in between the lines, at once or in spring.

Asparagus-cutting

Cutting asparagus is an operation of some delicacy. It should be cut with a saw-edged knife, having a straight, narrow, tapering blade, about 5–20 cm / 2–8 in long, and an inch broad at the haft, rounding off at the point. When the shoots are fit to cut, the knife is to be slipped perpendicularly close to the shoot, sawing it off aslant 8–10 cm / 3–4 in below the surface, taking care not to touch any young shoot coming out of the same crown.

ASTERS

Half-hardy annuals. The aster is indispensable in every garden where an autumnal display is desired.

All the varieties delight in a deep, rich, light soil, and in hot, dry weather should be mulched with well-rotted manure, and frequently supplied with manure-water. The plants benefit from being divided every other spring: divide live roots from dead ones and replant.

AURICULAS

Florists' flowers of great beauty, well deserving of cultivation. They may be propagated by offsets at any time during autumn, but the earlier the better. New auricula borders may be made in October, and old ones should then be carefully gone over and renovated. Let it be remembered that the auricula delights in shade, and will not bear excessive moisture. In planting offsets, be careful that the soil is well pressed round the roots. New sorts are to be obtained from seed, which must be raised in a gentle heat.

AZALEA

Beautiful flowering plants, azaleas are deciduous shrubs of the rhododendron genus, varying in height from 60 cm–1.8 m / 2–6 ft. The loftiest of them is the arborescens, which will grow from 3–4.5 m / 10–15 ft. The following are among the choicest named sorts:

Ambrosia – red, orange blotch.
Beauty of Flanders – fawn and pink, orange blotch.
Coccinea major – fine scarlet.
Honneur de la Belgique – bright orange.
Julius Caesar – dark crimson.
Nudiflora colorata – bright pink.
Pontica – large, yellow, very showy.

For conservatory decoration the Chinese and Indian azaleas are most important. After the growth is made, the plants should be gradually hardened off; and be placed during September full in the sun's rays out of doors, to thoroughly ripen their wood. Two parts of peat, two of loam, a sprinkling of sand, and one-sixth part of charcoal that has been steeped in manure-water suits them well. While growing, they will also require watering with clear weak manure-water every time that they become dry. Before housing them for the winter, examine the plants. There is an immense variety. The following azaleas are perhaps as good as any:

Admiration, Alba, Alba magna, Alba striata, Albertii, Amoena lateritii, Ardens, Beauty of Europe, Beauty of Reigate, Blondin, Broughtonii, Chelsonii, Coronata, Criterion, Danielsiana, Distinction, Duc de Nassau, Duke of Devonshire, Empress Eugénie, Exquisita, Exquisita pallida, Fulgens, Gem, *Gladstonesii, G. excelsa, G. formosa*, Glory of Sunning Hill, Grande Duchesse Hélène, *Formosa variegata, F. alba cincta, F. alba suprema, F. elegans*, Magnet, Mars, Optima, Petuniaeflora, Prince Albert, Queen of Whites, Queen Victoria, Leopold, Rosea punctata, Rosy Circle, *Smithii coccinea, Striata formosa*, the Bride, and Triumphans.

BALM

Hardy annuals. Sweet-scented plants, with ornamental foliage, very effective in mixed borders, and succeeding in any common garden soil.

Moldavian balm, *Dracocephalum moldavicum* – blue or white, 60 cm / 2 ft.
Lemon balm, *Melissa officianalis* – aromatic leaves, 50 cm / 20 in.

BEET

There are three sorts of beet for garden cultivation – the perpetual spinach beet, the leaves of which may be gathered throughout the summer and used as spinach: seakale beet, the mid-rib of the leaf of which is 5–8 cm / 2–3 in broad, very white and delicate in flavour. The edible-rooted beet is, however, the most useful variety. It may be cultivated in the following manner:

☛ PREPARATION OF THE SOIL: Select for this crop deep and rich, yet rather light and loamy soil, which has been well-manured during the previous season. If this cannot be done, the ground should be trenched 60 cm / 2 ft deep, and ridged up in autumn. A sprinkling of guano after the plants are up is preferable to manure, which often causes the roots to grow rough and forked.

☛ TIME AND MANNER OF SOWING: For the first supply sow a small quantity early in April, and the main crop the first week in May; but where small roots are desired, sow as late as the middle of June. Sow in drills about 2.5 cm / 1 in deep, and from 40–45 cm / 15–18 in apart, covering with friable soil.

☛ CULTIVATION AND AFTER-MANAGEMENT: Thin out the plants so that they are 15–20 cm / 6–9 in apart in the rows. Keep the ground free from weeds, and open by frequently stirring the surface. By the end of October the roots should then be taken up and stored in soil not over dry, crowns outwards. In pulling and cleaning, be careful not to wound the roots, or cut off any large fibres, as this would cause bleeding, which greatly injures the quality and tends to induce decay.

BEGONIA

There are no plants more worthy of admission into a conservatory or greenhouse than begonias, and the facility with which they may be cultivated is equal to their beauty. All they require is a good rich loamy soil, mixed with a little sand, and a little heat to start them. The chief requirements are heat, moisture, and shade.

Begonia fuchsioides – remarkable for its graceful habit.

B. odorata – remarkable for the fragrant odour, from which it derives its name.

B. nitida – an almost perpetual bloomer, one plant having had three or four cymes of flowers always open for three years.

B. octopetala – a tuberous-rooted winter flowering species, with large pure white blossoms.

B. griffithii, or *picta* – richly variegated, with colours shading beautifully into each other.

B. xanthia Reichenheimii – in which green bands follow the principal veins, the spaces between being pure white.

B. xanthia lazula – having copper-coloured leaves, shining with a fine metallic lustre.

B. Queen Victoria – a hybrid raised in Belgium; the leaf milky-white, except the margin of green dots, and a few central dots.

BERBERIS

Hardy shrub. The common berberis is a most elegant plant when trained to a single stem and then allowed to expand its head freely on all sides. So treated, the branches become drooping, and have a fine effect every spring, when they are covered with their rich yellow blossoms, and in autumn from their long red bunches of fruit. The following varieties are all hardy, and may be grown from seed.

Berberis bealei – yellow, very handsome, 120 cm / 4 ft.

— *dealbata* – yellow, evergreen with whitish foliage, 150 cm / 5 ft.

B. diversifolia – yellow, foliage distinct, 90 cm / 3 ft.

B. fortunei – yellow, evergreen, very handsome, 150 cm / 5 ft.

B. heterophylla – yellow, 120 cm / 4 ft.

B. japonica – yellow, handsome foliage.

B. Nepalensis – yellow, beautiful foliage, 90 cm / 3 ft.

BOX

The box used for the purpose of edging is *Buxus sempervirens*. It is readily propagated by dividing the old plants, and it will grow in any soil not saturated with moisture. The best time for clipping box is about the end of June. To form edgings of box properly is an operation in gardening that requires considerable care. Mrs Loudon gives the following excellent directions: 'First, the ground should be rendered firm and even: secondly, a narrow trench should be accurately cut out with the spade in the direction in which the edging is to be planted: thirdly, the box should be thinly and equally laid in along the trench, the tops being all about an inch above the surface of the soil: and fourthly, the soil should be supplied to the plants and firmly trodden in against them, so as to keep the edging exactly in the position required: the trench should always be made on the side next the walk, and after the soil is pressed down and the walk gravelled, the gravel is brought up over the soil, close to the stem of the box, so as to cover the soil at least an inch in thickness, and to prevent any soil being seen on the gravel-walk side of the box. This also prevents the box from growing too luxuriantly, as it would be apt to do if the trench were on the border side, when the plants would lean against the gravel, and the roots being entirely covered with soil, would grow with so much luxuriance that the plants would be with difficulty kept within bounds by clipping. A box edging once properly made and clipped every year, so as to form a miniature hedge, about 8 cm / 3 in wide at bottom, 8 cm / 3 in high and 5 cm / 2 in wide at top, will last ten or twelve years before it requires to be taken up and replanted; but if the edging be allowed to attain a larger size *Buxus sempervirens* say, 15 cm / 6 in wide at bottom, 15 cm / 6 in high and 8 cm / 3 in wide at top, it will last fifteen or twenty years, and probably a much longer period.'

BRACHYCOME

Half-hardy annuals. Beautiful free-flowering dwarf-growing plants, covered during the greater portion of the summer with a profusion of pretty cineraria-like flowers, very effective for edgings, small beds, rustic baskets, or for pot-culture; succeeding in any light rich soil.

Brachycome iberidifolia – blue, ½ ft.
B. iberidifolia albitlora – white, ½ ft.

BRACHYSEMA

A beautiful greenhouse climber, of a very ornamental character, exceedingly effective on low pillars or trelliswork; succeeds in any light rich soil.

Brachysema speciosum – deep red, very handsome.

BROAD BEANS

Beans, like peas, can be sown in October, where the soil is light, well drained, and well sheltered; where the ground is heavy, they may be raised in a pit or frame by sowing three in a 10-cm / 4-in pot, and planted out in March; but if the soil is cold, and no conveniences are at hand for starting in pots, they may be sown in the following manner: let the ground be laid in ridges 90cm / 3 ft wide, and 40 cm / 15–16 in high, sow the beans about 8 cm / 3 in apart. When about 25 cm / 10 in high, level the top of each ridge to the row of beans behind it: they will not require earthing up again. If sown in October, a succession may be sown in January, in the same manner; and so on once a month in June: they

113

do not bear well if sown after that. Those sown on level ground should have some earth drawn up to the roots when 8 cm / 3 in high: this induces them to emit fresh roots. They are sown in rows about 120 cm / 4 ft apart, which leaves room for a row of broccoli, spinach, or lettuce between. On light soils dib holes 10 cm / 4 in deep, planting a row each side of the line, 10 cm / 4 in apart, zigzag fashion; but in wet soils it is better to drill them in, laying boards along the row to stand on, so as to avoid clodding the ground by treading on it.

BROCCOLI

▶ PREPARATION OF THE SOIL: All the varieties of broccoli require a deep, rich soil, and the ground should be trenched to a depth of at least 60 cm / 2 ft, incorporating, as the work proceeds, abundance of rich manure.

▶ TIME AND MANNER OF SOWING: The early varieties, such as Purple Cape, Grange's White Cape, Walcheren, &c., should be sown from the middle of April to the middle of May, according to locality; and a second sowing of similar kinds should be made about a fortnight afterwards. These will succeed the cauliflowers, and will carry the supply on to Christmas. Two or three sowings of Snow's Winter White, put in from the beginning of April to the middle of May, will keep up the supply until the sprouting varieties are ready, and these again till the spring kinds come in. Sow the Purple Sprouting, and Lee's new White Sprouting early in March; and those intended to furnish the spring supply or main crop at the latter end of April or early in May. All the varieties should be sown in beds of well-pulverized rich soil. When the plants are sufficiently strong, and before they arc drawn by growing too closely together, transplant them into nursery-beds or lines, allowing about 10 cm / 4 in intermediate space.

▶ AFTER-MANAGEMENT: Plant in permanent situations as soon as the plants are sufficiently strong, in rows from 60–76 cm / 2–2½ ft apart, leaving about the same distance between the plants. Keep them well supplied with water until fairly established. Before severe weather sets in, the spring kinds should be laid over, with their heads facing the north. This operation checks the action of the roots, and the plants consequently become less succulent and better able to resist frost.

Division I For cutting during the autumn and early winter months:
Grange's White Cape – the best White Cape variety for succeeding the cauliflower.
Early Purple Cape – very useful, may be cut from August to December.
Early Purple Cape – new large-headed.
Walcheren – a very valuable variety for cutting in September and October.

Division II For cutting during the winter months:

Snow's Winter White – fine heads may be cut from this variety in November, December and January.

Early Purple Sprouting – a very fine sprouting variety, sometimes called Asparagus Broccoli.

Division III For cutting in March and April:

Adam's Earliest White – the earliest spring broccoli, sometimes ready in February.

Imperial Early White – a very superior variety, a fine succession to Adam's.

Beck's New Dwarf – a first-rate early variety, very dwarf.

Knight's Protecting – a very useful variety.

Sulphur or Brimstone – very useful, extremely hardy and produces fine heads.

Division IV For cutting in April and May:

Chappel's Cream – a fine variety, with large compact heads.

Howden's Large Late Purple – a valuable hardy variety.

Mammoth, or Giant White – the largest and best of this division.

Wilcove – a fine, large, late variety.

BROMPTON STOCKS

These are biennials. The seed should be sown early in May in a light sandy border with an eastern aspect. It succeeds best sown thinly in drills about 15 cm / 6 in apart. As soon as the plants show their second leaves they should be watered every evening with a fine rose pot. When about 8 cm / 3 in high they should be thinned out to at least 15 cm / 6 in apart and the other plants removed to another bed. The plants will require shading till they are established, and watering with liquid manure till they begin to flower.

BROWALLIA

Half-hardy annuals. Covered with beautiful flowers during the summer and autumn months; growing freely in any soil.

Browallia Czerniakowski – blue with white centre, beautiful, 1½ ft.

B. demissa – light blue, yellow and orange centre, 1½ ft.

B. elata alba – white, 1½ ft.

BRUGMANSIA

Magnificent conservatory plants, with a profusion of large trumpet-shaped highly odoriferous flowers; growing freely out of doors during summer. They require rich soil and plenty of space for their roots.

Brugmansia Knightii – white, splendid for winter decoration, 90 cm / 3 ft.

Brugmansia suaveolens – white; flowers 30 cm / 1 ft or more in length.

BRUSSELS SPROUTS

Brussels sprouts have the same treatment in the seed-beds as other Brassicae, early in April, or even March, being the best time for sowing in the open ground. Plant them in rows 60 or 45 cm / 2 ft or 18 in apart, keeping the ground loosened by hoeing; and as soon as the stems reach their full height and form a head, it is cut. This diverts all the strength into the sprouts on the stem.'

BUDDLEIA

Deciduous shrubs with butterfly-attracting flowers. Loamy soil suits them best.

BUGLOSS

The bugloss (anchusa) is a fine showy plant, mostly with large blue flowers. They may be propagated by dividing the roots into as many plants as there are heads, when they have done flowering, as well as by seeds saved in the autumn, and sown on a warm border in the spring.

BULBOCODIUM

A very pretty early-flowering plant; blooms about a fortnight before the ordinary crocus and, like it, may be cultivated indoors.

Bulbocodium vernum – pinkish-mauve.

BUSH FRUIT

Under this title are included gooseberries, the different kinds of currants – red, white, and black – and raspberries. It too frequently happens that bush fruit, from the readiness with which it yields a crop, is left to take care of itself; but the quantity and quality of the fruit produced will be found to depend very materially upon the good management of the bushes.

GOOSEBERRIES: Cuttings should be planted any time from October to March. Select for the purpose shoots of a medium size, not root-suckers, about 30 cm / 1 ft or more in length. Cut the base of the shoot square; no fruit canes should ever be planted with slanting heels; after this, remove with a knife every bud from the base to within 5 cm / 2 in of the top. If the cuttings are 40 cm / 15 in long, and four heads are left at the top, the future stem will be 30 cm / 1 ft high, which will be ample for a useful tree. The lower buds are removed in order to secure a clean stem and prevent the formation of suckers. Plant the cuttings in the shade 10 cm / 4 in deep, and fix the earth firmly about them. During summer, young growing shoots strike readily under a bell-jar on a shady border, and a season may frequently be saved in this way. The first season's growth of cuttings put in autumn should be very little interfered with. If any pruning is requisite, it is best done by rubbing off buds and by pinching in shoots which would interfere with the proper shape of the bush. At the end of the season, cut back all leading shoots to two-thirds of their length, so as to cause them to break next spring and form well-shaped bushes. At first, it is frequently desirable to plant cuttings only 8–10 cm / 3–5 in apart, and after the second year's growth to plant them out finally about 1.8 m / 6 ft apart. Each bush would then have about eight leading shoots to form a head, and must be kept in shape and order by yearly prunings. The best plan of protecting these from birds is by encircling the bush with wire netting, and covering the top with a piece of string netting.

With regard to the selection of sorts, we cannot do better than give the experience of so good a judge as Mr Shirley Hibberd. The best of the old varieties, he tells us, still hold their ground. There are none equal to the Champagne for flavour. The Red Champagne is of the same quality, differing only in colour. The old Rough is the best for preserving. For early work, take Golden Drop and Early Green Hairy. For the latest crop and for retarding, the best are Warrington, white; Viper, yellow; and Coe's Late Red.

CURRANTS, RED AND WHITE: May be pruned and treated in the same manner; black currants require a different treatment. In managing the cuttings, proceed as directed for gooseberries. Plant out the second year, when the cuttings have about 20 cm / 8 in of stem and about five leading shoots. The pruning of both red and white currants is very different from that of gooseberries. When the requisite number of branches has been produced, so as to form a uniform bush, the greater part of the young shoots should be taken off annually, leaving only those that may be required for new branches, and shortening these to 10–15 cm / 4–6 in with a clean cut just close to a bud. In pruning off the superfluous lateral shoots, take hold of each branch at its extremity with the left hand, and, with the knife in the right hand, remove every fresh lateral up the stem, leaving to each a short spur of 0.5–1 cm / ¼–½ in in length: from these spurs the bunches of fruit are produced. As the bush increases in age, it will be necessary to remove all old mossy wood, and also to thin out the spurs when they have become too crowded. To grow fine currants, make the plantation in an open sunny position, on a stiff, well-manured loam; plant the bushes 150 cm / 5 ft apart each way, and every autumn trench in a good dressing of half-rotten manure in such a way as not to injure the roots of the trees.

At autumn-pruning all the young shoots must be cut in to 5 cm / 2 in. The sorts which produce the largest fruit are White Blanche, with amber-coloured berries, and White Dutch. Of redcurrants, Cherry is the largest; La Fertile and Knight's Large Red are also excellent varieties.

BLACKCURRANTS: The cultivation of the blackcurrant is almost the same as the gooseberry, and the pruning is the same, only not so severe, as the black currant does not form so many young shoots. All dead and unproductive wood should be removed each year, and the shoots thinned so that light and air may freely enter the bush. The best varieties are the Naples Black and Ogden's Black; both of which, under good culture, are profuse bearers, and very large.

RASPBERRIES: Raspberries flourish in any good rich loam, and will grow to perfection in a dark unctuous soil. Before planting, the ground should be well trenched and manured; for though the roots lie near the surface, it is well to induce them to strike downwards in the event of a dry season. The second or third week in October is the best period for planting. Strong canes should be selected, and great advantage is gained if they be taken up with soil upon their roots. They may be put in singly, in rows, or in bunches of three canes each. In this latter case, it is desirable to cut the canes of different heights; the strongest may be 120 cm / 4 ft, the second 90 cm / 3 ft, and the third 60 cm / 2 ft. Staking will be necessary before the plants begin to grow in the spring, and great care should be taken that the ground is not trodden in wet weather.

The pruning of raspberries is an easy matter. In June the bushes should be gone over, and all suckers removed, except about six of the strongest. These, at a later period, may be reduced to four, and if the parent plant be weak, two or three will be sufficient. There is great benefit in cutting the canes of different heights, for as the top buds grow strongest, the young fruit-bearing shoots are more equally divided, and enjoy more air and light. The ground in which raspberries are grown should not be broken up, but have a top dressing of good rotten manure yearly.

The most useful varieties of the raspberry are the Red Antwerp, Fastolf, Prince of Wales, and Vice-President, the Yellow Antwerp, and Large-fruited Monthly. By a little management, raspberries may be made to bear a crop of fruit during the autumn. There are sorts called Double-bearing Raspberries, but the result is greatly due to pruning. For late bearing, as soon as root suckers show themselves in June, the old canes should be cut away entirely, so as to prevent summer fruiting; and encouragement should be given during July and August to such suckers as show blossom-buds, for these will bear fruit in autumn.

CABBAGES

Cabbages, or Brassicae, are the most exhaustive class of vegetables under the gardener's care. This important family of vegetables is biennial, triennial, and nearly perennial in some of the varieties. It may be divided into:

1. The cabbages proper, which have heads formed of the inner leaves growing close and compactly round the stem, which are thus blanched into a whitish yellow by the outer leaves.

2. Red, or Milan cabbage, which grows in the same form, but differs in colour.

3. Savoys, distinguished by their curly wrinkled leaves, but retaining the tendency to form a head.

4. Brussels sprouts, producing the sprouts, or edible part, from the stem in small heads, like very young cabbages.

5. Kale or borecole, of which there are many varieties, having a large open head with large curling leaves.

6. Cauliflower and broccoli, in which the flower-buds form a close fleshy head.

Of the first of these there are many varieties, some of them valuable for their precocity, which adapts them for early spring cultivation; others for more enduring qualities. They are all propagated by seed sown for main crops twice a year – namely, in April, for planting out in June and July, for autumn and winter use; and in August and September, for spring use; but it is usual to make sowings of smaller quantities every month for succession.

THE CABBAGE: Cover the seed to 0.5 cm / ¼ in with rich light soil, and rake it in: the after-cultivation will be gathered from the monthly calendars. The cabbage requires a rich retentive soil, and is improved by early transplanting. When about 5 cm / 2 in height, the young plants should be removed into nursery-beds thoroughly prepared by digging and manuring, and, if dry, by watering, where they are planted 10–13 cm / 4–5 in apart. Here they must remain till well rooted.

In final planting cut, the ground being trenched and well manured, a drill is drawn, 8 cm / 3 in deep, at a distance proportioned to the size and habit of growth of the variety; the small or early dwarfs at 30–40 cm / 12–15 in apart in the rows, the larger sorts, as Vanack, at 45 cm / 18 in. The subsequent culture is confined to weeding and occasionally stirring the earth during summer, and drawing it up round the stem when about 20–23 cm / 8–9 in high.

The best varieties of the white cabbage arc the Early York, Early Battersea, Early Dwarf Sugar-loaf, the Late Sugar-loaf, Vanack, the Portugal, or Couve

Trunchuda – of all of which there are many varieties; as Atkin's Matchless, Sutton's Dwarf Combe, Sutton's Imperial, Shilling's Queen.

CALANDRINIA

C. discolor and *C. grandiflora* have large handsome flowers, and are fine for edgings; *C. umbellata* is of a trailing habit, and produces profusely its glowing rosy violet flowers in bunches; is invaluable for rockeries and dry hot banks, or similar situations, where it will stand for many years. They succeed best in a light rich soil. They may be raised from seed.

Calandrinia discolor – rose-lilac, hardy annual, 30 cm / 1 ft.
C. grandiflora – rose-pink, hardy annual, 30 cm / 1 ft.
C. umbellata – rich rosy violet, hardy perennial 8 cm / ¼ ft.

CALCEOLARIA

Half-hardy perennials. The herbaceous varieties are remarkable for their large, finely-shaped and beautifully spotted flowers; these are cultivated exclusively for indoor decoration. The half-shrubby kinds grow more compact, have smaller flowers, bloom more profusely, and succeed in any light rich soil. The calceolarias mostly used for bedding are the different shades of yellow and brown. These admit of a very easy cultivation.

Take the cuttings early in October, and having prepared a piece of ground in a north border, the soil of which must be well drained, and made light with a large admixture of sand, place the cuttings in, and press the earth well round them, water them well and cover with a bell-jar, or place the cuttings in pots, and having sunk them in a north border, under a wall, place a bell-jar over the top of them. In this way they may be kept without further attention till the following spring. In the spring the cuttings should be repotted, and will soon turn into fine plants.

CAMELLIA

IN HOUSE: Favourite winter and spring-flowering shrubs of great beauty. Almost any soil will grow camellias. The best soil, however, appears to be two parts fibrous peat, one fibrous loam, one-sixth part sharp silver-sand, and one-sixth part rotten wood, or clean leaf-mould. Keep them in a temperature of 12°C / 55°F to 15°C / 60°F until their growth is made and flower-buds formed. During this period they should be frequently sprayed, and a humid atmosphere maintained. Towards the end of April gradually remove them by easy transitions, to a cool house or cold pit, and the last week in May to a sheltered situation out of doors, or they may continue in the same house or pit throughout the season. The pots must be placed on a hard bottom to prevent the ingress of worms, watered alternately with clean water and weak liquid manure, and finally removed under glass in October. With such treatment their blossoms will expand in November or December. As soon as the last flower has fallen, shift the plants into larger pots if the state of the roots require it.

Fine plants, from 45 cm / 18 in to 60 cm / 2 ft high, of the following or equally good varieties, can be purchased:

Alba plena, Albertus, Amabilis, Archduchesse Marie, Beata, Chandlerii, Elegans, Countess of Ellesmere, Countess of Derby, Cup of Beauty, De la Reine, Duchesse d'Orleans, Eximia, Fimbriata, Lady Hume's blush, Grand Frederick, Grandis, Imbricata, *Imbricata alba,* Jenny Lind, Mathotiana, *M. alba,* Marchioness of Exeter, Princess Royal, Prince Frederick William, Reticulata, *R. fiore pleno,* The Bride, Tricolor, Tricolor imbricata pleno, and Victoria magnosa.

☛ IN THE OPEN AIR: It may be useful to enumerate some of the sorts which are known to flourish and blossom freely against a north wall, or upon a north border, and to make one or two observations upon their culture and the soil best adapted for them. The sorts best-suited to open-air cultivation are Carolina (double white), Paeoniflora, Prince Leopold, Perfection, Eclipse, Dahlia-flora, *Imbricata alba,* Duchess of Orleans, and Bealii. The soil in which they are planted should be a mixture of peat, leaf-mould, and cow-dung, about 60 cm / 2 ft deep. Great care should be taken that the plants never suffer from drought. After flowering they should be freely watered with liquid manure, especially if the season be dry. The surface of the ground just round the stems of the plants may frequently, with very good effect, be paved with small stones, which assist in keeping the roots cool and moist.

As a general rule, the borders on which camellias are planted should not be disturbed more than is necessary to remove the surface weeds. A top-dressing of fresh soil may, with advantage, be given to them every winter. The snow should never be allowed to rest upon their branches. Some growers of camellias in the open ground bind straw round the stems of their plants, about 13–15 cm / 5–6 in from the ground, when winter sets in: this is found a very efficient protection against frost.

CAMPANULA or BELLFLOWER

A genus of exceedingly beautiful plants, some of them are remarkable for their stately growth, others for their close, compact habit; of the former, *C. pyramidalis,* produces a most striking effect. Of the dwarf varieties, *C. Carpatica* is a most valuable bedding plant.

CANDYTUFT

The candytuft, or iberis, springs up readily from seed sown in any light rich soil. Autumn is the best time for sowing.

Candytuft, Dunnettii, dark crimson, exceedingly beautiful hardy annual, 30 cm / 1 ft.
Candytuft, Normandy – lilac, 30 cm / 1 ft.
Candytuft – purple crimson, very fine.
—rocket, pure white, 30 cm / 1 ft.
—rose, 30 cm / 1 ft.
—sweet-scented, pure white, very fine, 30 cm / 1 ft.

CANNA

For the adornment of the conservatory, drawing-room, or flower-garden, these magnificent plants are unrivalled; their stately growth, combined with their rich and various-coloured flowers, and picturesque and beautiful foliage, render them the most strikingly effective of ornamental plants. Being of easy culture and rapid growth, no one need be without them. They may be propagated by dividing the roots or by seed. Steep the seeds for a few hours in hot water before sowing, then place the pot in a cucumber-frame, or some other warm situation; the plants will be ready to plant out in June, or to shift into larger pots.

CAPE BULBS

Charming in their foliage, abundant in their flowering, and of easy culture, these plants have but one fault – they are a very short time in flower.

In the open ground, a south border, sheltered by a north wall, is most suitable for their growth. It should be well drained, nothing being more prejudicial to them than a wet bottom; the soil turfy loam, a little peat or leaf-mould, and a little sand. The bulbs should be planted about 15 cm / 6 in deep any time in October, and during the winter months the bed should be covered a few inches thick with dry litter.

When grown in pots, the same soil will suit them; potted in October, they should be protected in a cold frame or pit. They will require little or no water till they begin to grow in spring. When they have made a little growth, they may either be planted out in a warm border, or placed on the shelves of the greenhouse near lights, and watered regularly to keep them in a growing state till the foliage shows signs of maturity; water must then be withheld. When at rest they should be kept quite dry.

CAPSICUMS

Pretty ornamental plants, especially in autumn, when covered with their light scarlet fruit. From the capsicum cayenne pepper is made.

☛ PREPARATION OF THE SOIL: These thrive best in a rich, yet light and free soil; and whether grown in pots or planted out, the soil should be of this description.

☛ TIME AND MANNER OF SOWING: The seed should be sown early in March, in well-drained pots filled with light sandy soil, and placed in a cucumber-frame, or wherever a temperature of about 18°C / 65°F is maintained. Cover the seed to the depth of about 1 cm / ½ in, and keep the surface constantly moist until the plants appear. When the plants are strong enough to handle, pot them off, placing two or three plants in a 13-cm / 5-in pot, and replacing them in the warmth. Keep them rather close until they become established, then shift into 18-cm / 7-in pots; and when they are fairly established in these, remove them, if intended for the open ground, to a cold frame, and gradually prepare them for planting out by a freer exposure to the air. Those intended to grow in pots under glass should be shifted into 25-cm / 10-in pots as soon as they require more space for their roots, and be stopped, so as to cause them to form bushy plants; they must be liberally watered and sprayed over head during droughty weather.

CARNATION

This flower is the cultivated *Dianthus Caryophyllus*, found wild in many parts of England.

The seed should be sown in May in pots of light rich soil, placing the pots in an airy, sheltered part of the garden. When the plants are up, and show five or six leaves, plant them out in beds in the same rich soil, and 25 cm / 10 in or so asunder; protecting them during winter. Many of them will bloom the following summer.

For layers, the propagating season is July and August. Having selected the shoots to be layered, and prepared pegs for pegging them down, and soil for their reception, add a little grey sand where the layers are to be placed. Prepare the shoot by trimming off all the leaves with a sharp knife, except five or six at the top; then with a thin-bladed knife make an incision half through the shoot, with an upward cut, beginning below a joint, and passing through it for 2.5 cm / 1 in or so; bend the layer down into the sandy soil prepared for it, pegging it down in that situation in such a manner as to keep the slit or tongue open, and cover it over with rich light compost. Two days afterwards, when the wound is healed, a gentle watering will be beneficial.

Cuttings are made by taking off shoots which cannot be conveniently layered, cutting them right through a joint with an oblique angular cut, and planting them in pots or beds prepared with mixed compost and sand.

In preparing compost for carnations, take two-thirds good staple loamy soil, the turfy top-spit in preference; add to this one-third of thoroughly rotted cow or stable dung, and one measure of drift sand or other sharp grit, to ten measures of the compost. The alluvial deposit from watercourses is an excellent substitute for the loam. In preparing the bed for carnations, having filled the bottom with sufficient drainage material, fill in the compost till nearly full. On this surface spread out the roots horizontally, and fill up with fresh compost, pressing the whole firmly.

The layers of carnations and picotees should be taken off as they begin to form fibre, and either potted or planted in a nursery-bed till October, in either case keeping them in a close frame till they have rooted. If potted, repot in October, and prune to a clean stem, leaving the lower pair of leaves 1 cm / ½ in from the soil, and removing all laterals over 2.5 cm / 1 in long: most of them will strike in the beginning of October, and bloom strongly the second year, if they do not bloom the first.

CARROTS

Sow broadcast on beds, and thin to 8–10 cm / 3–4 in for the smaller sorts: larger sorts are better sown in drills. If it is preferred to drill the seed, let the drills be 30–40 cm / 12–15 in apart, as shallow as possible, and sow the seed continuously along the drill, or three or four seeds at intervals of 15–20 cm / 6–8 in: this economizes the seed, and admits of going amongst the plants without treading on them. Light ground should be trodden before it is drilled: the seed hangs together, and should be separated by rubbing it up with soil. The seed is very light, so that a calm day should be chosen for sowing. It takes from one to three weeks to germinate. As soon as the plants are well above ground, use the small hoe unsparingly, and thin out to not less than 15 cm / 6 in apart. Carrots may be drawn for table as soon as large enough; but the main crop for storing should not be taken up till quite the end of October, or even later, unless severe frosts set in. There are many different sorts; but the Dutch Horn is generally used for forcing and early crops: Intermediate for second or late crop; the Altringham is good for main crop. To produce carrots and parsnips of an extraordinary size, make a very deep hole with a long dibble; ram the earth well round it while the dibble is in, and when it is removed, fill up the hole with fine rich earth. Sow a few seeds on the top, either parsnips or carrots, as may be required, and when up, draw out all except the one plant nearest to the centre of the hole.

CAULIFLOWERS

With us the cauliflower is treated as an annual, although it may be propagated from cuttings. In order to keep up a succession, three or four sowings should be made in the season, the first sowing being made on a slight hotbed in February, or very early in March. This is done by digging away 8–10 cm / 3–4 in of the soil, filling it up to 8–10 cm / 3–4 in above the surrounding soil with fresh stable-dung which has been well turned, covering the bed with the soil removed, raking it, and patting it smooth. On this bed sow the seed, sifting fine soil over it, and covering it when necessary.

Early in April a second and larger sowing should be made in the open ground, and a third and last sowing about the middle of August to stand through the winter. These sowings are made on beds of rich light soil, thoroughly pulverized by digging, and neither too dry nor too moist. In very dry weather, the seedbeds should receive a copious watering the night before sowing. When the plants are large enough to be handled, transplant them to nursery beds of rich soil, well-manured, pricking them out 10 cm / 4 in apart each way. In June, the April sowings will be fit to plant out where they are to grow; in September they will be heading, and will continue to improve up to the frosts of early winter.

Like all the Brassicas, the cauliflower requires a rich, deep soil and an open spot, but sheltered from the north. An old celery- or asparagus-bed, from which the plants have been lifted for forcing, is excellent. If none such is at liberty, let the ground be well trenched 90 cm / 3 ft deep, and manured with good rotten dung, thoroughly incorporated with the soil in digging. On the ground thus prepared plant the young seedlings 75 cm / 2½ ft apart each way.

The after-cultivation is very simple; careful weeding, stirring the soil from time to time with the hoe, and drawing the earth about their roots, and copious watering at the roots in dry weather, include the necessary routine.

The autumn-sown plants are usually pricked out under frames for protection during winter, keeping them clear, stirring the soil occasionally, and giving plenty of air in fine weather, protecting them from frost and rain.

When the heads begin to appear, shade them from sun and rain by breaking down some of the larger leaves, so as to cover them. Water in dry weather, previously forming the earth into a basin round the stem, and pour the water into the roots, choosing the evening in mild weather for so doing, and the morning when the air is frosty.

On the approach of winter, the plants in flower may be taken up with as much earth at their roots as possible, and planted, or rather laid in by the roots, on their sides, in a light sandy soil, in some warm, sheltered place, where the frost can be excluded.

CEANOTHUS

Half-hardy shrubs. An extremely handsome, free-flowering genus of highly ornamental shrubs, suitable either for conservatory decoration, or for covering fronts of villas, walls, or trellis-work in warm situations: they succeed best in peat and loam.

Ceanothus Americanus – white, 120 cm / 4 ft.
C. azureus grandiflorus – sky-blue, flowers in bunches, 120 cm / 4 ft.
C. Baumanii – 90 cm / 3 ft.
—*Californicus* – Blue, tinged with lilac, 120 cm / 4 ft.
C. caeruleus microphyllus – blue, small leaves, very pretty, 150 cm / 4 ft.
C. Delilianus – white, shaded pale blue, beautiful, 150 cm / 5 ft.
C. floribundus – dark blue, remarkably pretty, 90 cm / 3 ft.
C. Fontanesianus – blue, shaded red, 120 cm / 4 ft.
C. Hartwegii – blue, 1.8 m / 6 ft.

CELERY

The celery-plant, *Apium graveolens*, is a biennial in its wild state, although the mode of cultivation adopted makes it an annual, except when grown for seed. It may be sown in any month from Christmas to April. To get plants for the table in September, seeds should be sown in February in pans, which should be placed on a moderate hotbed: in about three weeks they will germinate, and, when about 5 cm / 2 in high, the plants should be pricked out under glass, either in a frame or in pots, in a compost of loam, and three parts well-rotted dung. If in pots, shift them in April, and at the end of May plant them in shallow trenches in a warm part of the garden. If the trenches are dug out to the depth of 75 cm / 2½ ft of hot dung placed in the bottom to stimulate the plants, the soil replaced, and the plants put in and covered with bell-jars, an early crop will be the result. A second sowing should be made in March, still on a hotbed; when fit to handle, they should be pricked out on a slight hotbed, or on a warm border. After a few weeks they should be again transplanted into a similar bed, and placed 10–13 cm / 4–5 in apart each way. In July the plants will be fit to plant out in trenches for autumn use; a third sowing in April, treated in a similar manner, will be ready for winter use, pricking them out in fresh loam and decomposed leaf-mould when large enough to handle. When ready to plant for good in the trenches, mark out the ground into 120 cm / 4 ft clear spaces between the trenches, allowing 40 cm / 15 in for the trench, if single rows, and 50 cm / 20 in if double rows, are to be planted. Dig in the trenches a good dressing of rotten dung. Let the young plants be taken up and planted with a trowel: they should be well settled in with water.

As frost sets in, a quantity of the crop for immediate use should be taken up; removing the roots and soil, and tying the leaves together, lay them in sand, not too dry. There are many kinds of celery in cultivation. Early dwarf, solid white, is recommended. Sutton's solid white, highly recommended for its colour and crispness. Seymour's white champion is recommended for its compact, blanched, and crisp heart.

CELOSIA

Half-hardy annuals. Elegant and free-flowering plants, producing in the greatest profusion spikes of the most beautiful flowers. Plants of the celosia flower freely if planted out in June in a warm, sheltered situation in rich loamy soil; grown in pots, they are the most graceful of greenhouse and conservatory plants. Favourite varieties are:

Celosia argentea – silvery white, shaded with bright rose, very handsome, 90 cm / 3 ft.
C. pyramidalis atrosanguinea – dark red, very handsome, 30 cm / 1 ft.
C. pyramidalis aurea – orange, exceedingly beautiful, 90 cm / 3 ft.
C. pyramidalis coccinea auraniaca – scarlet and orange, very handsome, 90 cm / 3 ft.

CHAMAEROPS

The chamaerops, or Fan Palm, is a splendid plant of oriental appearance, producing a striking effect if planted out in pots, and brought under glass during winter; it succeeds best in rich loamy soil.

CHELONE

A beautiful hardy herbaceous plant, with showy flowers; thrives in any rich soil.

CHRYSANTHEMUM

Unusual importance attaches to the cultivation of chrysanthemums, from the facility with which they may be grown in the very heart of large towns. The flower is of easy culture, and cuttings may be struck almost up to the time of flowering. Nothing is finer than the display of these flowers in October and November, ranging as they do from pure white to a deep orange, from a pale blue to deep red and crimson.

Cuttings of chrysanthemums should be potted pretty thickly together in sandy soil, and the pots plunged to the rim in a gentle hotbed. Nothing roots more certainly than the Chrysanthemum; and if rooted pieces of the old plant are taken instead of cuttings, propagation will go on without any trouble at all.

In order to give the plants every advantage, they must never be either root-bound or allowed to flag from drought. The blooming pots should generally be 25 cm / 10 in deep and 20 cm / 8 in in diameter at the top. Care must be taken that worms do not get into the pot, by placing them on bricks, slates, or coal-ashes. They should be turned round twice a week to prevent their roots striking into the material beneath the pots. Liquid manure may be supplied rather plentifully as the flower-buds begin to expand. The best compost consists of two parts light loam to one part of well-decomposed dung, freely mixed with sand.

The chrysanthemum, like other plants producing terminal flowers, has a tendency to send up one leading stem, which, if not interfered with, would produce a bunch of flowers at the top. This tendency is counteracted by stopping the terminal shoot, which produces a compact shrubby growth, and a great many more flowers. As a rule for the large-flowering kinds, stopping should cease in July. Early in September the best plants are selected, and repotted into 12-sized pots, using the compost as before, and giving ample drainage, and placing them under a south wall; the smaller plants being transplanted at the same time into 24-sized pots, and placed under an east wall. By the middle of October the earlier plants win be showing flower, and should be placed in a cold green-house, or cold-pit, where they can receive plenty of air, leaving those intended for late flowering under the east wall as long as the weather will permit. By the middle of November all should be housed, or at least provided with shelter, and a good supply of bloom for the next two months should be the result.

Large-flowering varieties

Adriane – cream, buff-tinted.
Aurora – very full; ochre-yellow.
Boadicea – creamy rose.
Cassy – orange and rose.
Chevalier Dommage – fine gold.
Cloth of Gold – fine; large.
Defiance – fine; incurved; white.
Etoile Polaire – deep yellow; incurved.
Excelsior – bright crimson; very full.
Fenestritum – primrose; fringed.
Golden Queen of England – canary, fine.
Guelder Rose – pure white; finely incurved.
Imbricatum album – incurved; white.
Novelty – large; blush.
Picturatum roseum – salmon; in curved.
Snowball – fine white.
Snowflake – very dwarf.
Vulcan – bright red crimson.

Pompon varieties
Adonis – rose and white.
Aigle d'Or – canary-yellow.
Apollo – fine; incurved; chestnut-yellow.
Bob – fine dark brown.
Brilliant – crimson-scarlet.
Diana – white; fine form.
Fairy – light lemon.
Fenella – bright orange.
Hendersonii – yellow; early flowering.
Indian Prince – carmine-red and gold; incurved.
President Decaisne – rosy carmine; scarlet.
Sacramento – golden yellow.

Large anemone-flowered varieties
King of Anemones – crimson.
Lady Margaret – pure white, with row of ground petals.

CINERARIAS

It is best to grow them annually from seed. The first sowing should be made in March, in pans filled with equal parts of peat and loam and one-sixth part sand. They should be well drained, made firm, and the seed slightly covered, and placed on a slight bottom-heat. Keep the pans and young plants, when they appear, partially shaded from the bright sun; put them into 8-cm / 3-in pots as soon as they will bear handling, return them to the same place, and renew the same treatment until they are thoroughly established in their pots. Then gradually harden them by giving plenty of air, and place them in a sheltered situation out of doors towards the end of May. As the roots reach the sides of the pots, shift them into larger, giving them their final shift in September. The first flower-stems should be cut out close to the bottom when large plants are desired. Towards the end of September, they should be returned to a cold-pit, and they will begin to flower in October. No soil is better for growing them than equal parts rich loam, leaf-mould, and thoroughly rotted sheep- or horse-dung, liberally mixed with sharp sand or charcoal dust, and used in a roughish state. They also luxuriate under the stimulating regimen of rich manure-water. Another sowing may be made in April, and a third in May, for very late plants. The treatment of old plants may be similar to this. Cut them down as soon as they are done flowering; shake them out, and pot each sucker separately in March; then proceed as above in every respect.

CLARKIA

Hardy annuals. Cheerful-looking flowers, growing freely from seed and bloom-ing profusely under almost all circumstances. When planted in rich soil and properly attended to, they rank amongst the most effective of bedding plants, more especially C. elegans alba, and amoena.

CLIANTHUS

A genus of magnificent free-flowering shrubs, with elegant foliage and bril-liantly coloured and singularly-shaped flowers, which are produced in splendid clusters. C. magnificus and C. puniceus blossom freely out of doors in summer, against a trellis or south wall. Seeds sown early in spring flower the first year; succeed best in sandy peat and loam. They may also be raised easily by cuttings.

Clianthus. magnificus – scarlet; beautiful, 120 cm / 4 ft.
C. puniceus – scarlet, 120 cm / 4 ft.

COLLINSIA

Hardy annuals. An exceedingly pretty, free-flowering popular genus, remark-ably attractive in beds, or mixed borders. C. bicolor, C. bicolor alba, C. bicolor atrorubens and C. multicolor marmorata.

COREOPSIS

The coreopsis, is one of the most showy, free-flowering, and beautiful of hardy annuals. Amongst the tall varieties, C. filifolia Burridgii is the most graceful and beautiful, and C. bicolor grandiflora the most showy and effective in mixed borders. All are hardy annuals except C. Ackermannii, which has a yellow, crim-son centre, and is a hardy perennial; 90 cm / 3 ft.

CROCUS

Culture indoors is the same as the hyacinth; but it is absolutely necessary, to ensure success, that they be kept well supplied with water and have abundance of fresh air, or they will produce leaves only.

Culture in the open ground – they can be successfully grown in almost any soil and situation. Plant 5–8 cm / 2–3 in deep, and not more than 5 cm / 2 in apart.

Crocuses, however, are very accommodating in reference to the depth at which they are planted. When planted in beds devoted to bedding plants, they will reach the surface and flower, if inserted four times that depth. Crocuses will flower freely for many years without being disturbed. The best growers, however, recommend dividing and replanting every third or fifth year. To secure perfect blooms, the foliage must be left to die down of its own accord.

CUPHEA

Profuse-blooming plants, equally valuable for the ornamentation of the conservatory and flower-garden. *C. eminens* is of a graceful branching habit, covered with splendid long scarlet and yellow tubular flowers and *C. ocymoides* with rich purple-violet flowers. The perennial species, if sown early, can be used for bedding-plants the first year; the annual kinds may be treated like ordinary half-hardy annuals.

CYCLAMEN

A genus of charming winter and spring blooming bulbous roots, with very pretty foliage, and flowers so easily cultivated withal, that any one may enjoy these either in the sitting-room window, conservatory, or greenhouse, from October to May, by a little management in the period of starting them into growth.

☛ CULTURE: Plant one bulb in a 13–15 cm / 5–6 in pot, using a rich soil composed of loam and leaf-mould, rotted dung, and a little silver-sand, and, to secure good drainage, place at the bottom of the pot an oyster-shell or potsherd, and over that some pieces of charcoal: the bulb should not be covered more than half its depth.

When the blooming season is over and the bulbs are at rest, plunge the pots in a shady well-drained border, and there let them remain till the leaves begin to grow, when they should be taken up, turned out of the pots, and as much soil removed as can be done without injury to the roots, and replaced with the compost already mentioned.

DAHLIA

☛ SEEDS: Seedlings are procured by sowing the seeds in shallow pans and plunging them into a hotbed, or by sowing on hotbeds prepared for the purpose, in March. The soil should be light and sandy, with a mixture of peat-mould. The seed should be chosen from the best varieties only; it should be lightly covered with soil. In April they will be ready for potting off either singly in the smallest-sized, or round the edge of 15-cm / 6-in pots: this strengthens them for final planting out. Towards the middle or end of August, if successfully treated, they will begin to bloom: at this time they should be examined daily, all single and demi-single blooms thrown away. When done flowering, the young bulbs are taken up and treated as old tubers.

▶ CUTTINGS: In February or March, and even as late as the first week in April, the tuber, which has been carefully wintered in a dry place, is put into soil placed over a hotbed, and in a very short time as many shoots as there are eyes in the tuber make their appearance. As soon as these are 5 cm / 2 in long, they are taken off just below the leaves, struck singly in small pots, and again placed in the hotbed. Some prefer cutting up the tuber as soon as the eyes are distinguishable, and replacing them either in the soil of the hotbed or in pots. As soon as rooted, they should be potted in 13-cm / 5-in pots, and again placed in a gentle heat, but with plenty of air. A week after they are potted they should receive a watering of liquid manure made from guano and powdered charcoal, well mixed with rainwater.

Early in May beds are prepared for the reception of dahlias. They will be best displayed in beds 90 cm / 3 ft wide, with alleys between. The beds being marked by stakes placed at each corner, 10 cm / 4 in of the surface-soil is removed, and 10 cm / 4 in of thoroughly-rotted manure put in its place, and the whole deeply dug, and the manure thoroughly mixed with the soil in digging. The plants are set 10 cm / 4 in deep, so that the crown of the plant is just above the surface. As the plant increases in growth, tying up commences; at the same time a diligent search should be made for slugs, earwigs, and other pests of the garden.

During June and July dahlias require careful attention in watering and stirring the soil about the roots. As the lateral shoots attain sufficient length, tie them up so as to prevent their breaking, placing other stakes for the purpose, should that be necessary. As autumn approaches, examine those tied up, slacking the strings where necessary, to prevent them from galling.

▶ DIVIDING THE ROOTS: Another and more common practice in gardens is to place the whole tuber in some warm place in March, and, when the eyes show themselves, cut up the tubers, and in May plant them at once 15 cm / 6 in below the surface, in the place where they are to bloom, and staking them.

In October the dahlia begins to fail. This then is the time to take care that seed from such as it is desired to propagate from is secured before they are injured by the frost. Provide also against severe weather coming on suddenly, by drawing the earth round the stems in a conical form, which will protect the roots from frost. Even in November, in mild seasons, the dahlia will remain fresh if the weather is open and clear. When the frost turns their foliage brown or black, take them up, cut off the roots, leaving them 15 cm / 6 in or so of stem attached, and plunge them into a box of ashes, chaff, or sand.

DAPHNE

Beautiful shrubs, remarkable for the elegance of their flowers and for their bright red poisonous berries. *D. Mezereum* is the most common variety. The dwarf daphnes are somewhat tender: they bear pink flowers very fragrant. There is a Chinese daphne, *D. odorata*, which is a great ornament in the greenhouse, or a warm, shady border.

DATURA

A tribe of highly-ornamental plants, hardy annuals, producing large sweet-scented trumpet-shaped flowers of the most attractive character, and succeeding in any light rich soil.

Datura ceratocaulon – satin-white, striped purple, very handsome, 60 cm / 2 ft.
D. fastuosa alba – pure white, double, 90 cm / 3 ft.
D. humilis flore pleno (*chlorantha fl. pl.*) – rich golden yellow, a magnificent, free-flowering, sweet-scented variety, 60 cm / 2 ft.
D. Knightii – white, splendid double flowers with exquisite odour, 90 cm / 3 ft.
D. quercifolia – lilac, oak-leaved 90 cm / 3 ft.
D. Wrightii (*meteloides*) – satin-white, bordered with lilac; an exquisite, sweet-scented plant, 60 cm / 2 ft.

DELPHINIUM

A genus of profuse-flowering plants of a highly decorative character. Planted in large beds or groups, their gorgeous spikes of flowers, of almost endless shades, from pearl-white to the richest and deepest blue, render them conspicuous objects in the flower-garden: they delight in deep, highly-enriched soil. With the exception of *D. cardiopetalum* they are all hardy perennials.

DEUTZIA

A beautiful hardy shrub, when in bloom covered with pretty snowdrop-like flowers, exceedingly valuable for the spring decoration of the conservatory.

Deutzia gracilis – pure white, very graceful, 90 cm / 3 ft.

DIANTHUS

A beautiful genus, which embraces some of the most popular flowers in cultivation. The carnation, picotee, pink, and sweet William (*D. barbatus*), all belong to this genus. *D. Sinensis* and its varieties may be considered the most beautiful and effective of our hardy annuals; the double and single varieties, with their rich and varied colours in beds or masses, are remarkably attractive; while the recently introduced species, *D. Hedewigii*, with its large, rich-coloured flowers, 8–10 cm / 3–4 in in diameter, close compact habit, and profusion of bloom, is unsurpassed for effectiveness in beds or mixed borders.

DIGITALIS or FOXGLOVE

Hardy perennials. Remarkably handsome and ornamental plants, of stately growth and easy culture. They thrive in almost any soil and situation.

DOG-TOOTHED VIOLETS

Pretty little plants, with beautifully spotted leaves. When planted as an edging to beds or borders, they are remarkably effective, and do well in any light soil. To prevent decay, surround the tubers with about an inch of silver-sand.

ECCREMOCARPUS

A half-hardy climber of great beauty; bearing rich orange-coloured flowers in profusion. It will grow in any common soil, and may be easily raised from seed.

Sow in autumn on a slight hotbed, and the plants, after two or three shiftings, will be ready for turning out in May. If cut down in autumn, and covered with dry leaves, the Eccremocarpus will live through any ordinary winter, and shoot up again vigorously in the spring.

ECHINOPS

The echinops, or globe-thistle, is a strong plant of considerable beauty, sown from April to May and divided in September. It grows freely in any soil.

Echinops bannaticus – blue ball, 90 cm / 3 ft.

ENDIVE

☞ PREPARATION OF THE SOIL: Trench the ground to a depth of 60 cm / 2 ft, mixing a very liberal dressing of rich and thoroughly-decayed manure. For crops intended to stand the winter, a light, dry soil is best, in a sheltered situation.

☞ TIME AND MANNER OF SOWING: Make the first sowing about the middle of May on a bed of well-pulverized rich soil, scattering the seed thinly, and covering it lightly. For the main crop sow in the middle of June, and again about the middle of July. Plants to stand the winter should be sown early in August. When the plants are about 5 cm / 2 in high, transplant into nursery beds upon rich well-prepared soil, taking special care not to injure the roots, as this, as well as want of water in hot, dry weather, very often causes them to run to seed.

☙ PLANTING AND AFTER-MANAGEMENT: When the plants are about 10 cm / 4 in high, transplant, lifting them carefully with as much soil as can be kept about their roots. Place them in drills about 8 cm / 3 in deep and 30–36 cm / 12–14 in apart, between the plants. Give a liberal supply of water immediately after planting, and as often as may be requisite to keep the soil moist. The plants will require no special attention till they are nearly full-grown, when means should be used to blanch them. In the case of the earlier crops this may be done by tying them up when dry, and drawing the soil about them so as to fill the drills in which they are planted, then ridging up the soil 5–8 cm / 2–3 in round each plant. But as late crops intended for winter use are liable to be injured by frost, these should be blanched by covering the plants with inverted pots. When severe weather is feared, a portion of the plants sown in July may be lifted with balls and planted closely together in pits or frames, where they can be protected from frost and wet, yet be fully exposed to the air when the weather permits. Tying or covering should be done at intervals, so as to have a continuous supply well blanched as they may be required for use. The August sowing should be planted out at the bottom of a south wall, or in some other sheltered situation.

Green Curled, extra fine French – very superior variety.
Batavian Green – smooth broad leaves.
Batavian White – large and very superior.

EPACRIS

These are heath-like shrubs. They all require a fine gritty peat soil, and flourish best in double pots, with moist moss between them. The pots should be well drained; but the roots of the plants must never suffer for want of moisture. Cuttings of the young wood strike easily in sand with a little bottom heat.

These plants should be freely cut back as soon as they have done flowering; and after the shoots have grown afresh, 5–8 cm 2–3 in long, is the best time for potting them. Place them in a close pit, but by no means warm, for a few weeks; gradually inure them to the air, plunge in a sunny situation: see that the wood is brown and hard by the end of September. Remove to conservatory-shelf in October, and you will have a charming profusion and succession of tiny tubes of colour.

ERODIUM

Charming little plants for rockeries, edgings, and flower-borders; succeed in any soil.

Erodium pelargoniaeflorum – white and rose, upper petals very prettily striped, 15 cm / ½ ft. Hardy perennial.

ESCALLONIA

Half-hardy, handsome evergreen shrubs, with rich glaucous leaves and bunches of pretty tubular flowers; they succeed against a south wall, if protected in the winter, and thrive best in sandy peat and loam. .

Escallonia floribunda – white, 90 cm / 3 ft.
E. macrantha – purple-scarlet, 90 cm / 3 ft.
E. macrantha carnea – flesh-colour, very beautiful, 90 cm / 3 ft.

ESCHSCHOLZIA

An exceedingly showy profuse-flowering class of Californian poppy annuals, quite hardy, remarkable for extremely rich and beautiful colours. *E. tenuifolia* is exceedingly neat for small beds, edgings, or rockeries; delights in light rich soil.

Eschscholzia Californica – bright yellow, with rich orange centre, 30 cm / 1 ft.
E. compacta – yellow and orange, 30 cm / 1 ft.
E. crocea – rich orange, 30 cm / 1 ft.
—— *alba* – creamy white, 30 cm / 1 ft.
—— *tenuifolia* – primrose, with orange centre, very compact, 15 cm / ½ ft.

EUCOMIS

A very ornamental half-hardy bulb; pot under glass, and set outside in sunny weather.

EUPHORBIA

Very ornamental, warm greenhouse evergreen shrubs; succeed in a mixture of peat loam.

Euphorbia regis Jubae – red, 90 cm / 3 ft.
— *splendens* – bright scarlet, 60 cm / 2 ft.
Euphorbia jacquiniflora.

FENNEL

Fennel may be raised from seed in April or May. The seed should be covered lightly with fine mould, and, when the plants are strong enough, they may be set out in a bed about a foot apart. A good bed of fennel will last for years; but to insure fine leaves, the flower-stalks should always be cut off as soon as they appear, so as never to ripen seed.

FERNS

Most ferns delight in a loose soil, abundant moisture, and a warm humidity in the air. Hardy sorts may be grown out of doors, and those that will stand a greenhouse temperature are great ornaments in the house.

FIGS (in the open air)

Almost any well-drained soil will suit the fig-tree if it is planted in its pot to restrict growth of the roots. Care, however, must be taken that it is not too rich, or the tree will not produce fruit. Three sorts of figs are usually grown, the Brown Turkey, Brunswick and Black Ischia: all require a wall and a sunny situation. The best mode of training is perpendicular. Fix as many permanent leaders to the wall as required, 25–40 cm / 10–15 in apart; remove all unnecessary wood by disbudding, and stop the fruit-bearing shoots at the end of August or beginning of September by merely pinching off or squeezing flat the terminal growing-point. The object of this is to induce the formation of fruit, and is a matter of much nicety. A too early stopping will cause a too early development of fruit, which will not survive winter frost. The fruit for next year must not be much larger than a pea when winter sets in.

FILBERTS

The trees may be introduced into orchards, shrubberies, plantations, or hedgerows. Planted close to each other, they form valuable screens or shelter in exposed situations. Filberts are not merely ornamental but edible. They will thrive almost anywhere, and are much improved by pruning.

FRAXINELLA

Handsome, aromatic, free-flowering, hardy herbaceous plants, perennials, suitable for mixed borders; succeed in any common soil.

Fraxinella – red, 60 cm / 2 ft.
— white, 60 cm / 2 ft.

FRENCH BEANS

🖝 PREPARATION OF THE SOIL: These delight in a deep, friable, and rich soil; and where the land is of a strong, tenacious character, it should be trenched and ridged as early in autumn as possible, well intermixing a liberal allowance of manure.

🖝 TIME AND MANNER OF SOWING: The seeds being liable to rot if sown early in wet, cold soil, the first crop had better be planted in boxes or pans. Place these in a cold frame, or under the shelter of a south wall, and protect them from frost. When the plants are in the rough leaf, and the weather considered safe, transplant in rows about 76 cm / 2½ ft apart on a warm and sheltered border. Transplanting induces early fertility, and may be practised with advantage even where the plants are raised in the open border. Sow for the principal crops early in May, June, and July; and on light dry soils in warm localities a small quantity may be sown towards the end of July. Cover the seeds with about 8 cm / 3 in of soil.

🖝 AFTER-MANAGEMENT: When the plants are about 10 cm / 4 in high, ridge the soil neatly up on either side. This will prevent their being blown about by rough winds: and while there is any danger of frost, the early crop should be sheltered by well-furnished branches of evergreens, stuck into the soil in a slanting direction on each side of the rows. Keep the ground between the lines well stirred and free from weeds. During dry, hot weather, an occasional soaking of water will be of service.

Canterbury White – very prolific, well known, 30 cm / 1 ft.
Chinese Long-podded – exceedingly productive, free-cropping variety, 30 cm / 1 ft.
Mohawk, or Early Six Weeks – a very good variety, 30 cm / 1 ft.
Newington Wonder – the best of all for forcing, very productive, 30 cm / 1 ft.
Speckled – a well-known prolific variety, 30 cm / 1 ft.

FRITILLARIA

Miniature Crown Imperials, with singularly marbled flowers. They are very interesting and pretty, with very individual growing conditions.

FUCHSIAS

Whoever has a glasshouse, or a window free from dust, may grow one or more fuchsias. Cuttings should be inserted in pots filled either with loam and leaf-mould, or peat and silver-sand, in equal parts, to within 3 cm / 1½ in of the top. Place over this 2 cm / ¾ in of silver-sand, and level the surface to make it firm;

then insert the cuttings – about 2.5 cm / 1 in long is the proper length, and plunge the pots in a bottom-heat of 15°C / 60°F. In three weeks they may be rotted in 8-cm / 3-in pots, and replunged in the same bed, keeping them at a temperature of from 10°C / 50°F to 15°C / 60°F. As soon as the roots reach the sides of the pots, the plants should be shifted into fresh pots, until they receive their final shift into 15-, 20- or 30-cm / 6-, 9-, or 12-in pots, towards the end of June. The size of the pot must be regulated by the period when they are wanted to bloom. If in July, a 15- or 20-cm / 6- or 9-in pot will suffice; if in September or October, a 30 / 12 will not be too large. During the period of growth, the plants will require stopping at least six times, care being taken never to stop the shoots immediately preceding or directly after the operation of shifting into larger pots. If the pyramidal form of growth, which is the best of all forms for the fuchsia, is adopted, the plants, from the first, must be trained to a single stem, and all the side-shoots stopped, to make the pyramid thick and perfect. If the bush form is wanted, the whole of the shoots should then be stopped at every third joint, until branches enough are secured to form the bush, and then be trained into the desired shape. A regular moist, genial temperature must be maintained during the entire period of growth, never exceeding 15°C / 60°F. Fuchsias will grow in almost any soil. Garden-loam and leaf-mould in equal proportions, with some broken charcoal and sand, do very well. It is better to feed them with manure-water than to mix dung with the soil. After they are well rooted, they should never be watered with clear water.

Hardy Fuchsias

Many large and beautiful varieties of fuchsias are hardy, and will stand our winters in the open ground, especially in a well-drained light soil having a large portion of peat in it; and a great many that are looked upon as tender varieties may be preserved if covered 8–10 cm / 3–4 in with dry cinder ashes at the first approach of frost. The dead branches should not be cut off, not should the ashes be removed until the fuchsias begin to shoot in the spring.

GAILLARDIA

These strong flowers are both annuals and perennials. The former are splendid bedding-plants, continuing in beauty during the summer and autumn: they thrive in any light rich soil.

Gaillardia alba marginata – white-edged, half-hardy annual, 45 cm / 1½ ft.
G. grandiflora hybrida – rich crimson and yellow, flowers remarkably large and attractive, half-hardy annual, 45 cm / 1½ ft.

GENTIAN

All the gentians are beautiful. *G. acaulis*, with its large deep mazarine-blue blossoms, looks well as an edging plant. It requires a pure air and rich light soil.

GERANIUM

These well-known floral favourites are not less indispensable in the garden. Plants to flower in May should be cut down by the end of the previous June; they should have broken, been reduced, repotted, and encouraged to grow 5–8 cm / 2–3 in in a close cold frame for a fortnight, and have received their final stopping by the end of July, and be potted by the 1st of November. Success depends upon their chief growth being completed before Christmas. No after-management can compensate for the neglect of early growth. Plants in general, and geraniums in particular, flower best when they are pot-bound.

Bedding varieties

Boule de Feu – fine scarlet.
Boule de Neige – white.
Comte de Mornay – rosy scarlet; blush edges, suffused with pink; fine.
Countess of Bective – deep salmon, with dark brown zone.
Defiance – large.
Emperor of the French – scarlet.
Frogmore scarlet.
Imperial crimson – mossy.
Lady Middleton – fine rose.
Madame Chardin – salmon-rose, white centre; large.
Minnie – pink; white spot on upper petals.
Rubens – fine salmon colour.
Shrubland – scarlet; fine large.
Tom Thumb – scarlet.
Tom Thumb's Bride – good scarlet.
Trentham rose – fine rose.

Silver and gold varieties, one thousand

Bijou – strong-growing scarlet flower; silver leaves.
Brilliant – slightly silvered; good scarlet; fine bedder; not a strong habit.
Cloth of Gold – unique.
Dandy – a neat silver-edged gem.
Lady Plymouth – a neat silver-edged gem.
Pink-flowered – ivy-leaved.
Scarlet-flowered – ivy-leaved.
Silver Queen – pink flowers; smooth foliage.
Silver – ivy-leaved.
White-flowered – ivy-leaved.

☛ CUTTINGS: Cuttings of all sorts of geraniums for bedding the following year should be struck early: from the last week in July to the end of the first week in August is very good time. They should be taken in dry weather, and they should be kept to dry twenty-four hours after they have been prepared for potting. They may be potted four or six in a pot, according to size. It is essential that the pots be well fitted with drainers, that the soil be light and sandy, and that it be pressed tight round the joint of the cuttings, which should be buried in it as flat as possible. When potted, they may be sunk in the ground on a south border, and well-watered in the evening, when the sun is off. If they grow too freely before it is time to take them in for the winter, the top shoots should be broken off, and in this way they will make strong bushy plants.

☛ PRESERVING OLD VARIETIES: Take them out of the borders in autumn, on a dry day. Shake off all the earth from their roots, and suspend them downwards, in a cellar or dark room. The leaves and shoots will become yellow and sickly; but when potted about the end of May, and exposed to a gentle heat, they will recover and vegetate luxuriantly.

Fancy Geraniums

Amy Sedgwick – rose; fine form and quality; clear white centre and edges.
Adèle – light rose, white belt on each petal; good form.
Bridesmaid – lavender-rose, edged with white; good form and substance.
Crimson King – crimson, dwarf and showy; medium size.
Delight – rosy crimson; upper petals bright cerise; delicate habit; light throat and edges.
Delicatum – white, with delicate rose blotch.
Emperor of Morocco – mulberry; lilac throat and edges.
Formosum – rich carmine; lower petals mot tled with white.
Princess Royal – silvery white lilac; rose-blotch on upper petals.
Undine – very large, rosy lake, with light throat and edges.

French or Spotted Geraniums

Bertie – deep rose; rich spots on lower petals; upper ditto carmine; fine good show variety.
Constellation – beautiful.
Eclipse – brilliant scarlet; fine dark spots.
Fairy Queen – rose-maroon blotch; white centre; fine.
Geant des Batailles – white, shaded with crimson-scarlet spots; fine large flower.
Imperatrice Eugenie – pure white; dark violet spot.
Leo – orange-rose spot on lower and blotch on top petals.
Pandora – scarlet, with light margin.
Salvator Rosa – rose, shaded violet; brown spots; white centre.
Scaramouch – fine exhibition variety.
Senior Wrangler – peach; maroon spots; shaded margin.

Zonale Geraniums

The following varieties, of thousands, are found to be good:

Annbrook Peaches, Brookside Primrose, Flaming Katy, Orion, Rigel, Samelia, Shocking Violet.

GLADIOLI

The varieties of gladioli may be divided into two sections – summer- and autumn-flowering; Ramosus and its seedlings representing the former, gandavesis and its seedlings the latter. The flowers of each are extremely beautiful.

The ramosus varieties bloom in July and August; the gandavensis in August and September, and with a little management in successional planting, even the months of October and November may be enlivened with the brilliant colours of this floral gem.

Early-flowering Ramosus seedlings

CULTURE IN POTS: for the decoration of the orchard-house or conservatory, and for an early summer bloom out of doors: plant in November, December, or January, three bulbs in a 15- or 18-cm / 6- or 7-in pot, using a compost of equal parts of peat, leaf-mould, loam, and sand; make the soil somewhat firm about the bulbs, and withhold water till the plants appear; then give it very gradually. The pots should be plunged in ashes or cocoa-fibre in cold pits or frames, where they may remain till May, when the plants should either be planted out, or if intended for indoor decoration (for which they are admirably adapted), placed out of doors in a shady situation, the pots plunged in ashes or cocoa-fibre, and attended to with water till showing for bloom, when they should be placed in the conservatory.

CULTURE OUT OF DOORS: Plant for succession in December, January, February, and March. Should the soil be well drained, it will simply require deep digging and well working; adding as the work proceeds plenty of thoroughly rotted manure; should it be wet, or of an adhesive character, besides deep digging and well-working, it should be raised 5–8 cm / 2–3 in above the general level. Plant the bulbs 15 cm / 6 in deep and 23 cm / 9 in apart, surrounding each with an inch of river-sand or a handful of cocoa-fibre; when planted in February or March, 8–10 cm / 3–4 in will be sufficiently deep. The first plantings should be protected by placing on the surface 2.5–5 cm / 1–2 in of newly-dropped leaves or cocoa-fibre; the former must be removed in March or April. When the ground intended for these is occupied with spring-flowering bulbs, or is unusually wet and cold, first plant in pots, and when the time comes for turning the plants out, be careful not to disturb the roots. In dry seasons much disappointment would be avoided by mulching the plants with manure or cocoa-fibre.

Autumn-flowering gladioli

☛ TIME OF PLANTING: On light well-drained soils the bulbs may be planted as early as the end of March; but on stiff soils, and such as are somewhat damp, the end of April or beginning of May would be early enough, unless required to be in flower early in July. To accomplish this, plant three bulbs in a 15- or 18-cm / 6- or 7-in pot, and treat them as if they were intended to blossom without removal. In May, transfer them from the pots to the place in which they are intended to bloom, without disturbing the roots.

GLOXINIA

A superb genus of greenhouse plants, producing, in great profusion, flowers of the richest and most beautiful colours; thrive best in sandy peat and loam.

GORSE or FURZE

Ulex is the botanical name for the gorse or furze, of which there are several varieties. All are free-flowering evergreen shrubs with yellow blossoms: they may be propagated by cuttings, and most of them from seed, which they produce and ripen freely. The double-blossomed furze is singularly beautiful and very useful for hedges. Where furze of any kind is used for this purpose, the best plan is to raise a bank the height desired, wider at bottom than at top, and along the ridge to plant the cuttings, or sow seed.

GRASSES

Flowering Grasses

That splendid importation *Gynerium argenteum*, or pampas-grass, resists the cold of our ordinary seasons. The old leaves should not be removed until the end of April, as they afford the best possible protection as far as it goes; experience, however, shows the necessity of a little extra litter. A rich alluvial soil, at least a yard deep, abundance of space to unfold its large, graceful leaves, and throw up its flower-stems, and an unlimited supply of water, are all the conditions its successful culture demands. With liberal treatment, seedlings will flower the third or fourth year. By sowing thinly in February or March in pots, and planting out in prepared beds in May, a season may almost be gained in the growth of the plants. Like all the grasses, the seed should be barely covered with soil, and the surface kept moist, until germination is insured. If the flower-stem is cut before it begins to fade, it looks almost as noble when dry. The pretty millet-grass (*Millium effusum*), and the several varieties of briza, or quaking grass, should be sown either in pots or on a rather sheltered bed out of doors. *Bromus brizoformis* is useful for bouquets. The two feather-grasses, *Stipa pennata* and *S. gigantea*, hardy perennials, and the hardy biennial foxtail barley, *Hordeum jubatum*, are also most useful for mixing with other flowers, and very elegant in themselves. The smallest feather-grass almost rivals the *Festuca glauca* for edgings. The handsome silver foliage of the *Festuca* contrasts beautifully with gravel walks. It is neat, graceful, and easily kept, the only attention required being to cut off the flower-stems in summer, which maintains the leaves in health and beauty.

HEARTSEASE or PANSIES

The common *Viola lutea*, with *Viola grandiflora* and *Viola amoena*, are the joint parents of the many beautiful flowers known to us in these days under the general name of heartsease or pansies. Heartsease require little attention during the autumn months; indeed, those not intended for propagation may be dug up as soon as flowering is over. The choicer varieties must be taken care of, in order that their roots may be divided, or cuttings taken from them in April or May; for it is only by such an annual renewal that degeneration can be prevented.

About the first week in October is a good time to make a selection of plants for potting. These should be vigorous, healthy plants. The bed for their reception may be prepared by digging out the soil for about 46 cm / 18 in, and filling it up, after providing proper drainage, with compost properly mixed: a better plan is to make a raised bed for the purpose. This may be done by placing a row of bricks, 46 cm / 18 in high and 120 cm / 4 ft wide, or wood, supported by stakes at each end, of the same height, and of a length suited to the number of plants required. This bed should be filled with compost, consisting of well-decomposed turfy mould, leaf-mould, and thoroughly decomposed cow-dung; or, failing that, stable-manure; where the loam is stiff, a little well-washed river-sand should be added; where it is light and sandy, equal parts of earth should be added.

Set the plants in rows 30 cm / 12 in apart, and protect them from frost, which is easily done in the raised bed: occasional examination for their great enemy the wire-worm, and the removal of dead leaves, is all the care they require during winter; in the spring, copious watering, and in summer, mulching, to prevent radiation.

HELICHRYSUM or CURRY PLANT

Hardy annuals, everlasting. The yellow flowers, if cut when young, make pretty winter bouquets. *H. italicum* smells strongly of curry. Succeeds in any rich garden soil.

HELIOTROPES

Half-hardy perennials. Profuse-flowering and deliciously fragrant plants, valuable for bedding and pot-culture; seeds sown in spring make fine plants for summer and autumn decoration; succeed in light rich soil. Obtained from cuttings in the same way as verbenas and bedding calceolarias. All are very sensitive of frost.

HOLLYHOCK

There is no finer ornament of the autumnal flower-garden that the hollyhock: its noble tapering spike-like stem and rich rosettes of flowers clustering round the footstalks of the leaves, their variety of colour renders them also most attractive objects. Hollyhocks may be propagated by seed and by cuttings.

The seed of the hollyhock should be gathered only from the most perfect plants. About the middle of March, or not later than the first week in April, the seed-bed should be prepared. Trench the bed 60 cm / 2 ft deep, throwing the top spit to the bottom, and bringing the second spit to the surface, breaking up the surface thoroughly. On this bed, raised smooth, sow the seed so thickly as to come up 2.5 cm / 1 in apart, and sift over the seeds some rich dry soil, so as to cover them for about the same. When they come up and begin to grow, vigorous growth must be encouraged by watering in dry weather. If they are intended to bloom in rows where they stand, every other plant must now be removed, so as to leave them 30 cm / 1 ft apart all over the bed; here they may be supported by strong stakes placed at both ends of each row, and a strong cord carried from one to the other, to which the plants are to be tied.

In propagating by cuttings, as soon as the first flowers of an old plant open sufficiently to judge of the flowering, the superfluous side-branches having no flower-buds should be taken off, with two or three joints and leaves. Cut the shoot through with a clean cut, just under the lower joint, leaving the leaf entire; cut it also at about 5 cm / 2 in above the joint: either joint will do, provided they have growing eyes, with a leaf and piece of ripened wood to support the bud until roots are formed. These cuttings, planted in a light sandy soil, placed under a bell-jar, and watered occasionally, and shaded from the sun, will require little further care except keeping clear of weeds and dead leaves. When rooted, pot them off in a cold frame where they can remain during the winter. In spring plant them out in the open ground, taking care to furnish the roots with the proper soil.

The old plants in autumn furnish another source for new plants. When the flowers are becoming shabby, cut the plants down, and, beginning at the bottom joints, continue to make cuttings, as described above, until the fibre gets too soft for the purpose – each joint having eyes will furnish a plant: these struck under a bell-jar, on a very slight hotbed, will grow vigorously, the soil being gritty sand, loam, and leaf-mould, in equal proportions. Sprinkle the cuttings slightly with water every day in fine weather.

Three flowering-spikes should only be allowed to the strongest plants – to weakly ones only one. When 45 cm / 1½ ft high, stake them, placing two to each plant, one of these stakes being driven in on each side of the plant, the stakes being 150 cm / 5 ft long and driven 75 cm / 2½ ft into the ground.

White and blush-colour – Vista; Celestial.
Buff, fawn, and salmon – Empress; Queen of the Buffs.
Lemon – Alcea Chaters.
Pink – Alcea Rosea.

Humea elegans – red, 2.5 m / 8 ft, half-hardy biennial.

HUMEA

A remarkably handsome plant, invaluable for decorative purposes, whether in the conservatory, or dispersed in pots. Planted in the centres of beds or mixed borders, its majestic and graceful appearance renders it a most effective and striking object. The leaves, when slightly rubbed, yield a powerful odour. When well grown, we have seen it 2.5 m / 8 ft high and 120 cm / 4 ft in diameter. Succeeds best in light rich soil.

HYACINTH

In the conservatory or sitting-room it is equally at home and in the most confined streets of London the hyacinth may be seen blooming as magnificently as if surrounded by all the advantages of the open country.

☛ TIME OF PLANTING: Nature has undoubtedly declared herself in favour of planting the hyacinth in October and November; yet we would say to the lovers of this flower, make your first planting as near the 1st of September as possible, and your last about the 31st of December. You may then have the glowing beauty of the hyacinth from Christmas till April or May.

PLANTING OUT OF DOORS: In the open ground we have planted hyacinths as late as the beginning of March, and have been rewarded by some very good blooms; others planted early in February blossomed beautifully. We do not, however, recommend planting later than the beginning of January. If the soil be light or medium, it simply requires to be deeply dug and well worked; if heavy, besides deep digging and well working, the bulbs should be surrounded with sand, or, better still, two good handfuls of cocoa-fibre. When manure is added, thoroughly rotted cow-dung or leaf-soil is best; and when winter protection is given, long straw laid loosely on the bed, and hooped down to prevent its littering the garden, or cocoa-fibre, both are unequalled; but they should be removed as soon as the plants begin to show.

In planting, the crown of the bulb should be 10 cm / 4 in under the surface, and for a very effective display the bulbs should be planted 15 cm / 6 in apart.

At the time of planting, groups of crocus, snowdrops, winter aconites, or *Scilla sibirica*, can be planted in masses – these will bloom before the hyacinths; or in spring, autumn-sown annuals can be pricked in all over the bed – these will succeed the hyacinths.

PLANTING IN POTS: To cultivate the hyacinth successfully in pots, a free porous soil is indispensable, and one composed of equal parts of turfy loam, rotted cow-dung, and leaf-soil, adding about one-eighth part of silver-sand, and thoroughly incorporating the whole and passing it through a rough sieve, is undoubtedly the best compost. Cocoa-fibre and charcoal, mixed with rotted cow-dung and loam, makes a fine mixture if used in equal parts.

The size of the pot must be regulated by the accommodation and requirements of the cultivator; for one bulb a 10- or 12-cm / 4- or 4½-in pot will grow the Hyacinth well; for three bulbs a 14-cm / 5½-in pot will be sufficient (and here we would remark, hyacinths cultivated in groups are much more effective than grown singly). At the bottom of the pot place over the hole a piece of potsherd and some charcoal, and on this some rough pieces of turfy loam to insure good drainage; then fill the pots with the prepared soil to within an inch of the top, placing the bulb in the centre, or if three, at equal distances apart, pressing them well into the soil, and filling up, leaving only the crown of the bulbs uncovered; moderately water, and place them anywhere out of doors, on coal-ashes or anything that will secure good drainage and at the same time be objectionable to worms; then with coal-ashes, leaf-soil, or better still, common cocoa-fibre, fill up between the pots, and cover over 5–8 cm / 2–3 in. In five or six weeks the pots will be full of roots, and may then be removed at pleasure.

To maintain the succession, a portion of the newly-potted bulbs, intended for late blooming, should be placed under a north wall, while those for early blooming should be arranged under a south wall, and every fortnight a part of these should be brought indoors.

🐾 PLANTING IN SAND: Besides the advantage which sand offers in being independent of drainage, it may be procured in various colours. The different shades may be arranged either in geometrical figures or fanciful designs, with very charming effect. As soon, however, as the plants appear, the surface should be covered with green moss.

To insure an effective display, it is necessary to plant thickly. Push the bulbs into the dry sand, leaving only the top visible, and to fix the sand, the vessel should be immersed in a pail of water; also, to prevent any subsequent displacement of the sand, and to secure for the plants a sufficient supply of moisture, this operation must be repeated once a week, a bath of two or three minutes' duration being sufficient; and if the water used be tepid, it will be all the better, as it encourages the development of the flower. An occasional watering of tepid water overhead, through a fine rose, will free the plants from dust. Cocoa-fibre and charcoal is a much better medium than sand.

HYDRANGEA

The common hydrangea is a Chinese shrub, half-hardy, imported into England about the year 1790, by Sir Joseph Banks. It thrives best in a rich soil, and requires plenty of water. When the plant has done flowering, its branches should be cut in. Blue hydrangeas are much admired. It is some soil containing aluminium which produces this variety. Blue flowers may in general be procured by planting in a strong loam and watering freely with a solution of alum or nitre.

IMPATIENS or BUSY LIZZIE

Also called *Noli me tangere*, from a curious property in the seed-vessel, which springs open as soon as touched. They thrive in rich loamy soil.

Impatiens tricornis – yellow and crimson, half-hardy annual, 75 cm / 2½ ft.
Impatiens flaccida – lilac, very handsome, 75 cm / 2½ ft.

INOPSIDIUM

Charming profuse-blooming hardy annuals, growing freely, in any damp rich soil, or upon the shady side of rockeries; they make remarkably neat edgings in shady situations, and are valuable for pots and vases.

Inopsidium aculae – sky blue, 4 cm / 1½ in.
I. album – white, 4 cm / 1½ in.

IPOMOEA or MORNING GLORY

Beautiful climbing plants. The seed should be raised under glass in April and the young plants set out in May. They require a rich light soil. In some situations the plants will shed their seed and come up from year to year in the open ground.

IRIS

Amongst the many forms of floral beauty which adorn the flower-borders in June, few assert their title to admiration more effectively that the Iris. The height of the plants is from 46–60 cm / 18–24 in, while its cultivation is unusually simple, succeeding in any ordinary light rich garden soil. The Iris should be planted in clumps of three or more, and if allowed to remain undisturbed, they will each succeeding year become more effective.

IRISH IVY

The Irish Ivy, *Hedera canariensis*, or, as it is sometimes called, the Giant Ivy, is very ornamental and grows very rapidly. It requires to be clipped once or twice a year freely.

ISMENE

A genus of free-flowering handsome sweet-scented summer-blooming plants. They grow freely on a south border in a mixture of light loam and rich vegetable soil; they make also handsome plants for indoor decoration. Culture the same as recommended for amaryllis.

Ismene Illyricum – white.
— *maritimum* – white.
— *undulatum* –white.

IXIA

An exceedingly pretty Cape flowering bulb, producing its graceful flowers in long slender spikes, and in the greatest profusion; succeeds well on a warm south border, in a mixture of sandy loam and leaf-mould, or peat.

JASMINE

Of the fragrant free-flowering shrubs called jasmines, there are many hardy varieties. The most common are *Jasminum officinale*, which has white blossom, and *J. Revolutum*, yellow. There are several hothouse varieties extremely beautiful, as *J. grandiflorum* and *J. odoratissimum*. All the jasmines are easily propagated by cuttings in sandy soil, covered with a bell-jar.

JERUSALEM ARTICHOKE

☞ PREPARATION OF THE SOIL: These useful vegetables will grow and yield plenty of tops in almost any soil or situation; but to secure an abundant crop of large and good-flavoured tubers select a deep light sandy loam. The ground should receive a moderate allowance of manure in autumn, and be trenched to a depth of 60 cm / 2 ft at least, ridging it up roughly for the winter.

☞ TIME AND MANNER OF PLANTING: Plant early in March, in lines 3 ft asunder, and about 46 cm / 18 in apart in the lines. The tubers may be dibbled in, as is often done with potatoes; but we recommend the making of a narrow trench, about 15 cm / 6 in deep, in which the tubers can be placed at equal depths with greater certainty; the soil placed over them should be left in a loose open state.

☞ AFTER-MANAGEMENT: Thin out the shoots when a few inches high, not leaving more than two or three from a tuber. This, however, will be unnecessary where the soil is light and somewhat dry. Keep the ground free from weeds by frequent deep hoeings. The tubers may be left in the ground till wanted for use, or they may be taken up towards the end of November, and stored in sand or soil; but light and air must be effectually excluded, otherwise they will be of a dark colour when cooked.

KALE

☞ PREPARATION OF THE SOIL: To secure heavy crops of this hardy useful winter vegetable, a deep rich soil is essential. The ground should be trenched 60 cm / 2 ft deep and liberally manured.

☞ TIME AND MANNER OF SOWING: For the main crops, sow about the middle of March, covering the seeds thinly and evenly. Another sowing may be made about the middle of May, which will furnish plants for filling spare ground in August.

☞ TIME AND MANNER OF PLANTING: The Cottager's kale, which is one of the best and most useful of this tribe, should be planted in rows not less than 76 cm / 2½ ft apart, allowing the same distance between the plants. Unless these are properly cared for, and planted out as soon as they are sufficiently strong, they will not, in cold localities, furnish sprouts until spring. A moderate breadth of the

Dwarf Feathered, and any other esteemed sorts, should be got out as early as circumstances will permit.

Spare ground may, however, be planted with these as late as the middle of August, and although the crop will not be so abundant as from the June planting, they may yield a fair produce at a time when vegetables are scarce, about 10 cm / 4 in apart, so as to have them strong and stocky. Keep the ground between the rows open and clear of weeds, by frequent stirrings. The tall-growing varieties will be benefited, particularly in exposed situations, by ridging the soil up about their stems. Water occasionally until the plants get fairly established. The best varieties are:

Chou de Milan; Cottager's Kale; Feathered, or Fine Dwarf Curled German Greens; Imperial Hearting.

KALMIA

This beautiful shrub, known also by the name of the Calico Laurel, is a native of North America, and should be treated as rhododendrons, &c., with acidic bog earth. The kalmias are quite hardy in full sun. They may be propagated by seed or by layers.

KAULFUSSIA

These are little free-flowering plants, of good compact growth. They grow freely in any soil.

Kaulfussia amelloides – bright blue, 15 cm / ½ ft.
K. rosea – rose, with mauve centre, 15 cm / ½ ft.

LANTANA

Half-hardy perennial. A genus of dwarf bushy shrubs, from 30-45 cm / 12–18 in in height, thickly studded with pretty miniature verbena-like blossoms of varied colours and changing hues – from snow-white with primrose centres to delicate pink and rose with white discs, and from bright rose-lilac to orange and scarlet with creamy centres. For the conservatory and flower-garden they are alike valuable. Seeds sown in March make fine summer and autumn blooming plants. They succeed best in dry, warm situations, and in light rich soil.

LARKSPUR or DELPHINIUM

Hardy annuals. One of the most generally-cultivated and ornamental genera of plants, combining unusual richness with an endless variety of colours. The tall

151

stock-flowered variety is of the same style as the branching, but with more compact spikes and larger and more double flowers. The tall-growing varieties scattered in shrubbery borders produce a charming effect when backed by the green foliage of the shrubs. Water liberally and mulch once a month. (See also delphinium.)

LAVATERA

Very profuse-blooming showy plants, which are attractive as a background to other plants, or for woodland walks and wilderness decoration, growing freely in any soil.

Lavatera trimestris – rose, pink-striped, 90 cm / 3 ft, hardy annual.
L. trimestris alba – white, 90 cm / 3 ft, hardy annual.
L. arborea (Tree Mallow) – violet, 150 cm / 5 ft, hardy biennial.

LEEKS

Leeks, for the main crop, are usually sown in April, about the same time as onions. Some gardeners sow them with a small sowing of onions, the latter being drawn young for salading, and the leeks being left on the bed, or planted out. Some sow them in drills 45 cm / 18 in or even 60 cm / 2 ft apart, and thin them to a foot or so apart in the row, planting the thinnings at the same distance. Sow very shallow, tread, and rake, provided the ground admits of it: water in dry weather. This crop delights in a light rich soil, and in moist seasons grows very large.

LEPTOSOPHON

A charming tribe of hardy annuals. *L. densiflorus*, with its pretty rose-lilac flowers, and *L. densiflorus albus*, with its pure white blossoms, are exceedingly attractive in beds. *L. hybridus* and *L. aureus* are very suitable for rockeries; they all make nice pot plants, and succeed in any light rich soil.

LETTUCES

▬ PREPARATION OF THE SOIL: A rather strong and highly-enriched loamy soil is best; but ordinary garden soil, with plenty of old rotten manure, will produce very fine lettuces.

▬ TIME AND MANNER OF SOWING: For an early crop sow under glass in February, and transplant on a well-prepared bed, in some sheltered corner, in April. For successional crops sow, in beds of well-pulverized soil, early in March, and at intervals of about a fortnight until the end of July. The crop intended to stand the winter should be sown in the second week of August and first week of September, using some approved hardy sort. Make the surface of the beds fine, sow thinly, and cover the seeds lightly with fine soil. The plants for the main summer crops may be transplanted with advantage into nursery lines, in beds of light rich soil, and if not transplanted, they must be thinned out in the seed-bed early, so as to afford them ample space to grow strong and stocky. They must be lifted carefully in transplanting, injuring their roots as little as possible. The August and September sowings should be planted about 5–8 cm / 2–3 in apart, in sheltered situations, transplanting them again early in spring. In many localities it may be necessary to winter them under frames or bell-jars, planting them out in sheltered situations in the spring.

☛ PLANTING AND AFTER-CULTIVATION: Plant in lines about a foot apart, allowing the same distance between the plants. In hot, dry weather give a good soaking of water immediately after planting, and keep the ground moist afterwards. A north border is a good situation in which to plant during the summer months, as the plants are less exposed to the sun, grow stronger, are more succulent and crisp, and are longer before they run to seed. Some varieties require tying up in order to get them properly blanched, and this should be done when the plants are a fair size, and a week or ten days before they are wanted for use, selecting first the strongest plants, continuing to do this as they are wanted. Where lettuce is wanted for the winter, a portion of the plants from the sowing made at the end of July should be covered. By thus protecting them from frost and yet and giving air freely, they will, if not too large, keep in good condition for a long time.

LILIUM

The lily in all its varieties is equally adapted for ornamenting the conservatory and the sitting-room as it is for the flower-borders.

☛ CULTURE INDOORS: Use a good mellow soil, composed of equal parts of leaf-mould and loam, with a little peat, and one-sixth of silver sand. A 30-cm / 12-in pot, with six bulbs planted in it, will furnish a group of no ordinary beauty: smaller-sized pots will require fewer bulbs. Place at the bottom of the pot a piece of potsherd, and over it some pieces of wood charcoal and rough fibrous soil to secure good drainage, then fill up with compost. When planted, the bulbs should be covered 2.5 cm / 1 in, and the soil made close by pressure: they should be treated in their first stage of growth precisely as hyacinths grown in pots, except that they should remain buried in ashes or cocoa-fibre till they begin to indicate a top-growth. Those intended to flower early should be placed under glass, while such as are for late blooming should remain out of doors in a sheltered situation, the pots plunged to the rim in ashes or cocoa-fibre.

🏶 CULTURE OUT OF DOORS: If the land be of an adhesive nature, it should be removed to the depth of 60 cm / 2 ft, and replaced with a rich free soil, or else the bulbs should be planted in 13-cm / 5-in pots, and early in May turned out where intended to bloom. Light or medium soils will only require deep digging and well working, with the addition of some thoroughly-rotted manure. Plant the bulbs 13 cm / 5 in deep, and for the first winter place on the surface a few dry leaves. The bulbs should not be disturbed oftener than once in three years, as established patches bloom much more profusely than those taken up and divided annually.

The varieties best-adapted for indoor culture are:

Astrosanguinium maculatum, Lancifolium album (Tiger Lily), *L. Punctatum and roseum, L. Rubrum and longiflorum*. The Martagon varieties are very effective in borders; so also are the common White Lily and Chalcedonicum, or Scarlet Turk's Cap.

LILY OF THE VALLEY

To grow these spring favourites to perfection, the roots should be set in bunches 30 cm / 1 ft apart and covered with a dressing of well-rotted manure before the winter sets in. They can hardly be treated too liberally. If grown in pots for the greenhouse, by a little management a succession may be kept in bloom till June. Keep the pots perfectly dry and in a cool shady place until their natural season is past, and by watering they soon come into foliage and flower.

LINUM

A fine genus of free-flowering plants, among which stands distinguished for its beautiful saucer-shaped flowers of rich crimson-scarlet with crimson-black centre, *Linum grandiflorum coccineum*, one of our most effective and showy bedding plants; its habit of growth is slender and delicate, and it produces flowers in profusion for many months. *L. flavum*, with its golden-yellow blossoms, profusion and duration of bloom, forms a valuable contrast and companion to the above. The plants succeed best in a light rich soil.

LOBELIA

Exceedingly pretty profuse-blooming plants: the low-growing kinds make the most beautiful edgings. *L. speciosa* forms a delightful contrast to *Cerastium tomentosum* and the variegated alyssum; all the varieties of *L. Erinus* are valuable for hanging-baskets, rustic-work, or vases, over the edges of which they droop in the most graceful and elegant manner. All the varieties grow freely from seed, and most of them from cuttings.

LOTUS

The hardy varieties of this plant are well suited for ornamenting rockeries or dry banks. *L Australis*, with its splendid spikes of rose-coloured flowers and dwarf habit, grows freely in light soil. Other varieties are:

Lotus corniculatus – trailer.
L. Jacobaeus – dark brown, 60 cm / 2 ft; half-hardy perennials.
L. Jacobaeus luteus – yellow, 60 cm / 2 ft; half-hardy perennials.

LUPINS

Free-flowering garden plants, with long graceful spikes of bloom, colours rich and beautiful. Many of the varieties are of a stately, robust growth, which makes them exceedingly valuable for mixed flower and shrubbery borders, while the dwarf varieties make neat, trim bedding-plants, Amongst the most distinguished, we may mention *L. Hartwegii* and varieties, *L. hybridus* and varieties, *L. magnificus*, *L. pubescens elegans* and *L. subcarnosus*.

MARROW

PREPARATION OF THE SOIL: These require a very deep, light, rich soil, and if planted in the open ground, a sheltered and warm situation. Dig pits 60 cm / 2 ft wide and deep, and fill with well-prepared fermenting manure, and cover about a foot deep with soil. The pits should not be less than 25 cm / 10 ft apart, and should be prepared about a week before planting, so that the soil may be properly warmed by the heat from the manure. The tops of compost-heaps, and hills of decaying leaves, manure, &c., will, however, afford the best possible situation for their growth.

SOWING AND PREPARATION OF THE PLANTS: Sow early in April, in a pot or pan, filled with light soil, covering the seeds about half an inch; place in gentle heat, and as soon as the plants are sufficiently strong to handle, pot them off into 18-cm / 7-in pots, putting two plants in each, and replace them near the glass in the warmth. When well established, remove to a cold frame, and gradually prepare for planting out.

PLANTING AND AFTER-MANAGEMENT: Towards the end of May, or as soon as the weather is warm and appears to be settled, and the plants ready, plant them out, and protect them for a time and attend to watering until the roots get hold of the soil. Train and regulate the shoots, so as to prevent them from growing too closely together, and stop them if necessary, to forward the growth of the fruit. Do not allow the plants to feel the want of water at the roots, but if planted in suitable situations, watering will seldom be necessary.

MESEMBRYANTHEMUM

Half-hardy annuals. A brilliant and profuse-flowering tribe of extremely pretty dwarf-growing plants, strikingly effective in warm sunny situations; also for indoor decoration: succeed best in a dry loamy soil.

MIGNONETTE

If well thinned out immediately the plants are large enough, they will grow stronger, and produce larger racemes of bloom: the seed should be scattered about shrubberies and mixed flower-borders, where it grows readily. The scent will last for months when the flowers are cut and dried.

Mignonette – 30 cm / ½ ft.
—*grandiflora* – 30 cm / ½ ft.

Mignonette Tree

The tree mignonette is formed by training a vigorous plant of common mignonette for about three years. Sow the seed very thin in April, draw out to a single plant. Next autumn remove all the lower shoots and shape the plant into a tree. Keep it in a warm greenhouse and in a growing state, carefully removing all flowers. In the spring, it will appear woody. Treat it in the same manner the next year, removing all branches except those that are to form the head of the tree. By the third year it will have bark on its trunk; and by stopping the flowers as they appear during summer and autumn, it may be made to blossom freely during winter and spring for many years in succession.

MIMOSA

Half-hardy annuals and perennials. Very curious and interesting plants: the leaves of *M. pudica* (the Humbleplant) and of *M. sensitiva* (the Sensitive-plant) close if touched or violently shaken. They succeed out of doors in a warm situation, growing freely in peat and loam.

MIMULUS or MONKEY FLOWER

A genus of extremely handsome profuse-flowering plants, with singularly-shaped and brilliantly-coloured flowers, which are distinguished by their rich and strikingly-beautiful markings. Seed sown in spring makes fine bedding plants for summer blooming, and seed sown in autumn produces very effective early-flowering plants for greenhouse decoration, &c.

Mimulus cardinalis – scarlet, 30 cm / 1 ft.

MISTLETOE

Mistletoe may be cultivated by attending to the following directions – make an incision in the bark of an apple-tree (many other trees, as the pear, oak, whitethorn, and even laurels, will answer equally well), and into this incision, in the spring of the year, insert some well-ripened berries of the mistletoe, carefully tying the bark over with a piece of mat, or woollen yarn. This experiment often fails, from the birds running away with the berries from the place where they have been inserted, for they are very fond of them. To prevent this, the incision in the bark should be made on the underside of a hanging branch.

NARCISSUS

The Double Roman narcissus, planted early in September, would bloom indoors before Christmas, while the Paper-white, combined with the other varieties for indoor culture, if planted in succession from the 1 September to the 31 December, would maintain a rich floral display till the end of April.

☛ CULTURE INDOORS: is similar to that recommended for the hyacinth. The bulbs of the polyanthus narcissus: being large, a 13-cm / 5-in pot will be needed for one bulb, and a 15-cm / 6-in pot for three; a group of six in a 20-cm / 8-in pot will produce an exceedingly beautiful effect.

☛ CULTURE OUT OF DOORS: is exactly the same as that for the hyacinth, except that the crown of the bulb should be at least 13 cm / 5 in under the surface, and for winter protection should be covered with about an inch of newly-dropped leaves, or 8 cm / 3 in of cocoa-fibre. September is the time for sowing seed.

Jonquil

The jonquils admit of the same culture as the other narcissi. They are hardy bulbs, and may be left in the ground several years without any injury; care, however, must be taken not to shorten or cut off their leaves. Planted four or six in a pot, they are very useful in a conservatory.

NASTURTIUM

The dwarf improved varieties of nasturtium are amongst the most useful of garden flowers; and rank with the geranium, verbena, and calceolaria; their close, compact growth, rich-coloured flowers, and the freedom with which they bloom, all combine to place them among first-class bedding plants. The scarlet, yellow, and spotted Tom Thumb are distinguished favourites, as are also the old crimson, and the Crystal Palace Gem. The peppery flowers may be eaten fresh in salads.

NEMOPHILA or BABY BLUE EYES

This is perhaps the most charming and generally useful genus of dwarf-growing hardy annuals. All the varieties have a neat, compact, and uniform habit of growth, with shades and colours the most strikingly beautiful. *N. maculata* and *N. phacelioides* are distinct; the latter is a beautiful hardy perennial; the former is more robust in growth. They all grow well from cuttings and seeds.

ONIONS

☞ SELECTION AND PREPARATION OF THE SOIL: A rather strong, deep, and rich loamy soil is most suitable for this crop. Onions grown in a strong soil are much less liable to be attacked by the fly or maggot than in light, dry, sandy soils. The ground should be heavily dressed with rich well-rotted manure, trenched deeply, and ridged up early in autumn. If the soil is light and sandy, cow manure will be most suitable.

☞ TIME AND MANNER OF SOWING: The main crop should be sown as early as the ground may be in working condition, and whether this occurs in February or early in March. After levelling down the ridges, if the soil is light, tread the ground regularly and closely over, then rake and well pulverize the surface, making it as fine as possible. Draw drills 1–2.5 cm / ½–1 in deep, 15 cm / 6 in from each alley, and 23 cm / 9 in apart. Sow the seeds thinly and regularly, and cover with the soil displaced in making the drills. A sowing should also be made about the middle of August, to furnish a supply of young onions during winter, and bulbs for use in summer before the main crop is ready. Where small bulbs such as are used for pickling, are required, sow the Silver-skinned thickly early in May, upon the poorest soil, and in the driest situation at command, and thin out very sparingly.

AFTER-MANAGEMENT: The ground must be kept clear of weeds by frequent hoeings, and the plants thinned early, to 15–20 cm / 6–9 in apart. In dry, warm situations, strong manure-water may be given freely during the summer; but where there is any danger of the crop running to 'thick necks', or not forming bulbs, watering should not be practised, except when the weather is very warm and dry, and then not after July. Towards the end of September the bulbs should be well formed, and the tops show indications of ripening; where this is not the case, go over the crops, bending or breaking them down with the back of a wooden rake, and repeat this as often as may be necessary to check the growth of the tops effectually. As soon as the bulbs seem to be properly matured, which will be known by the decay of the leaves, &c., take them up, spread them in an airy shed, or sunny situation in the open air, until thoroughly dried, and then store in a dry, cool place till wanted for use. The Lancashire method of wintering onions is, perhaps, the best. There they tie up the bulbs in what are called ropes, and hang them on an outside wall, not facing the sun, and protect them from wet by placing a board against the wall overhead. They keep sound longer by this than by any other method. The best varieties are:

White Spanish – the mildest in flavour, and most useful for main crop.
Deptford, or Brown Spanish – similar to the above, but brown; a useful and good keeping variety.
Brown Globe – a hardy useful kind.
White Globe – a mild-flavoured good keeping variety.
Giant Madeira – grows to a great size, and particularly mild-flavoured.
Blood-red – a very useful hardy salad onion.
James's Long-keeping – keeps longer than any other variety.
Silver-skinned – the best for pickling.
Tripoli Large flat Italian – the best variety for autumn sowing.
Tripoli Large Globe – very fine for autumn sowing.
While Lisbon – the variety sown in autumn for spring onions.

OXALIS

A genus of exceedingly pretty bulbous plants, all of which have beautiful green foliage, which forms a fine contrast to their richly-coloured blossoms. They are admirably adapted for pots, borders, and rockeries, succeeding in any light soil.

Oxalis bipunctata – lilac.
— *Bowiei* – crimson, large trusses.
— *cernua* – yellow
— *floribunda rosea* – rose.
— *grandiflora alba* – white.
— *hirta rosea* – rose.
— *rubella* – red.

— *speciosa* – rosy-purple, very showy;
— *tetraphylla* – purple;
— *versicolor* – scarlet and white.

PAEONIA or PEONY

For late spring or early summer flowering few plants are more useful than paeonias. Every flower-garden should have some of them. They are mostly very hardy, and in colour vary from pure white, blush, salmon, and rose, to the most intense and brilliant scarlet. The Chinese tree varieties (*Paeonia Moutan*) are also hardy and early flowering. Bedded upon lawns they have a beautiful effect. In a shrub-like form they rise from 90–150 cm / 3–5 ft in height, and branch out in a good rich soil to 3–5.5 m / 10–18 ft in circumference.

PARSLEY

Full crops of parsley should be sown in the spring along the edges of one of the borders. In preparing the beds, remove the soil to the depth of 15–20 cm / 6–8 in, and fill in the bottom with the same depth of stones, rubble, and similar loose material. Over this prepare the bed of light rich soil, which will thus be raised considerably above the level of the ground, the bed being raked smooth and level. Towards the end of May, sow some seed, either in shallow drills, slightly covered with fine soil, or thin broadcast raked in. If the weather continue dry, water frequently: in five or six weeks the plants will have appeared; when large enough, thin them out, so that they may be 10–13 cm / 4–5 in apart. By the end of autumn they will be large and vigorous plants. At this time, drive a row of stakes or hoops into the ground, on each side of the bed, so as to form arches strong enough to support a covering of mats, which should be laid over them as soon as frosty or wet weather threatens to set in. During intense frosts, increase the protection, removing it on fine days, and removing it entirely in mild weather. The soil should be kept dry, and all decayed leaves carefully removed: in this manner this useful vegetable may be available all the winter, until it seeds.

PARSNIPS

☞ PREPARATION OF THE SOIL: Parsnips succeed best in a deep, free, rich soil, and as the application of fresh manure tends to the production of forked and badly-formed roots, ground in high condition (having been heavily manured for the previous crop) should be selected. If manure must be applied, let it be well decomposed, or use guano. The ground should be trenched 75 cm / 2 ft 6 in, and ridged up as long as possible before sowing.

☛ TIME AND MANNER OF SOWING: Sow in lines 40–46 cm / 15–18 in apart, as early in spring as the ground can be found in fair working condition, scattering the seeds thinly, and covering them 1–2.5 cm / ½–1 in with the finest of the soil.

☛ AFTER-MANAGEMENT: When the plants are about 5–8 cm / 2–3 in high, thin them out, leaving 15–20 cm / 6–8 in between them. Keep the ground free from weeds, and the surface open by frequent deep stirrings with the hoe. Towards the end of November take up the roots, and, after cutting off the tops, &c., either store them in damp sand, in a cellar, or pit, as is done with potatoes.

Sutton's Student – This variety has been ennobled from the wild parsnip of Great Britain, and is considered an important acquisition: the flavour is very superior and the roots are clean and handsome.

Hollow Crown Improved – The most useful for main crop.

Jersey – A large valuable sort.

PASSIFLORA or PASSION-FLOWER

A genus of magnificent ornamental twining shrubs, with flowers at once interesting, beautiful, and curious, which are produced in the greatest profusion and in succession during the greater part of the year under glass, and out of doors (during summer and autumn. They are among the most important and effective of plants for training in conservatories or covering the fronts of cottages and villas in town or country. For indoor culture, *P. Contessa* 'Clara Gigliucci' is one of the most important, and for outdoor decoration *P. caerulea*.

PEARS

These are best grown dwarf. The varieties of the Pear are very numerous.

Beurré Giffard – ripe in July; suitable for a standard.

Citron des Carmes – ripe in July.

Epargne – in July and August, suited for espalier on an east or west aspect. Does not make a good pyramid.

Louise Bonne de Jersey – an espalier on free stock; east aspect; ripe in October.

Beurré Gris – an espalier on free stock; east and west aspect; ripe in October..

Beurré de Capiaumont – espalier on free stock; east and west aspect; ripe in October and November.

Duchesse d'Angoulême, - as an espalier on east, west, or north aspect; ripe in October and November.

Jargonelle – ripe in August.

Bon Chretien, Williams's – a standard, grafted on a free stock; ripe in August and September.

Seckle – ripe in October.

Beurré Diel – an espalier on east, west, or north aspect; ripe in November and December.

Beurré passe Colmar – espalier on free stock, for east, west, or north aspect; ripe in November and December.

Glou Morceau – in December and January.

Easter Beurré – in March; keep till March.

Beurré de Rance – espalier for east, west, or south aspect; ripe in February and March.

PEAS

🖝 SELECTION OF SOIL AND SITUATION: For heavy crops of this prime esculent a deep loamy soil must be secured; but ordinary garden soil, if properly prepared and well-manured, will yield abundantly. For an early crop, plant in the warmest and most sheltered situation; but for the main crops choose an open airy situation; and instead of devoting a portion of the garden to peas alone, as is usually done, plant them in single lines amongst other crops: the plants will thus get more sun and air, and bear much longer and more abundantly.

🖝 PREPARATION OF THE SOIL: Trench to the depth of 60 cm / 2 ft, and ridge up roughly, exposing as large a surface as possible to the action of the weather; and this should be done as long before sowing as convenient. The summer and autumn crops will require abundance of well-rotted manure; but the early crop will come sooner into bearing if planted in poorer soil, which should be deep and well pulverized.

🖝 TIME AND MANNER OF SOWING: Sow the first crop about the middle of November, the second early in January, putting in a small breadth of a second early variety at the same time; and to secure a constant succession, sow once a fortnight from this time till the end of June, or yet later. After the beginning of March sow the best kinds of wrinkled marrows; but for the last two so wings use a free-cropping early, or second early variety, and when the ground is sufficiently dry to work kindly, sow in drills 5 cm / 2 in deep and 10 cm / 4 in wide, covering the seed with friable soil. If sown in successive lines, let the intervening space exceed the reputed height to which the variety grows by 15–30 cm / 6–12 in. As the seed for the earlier crops will be some time in the ground exposed to the depredations of mice, &c., it should be sown thickly. The strong-growing branching kinds, which are used for the main crops, succeed better if sown thinly, but it is prudent to guard against loss from various causes by sowing all rather thickly.

🖝 AFTER-MANAGEMENT: When the plants are about 5 cm / 2 in high, draw the soil neatly towards them, and apply stakes of about the height to which the variety grows. Spruce fir or other evergreen branches will afford a useful shelter to early crops. Keep the ground between the rows well-stirred and free from weeds. In dry weather mulch with manure for 46 cm / 18 in on each side the rows, giving a liberal supply of water when necessary, to keep the plants vigorous, and to prevent mildew: the growing crops should never be allowed to feel the want of water.

PELARGONIUMS

June and July are the best months for increasing pelargoniums for ordinary purposes. Cuttings struck at this season from plants which have been forced, and the wood thoroughly ripened, produce fine plants for autumn flowering and early spring forcing, supplying the want of flowers in the conservatory in winter and spring. The pots being prepared in the usual manner, and well supplied with drainage and other loose material for one-third of their depth, fill up with a compost composed of equal parts turfy loam and silver-sand well mixed and sifted, so as to keep back the large lumps. Select cuttings from strong short-jointed shoots 8–10 cm / 3–4 in long, removing the lower leaves so as to leave the base of the cuttings clear; place them round the edge of the pot about 2.5–3.5 cm / 1–1½ in deep. When planted, water freely to settle the soil round them, and place them in a cold pit or frame. Sprinkle them occasionally overhead till rooted; afterwards give air gradually to harden them for potting off into 8-cm / 3-in pots.

When well established in the small pots and about 15 cm / 6 in high, stop them that they may throw out lateral or side shoots. When they have made their shoots, repot them in equal parts turfy loam, peat, and decomposed cow or stable dung, with a good proportion of road or river sand, the pots being thoroughly drained with potsherds: thin out the leaves and small shoots occasionally, to throw the whole sap into the shoots which are to produce flowers. When plunged into the border to flower, these plants will be benefited by being lifted occasionally to prevent them from rooting through the bottom of the pots. Those for spring forcing will require a further shift in September; and the fancy varieties, being more delicate growers, will require more drainage.

PETUNIAS

Highly ornamental and profuse-flowering half-hardy perennials, easily cultivated both from seed and cuttings. The brilliancy and variety of the colours, combined with the duration of the blooming period and the capability of the flowers to bear the atmosphere of large towns, render petunias invaluable. Seed sown in March or April makes fine bedding-plants for a summer and autumn display: they succeed in any rich soil. The following are good:

Brilliant – fine velvety rich crimson.
Eclipse – distinct and novel.
Crimson King – a good bedder.

PHLOXES

This magnificent genus of plants, both annual and perennial, is unrivalled, for richness and brilliancy of colours, and profusion and duration of blooming. The *P. Drummondii* varieties make splendid bedding and pot plants; the *P. decussata* produces a fine effect in mixed border. They succeed best in light rich soil.

PICOTEES

These are a kind of carnation, distinguished by a narrow dark-coloured edging to the petals, or by the petals being covered with very small coloured dots. The cultivation is in every respect the same as the carnation.

PLUMS

The most useful varieties for small gardens are, for early fruiting, the Goliath, Greengage, Victoria, and River's's Prolific; for late fruiting, Magnum Bonum, Coe's Golden Drop, and Damson. The Reine Claude is an excellent plum upon a warm wall or under glass.

POLYANTHUS

Late in autumn is the time for sowing; for moderate sunlight only is required to bring up the seed, and the young plants will not stand the scorching sun of summer. Sow in boxes, or pans well-drained, filled with light rich mould. The seed must be very lightly covered – indeed, it may almost lie upon the surface. The boxes should be placed under glass, and sparingly watered. They require no artificial heat.

Divide the roots of the best plants intended for preservation. This operation must be performed every year, or the flowers will soon degenerate. Fresh soil and continual division is the only plan with all flowers which give out offsets.

POTATO

☞ SELECTION AND PREPARATION OF THE SOIL: A deep, thoroughly drained, light sandy loam, or peaty soil, is most suitable for the potato. The application of manure is now generally held to increase the liability to disease, to bring it on at an earlier period, and to produce large crops of imperfectly matured tubers, which if they escape the disease while in the ground, are more liable to be attacked after they are lifted. The ground selected, therefore, should be in fair condition, from having been moderately manured for some exhausting green crop in the previous season. The ground should be trenched two spades deep, and ridged up early in autumn; if manure is applied, this should be well mixed with the soil. Charred vegetable refuse may be applied about the sets when they are planted.

☞ TIME AND MANNER OF SOWING: We have no hesitation in saying, that early planting has hitherto proved the best preventive against the attacks of disease. Plant, therefore, as early in January as the ground can be found in fair working condition. A small breadth of the ash-leaved kidney should be planted on a south border, or in the warmest and most sheltered situation at command, to furnish an early supply. In planting, let the ground be neatly levelled, then, beginning at one side, dig it over about 15 cm / 6 in deep, and put in the sets in the openings at proper distances, which must be regulated by the growth of the variety. The lines for the early kinds, as ash-leaved, &c., which form but small tops, may be about 50 cm / 20 in apart, leaving about 23 cm / 9 in between the sets, but for the second early varieties 60 cm / 2 ft should be allowed between the lines, and 25 cm / 10 in between the sets. The late kinds will require an additional 15 cm / 6 in between the lines. The sets should be covered about 15 cm / 6 in, leaving the soil over them as open and loose as possible. On strong heavy land the ash-leaved and other weakly growers should not be covered more than 10 cm / 4 in.

☞ PLANTING in autumn has been strongly recommended, and on light, well-drained land, it may safely be practiced – the crop will probably be both earlier and more abundant than from spring planting. All things considered, we think that planting early in spring is to be preferred.

☞ AFTER-MANAGEMENT: When the tops are 10–15 cm / 4–6 in above the ground, ridge the soil up neatly about them. In the case of the early varieties, which may be in danger of suffering from the frost, the soil should be kept ridged up round the shoots as soon as they appear above the ground, keeping them covered until all danger of frost is past. Before earthing up, fork the ground lightly between the lines, so as to pulverize the soil, then draw it to the plants with a hoe or spade. Keep the ground clear of weeds. When the crop attains maturity, lift and store.

Potatoes in frames

When potatoes are grown in a frame, the treatment is much the same as before; but they are also grown very successfully in this manner – the frame being placed on a level piece of ground, the soil within is dug out to the depth of 60 cm / 2 ft, and banked round the outside of the frame. The pit thus formed is then filled with prepared dung; and on this 8 cm / 3 in of soil is placed; then the potatoes; then 15 cm / 6 in more soil. The potatoes, when planted, should be just starting into growth; but the shoots should never be more than half an inch from the tuber, or they do not grow so strong. It is advisable to pick off some of the shoots: three on each tuber are sufficient. They may also be forced under the stand in a greenhouse or hothouse, the potatoes being planted singly in large pots of very rich light soil. Each pot ought to yield a good dish.

PRIMULA

This genus is a very large one, including, as it does, some of the most popular florists' flowers; viz., the auricula, the polyanthus, and the primrose. With mulching when planting in autumn or spring, and regular watering with clear manure-water, these plants tend to thrive under any care.

PUMPKINS

These are used, when young, as a vegetable. When ripe they form a valuable esculent for soups and pumpkin pies in winter. The young shoots in summer are an excellent substitute for asparagus. Big Ben and Mammoth are successful varieties.

RADISH

🐾 PREPARATION OF THE SOIL: Deep, light, and rich soil – not made so, however, by the application of manure – should be chosen. It should be carefully dug or forked deeply, making the surface soil fine and level before sowing.

🐾 TIME AND MANNER OF SOWING: Sow early in January, on a warm sheltered border, and at intervals of three weeks until May; afterwards every fortnight during the summer, and at longer intervals when the weather becomes cold in autumn. Radishes are often sown much too thickly, and this causes the roots to be small, hard, stringy, and disagreeably hot in flavour. Sow broadcast, in beds of convenient size, and cover the seeds evenly and lightly with fine soil. The early sowing will require to be protected from frost by a covering of litter, but this must be removed every mild day, as soon as the plants appear above ground. Water the beds well, and keep the soil moist until the crop is finished. With the convenience of a frame and a little fermenting material, a supply may be obtained considerably earlier than in the open border, and with much less trouble. If grown in this way, cover the manure with 15 cm / 6 in of light rich soil, and sow when there is no risk of the bed overheating. The Spanish varieties should be sown in drills, about 30 cm / 1 ft apart, and thinned out when sufficiently strong to draw, so as to stand from 4 to 6 apart in the rows.

For a winter supply of these, sow from the middle of July to the middle of September, regulating this by the locality, and the size at which the roots may be most esteemed. Fair-sized roots, however, will be obtained in most localities from sowings made about the middle of August. These may be taken up before severe weather sets in, and stored in damp sand, in a cool cellar or shed, for winter use.

RAMPION

This is a campanula, and very good as a vegetable, to be used like radishes.

🐟 PREPARATION OF THE SOIL: This plant will be found to thrive best in well-pulverized, deep, rich soil, such as is recommended for carrots; well decomposed manure may be added, if necessary. If grown in a warm, dry situation, the roots are liable to be hard and stringy; therefore the main crop should be sown in a cool situation and watered liberally during droughty weather.

🐟 TIME AND MANNER OF SOWING: If to be used for salad or for cooking, in a small state, sow at intervals, to be regulated by the size at which the roots may be most esteemed. For winter use sow in April or early in May, in lines a foot apart, covering the seeds very lightly with fine soil, and thin the plants out, so that they may stand 10 cm / 4 in apart in the lines.

RANUNCULUS

Ranunculus may be planted from October to the end of March, some preferring one period and some another: perhaps no better time could be chosen for planting than the beginning or middle of February. As soon as the beds are in a fit state, lose no time in planting, if the weather be favourable; waiting a day, or even a week, is nothing in comparison with placing the roots in soil in an unfit state to receive them. They are best cultivated in beds of rich loam mixed with one-fourth part of decomposed cow-dung. The soil should be dug from 60–75 cm / 2 to 2½ ft deep, and if the situation is moist and partially sheltered, so much the better. The roots should be planted about 5 cm / 2 in deep and 15 cm / 6 in apart; their claw-like extremities should be pressed firmly into the earth, and the crowns be covered with an inch of sand previous to another inch of soil being spread over them; the beds may then be covered with a layer of spruce branches, straw litter, or leaf-mould, to protect them from the frost: this will, of course, be removed before the appearance of the plants above ground. Ranunculuses are increased by offsets, dividing the tubers, and seed. Offsets is the usual mode of increase, and they are generally sufficiently strong to flower the first year.

Choice sorts may also be divided into several plants; every little knot that appears on the top of a tuber will form a plant if carefully divided, so as to insure an accompanying claw. Seed is the most rapid mode of increase. Perhaps the best time for sowing is the month of January, and the best place a cold frame. Sow either in the frame or in pots or boxes, on a smooth surface, and barely cover the seed with soil. Exclude the frost, and keep the frame close until the plants show two seed-leaves; then gradually inure them to more air, until the light may be entirely removed in May. The little tubers may be taken up when the foliage is quite ripened off.

Some prefer sowing the seed on beds out of doors in the autumn or spring months. Generally ranunculuses will have died down, and be fit for taking up and storing, by the end of June or beginning of July. The place for storing should be dry; a drawer with a bed of sand being the most convenient.

RHODANTHE

Half-hardy annuals. Everlastings of great beauty; valuable alike for the decoration of the conservatory and flower-garden. Succeed best in a light rich soil and warm sheltered situation.

Rhodanthe Manglesii – bright rose, with silvery calyx, 30 cm / 1 ft.
R. maculata – flowers nearly 5 cm / 2 in diameter, and of a bright rosy purple, with yellow disc, surrounded by a conspicuous dark crimson ring.

RHODODENDRONS

Nothing equals the common Ponticum for underwood in plantations. There are many varieties of this class alone, including almost every shade of colour. The splendid Catawbiense variety has been almost equally fruitful in hybrids.

All rhododendrons require bog and prefer acidic soils. They bear frequent removal; but care must always be taken not to break the ball of earth or loosen the soil from the stem. Never use lime or any other alkaline substances. Rain-water is to be preferred over tap-water.

RHUBARB

Directions for the cultivation of rhubarb will be found in the monthly calendars. It will grow without forcing; but is far better forced. If rhubarb be forced on the ground where it grows, nothing more is required than to cover with large pots and stable manure – by this method it is blanched; but when forced in a frame, or otherwise, it is unnecessary to exclude the light, as there is no advantage in blanching it. Rhubarb may be planted at any time of the year, although mild weather in autumn or early spring is best: it should be planted on a clear open spot on good soil, which should be well trenched 90 cm / 3 ft deep. The plants should be not less than 120 cm / 4 ft apart; or, where it is intended to take up some every year for forcing, a distance of 90 cm / 3 ft will be sufficient. Before planting, a good substance of very rotten manure should be worked into the soil. When the plants are to be increased, it is merely necessary to take up large roots and divide them with a spade: every piece that has a crown to it will grow; and as it grows very quickly, this is a good method of propagating it. To insure fine rhubarb, a large dressing of well-rotted manure should be dug in about the roots, as soon as you have finished pulling the leaves. It is not right to wait till the winter before the plants are dressed.

ROCKETS

Very pleasing early-spring-flowering hardy perennials, with deliciously fragrant flowers; grow freely in any soil.

Rocket, Sweet – purple, 45 cm / 1½ ft.
—— white, 45 cm / 1½ ft.
—— mixed, 45 cm / 1½ ft.

ROSES

Propagation

☞ BY CUTTINGS: Most roses may be increased by cuttings; but all are not alike calculated for being thus propagated, bottom-heat of last year's wood attached, and cut into lengths of 13–15 cm / 5–6 in, selecting such as have two lateral shoots, with five or six leaves to each. An inch of the old wood should be inserted in the soil, leaving at least two leaves above. From four to six of these cuttings may be placed round the inside of a pot, in soil consisting of equal parts of leaf-mould, turfy loam chopped fine, and silver-sand, watering them well, to settle the earth round the roots. When the water is drained off, and the leaves dry, remove to a cold frame, or place them under bell-jars, shade them from the sun, excluding the dew, and sprinkling them daily for a fortnight. If threatened with damping off, give air and sun. In a fortnight callus will be formed. At this time they are greatly benefited by bottom-heat; they root more rapidly, and may soon be shifted singly and removed back to the cold frame for planting out in August, without bottom-heat. They must be kept in the frames till the spring.

🪶 GRAFTING: Grafting is performed by cutting the top of the stock to a proper height by a clean horizontal cut; then make a longitudinal V-shaped cut down the centre, 2.5–8 cm / 1–3 in long, according to the size of the stock. In this slit place the graft, after having cut the lower end of it to fit the cut in the stock. Having inserted it, bind the whole up with clay or grafting-paste, as directed in budding.

The best time for grafting roses in pots is January; and July, in ordinary seasons, is the best month for budding; but that depends upon the season. Some operators prefer a moist gloomy day for the operation.

🪶 BY SUCKERS: Roses – some kinds much more than others – push their roots in a lateral direction under ground, and throw up young shoots or suckers from them; these suckers, separated from the parent root by the cut of a sharp spade, form flowering plants the same season, if separated in the spring and transplanted to suitable soil.

Ayrshire Rose

The Ayrshire is the hardiest of climbing roses, and its cultivation and management is very simple. Layers of its long pendulous shoots root readily, and it strikes easily from cuttings; it will grow rapidly where other roses will scarcely exist, and when placed in good rich soil, its growth is so rapid that a large space is covered by it in the second season of planting. It forms an admirable weeping rose when trained on wires. It is useful for trellis, verandah, or alcove, as well as in rough places of the park or shrubbery. Like the other roses, the Ayrshire has yielded many hybrid varieties:

Ayrshire Queen – dark purple-crimson.
Bennett's Seedling – pure white; forms a beautiful pendulous tree as a half-standard.
Dundee Rambler – white, edged with pink; well adapted for a half-standard for the lawn.
Ruga – pale flesh.colour: very fragrant: a hybrid between Ayrshire and a tea-scented rose.
Splendens – creamy white, approaching flesh-colour when full; crimson in the bud;
large, double, and globular; one of the finest pendulous roses.
Alice Grey – creamy salmon-blush.

Banksia Rose

The flowers of this elegant rose are produced in small umbels, each of three, four, and up to twelve flowers, at the extremities of small lateral shoots, branches of the preceding year's growth. The peduncles or stalks are slender and smooth, and the flowers have a drooping habit when fully expanded. The scent of the flower is agreeably fragrant, not unlike to that of the sweet violet. Vigorous growth and bloom is produced by planting the rose in a rich sandy loam, and against a wall with a south or west aspect, nailing its shoots close to the wall; and when the wall is covered to the extent proposed, cutting away all the strong shoots as they appeared, leaving only those intended to produce flowers in the following spring. From August to February the only care required is to nail in all young shoots, only removing those that are super-abundant.

Bourbon Rose

The distinguishing characteristics of Bourbon roses are brilliancy and clearness of colour, large and smooth petals, falling in numerous and graceful folds. They are perfectly hardy, and thrive under the ordinary culture, delighting in a rich soil, like most of the roses, and requiring close pruning, except the more vigorous kinds. They are of slow growth, however, in spring, and thus they are best adapted for autumn-flowering roses. The following list embraces the best varieties of the Bourbon rose:

Mrs Bosanquet – creamy white; a profuse bloomer from June to November; moderate grower. This rose appears to be intermediate between the Chinese and what are called Bourbons. Will form a small clump, if possible more unique and beautiful than any other variety. A truly splendid rose.

Bouquet de Flore – brilliant carmine; opens freely, and blooms profusely from June to November; a strong, vigorous grower, and admirably adapted for massing. A China striking rose, and suitable for pot-culture.

Armosa – deep pink, of full form and medium size, partaking of the Chinese; suitable for a standard or for pot-culture.

Amenaide – flowers lilac rose-colour, produced in clusters; large, full, and cupped, partaking of the Noisettes.

Apolline – flowers silvery rose-colour, shaded: large, full, and cupped. A fine autumnal climbing rose.

Georges Cuvier – rosy-crimson, tinted with light purple; fine shape, expands its blooms freely; a moderate grower. Distinct autumnal rose, with large, full, and compact flowers, with beautiful foliage.

Grand Capitaine – velvety fiery scarlet, very brilliant; opens its flowers both in summer and autumn. Not very double; dwarf habit; well adapted for a small bed, where the intense brilliancy of its flowers will show to advantage.

Pierre de St Cyr – glossy rose; fine, large, double-cupped flower; expands well, and blooms profusely; a most robust grower. Will form a splendid clump to contrast with any of the strong-growing hybrid perpetuals. As a weeping rose it forms a splendid umbrageous tree, blooming through the summer and autumn.

171

Queen – fawn-colour, shaded with salmon; very sweet-scented flowers; large, double, and cupped. One of the first and last in bloom, invariably expanding its flowers well, which appear in profusion. Rather dwarf habit.

Souvenir de la Malmaision – white at the margin, approaching to flesh-colour, or fawn in the centre. Very large and magnificent flower, with very thick petals, blooming freely through the summer and autumn; a strong grower.

Boursault Rose

The Boursault rose is a cultivated variety of the Alpine rose; the shoots are very long, flexible, and smooth, in many instances entirely without spines, and the eyes are further apart than in most other kinds. The flowers are produced in clusters suitable for pillars, and from their naturally pendulous habit they may be trained to form weeping roses. They should be well thinned out in pruning, but flowering-shoots should only have the points cut off. The following bloom from May to July:

Amadis – deep crimson-purple, shaded with lighter crimson; large, semi-double, and cupped; the young wood whitish-green.

Black Boursault – flowers whitish-blush, with deep flesh centre; very double and globular, of pendulous habit, excellent as a climbing rose in a good aspect.

Drummond's Thornless – opens a rosy carmine, changing to pink; flowers large, double, and cupped; habit pendulous.

Elegans – flowers in clusters of semi-double rosy crimson; sometimes purplish, often streaked with white; erect in habit, and suitable for a pillar.

Gracilis – flowers early; cherry, shaded with lilac-blush; full-formed and cupped; of branching habit; spines long and large; foliage a rich dark green.

Inermis – rosy-pink, becoming pale when expanded; large and double, and of branching habit; shoots spineless.

Old Red Boursault – opens a bright cherry; becoming paler gradually; large and semi-double; of pendulous habit, a showy pillar or weeping rose.

China Roses

The first introduction of the Chinese roses dates from 1789, in which year both the monthly rose and the crimson Chinese were introduced. They have been hybridized extensively with the tea-scented. Unlike other roses, also, the Chinese roses get a deeper and more brilliant tint by exposure to the sun.

The common and Crimson China are very beautiful, either grown in beds or on walls. Towards the end of Mayor beginning of June, they will be in full beauty, and the mass of blush pink is peculiarly soft and beautiful. By cutting off the flowering-stems as soon as they begin to fade, a succession of flowers will be secured throughout the summer.

Cramoisie superieure – bright crimson.

Prince Charles – bright carmine.

All the China roses require some protection in the winter months. Nothing is better than some coal-ashes over the roots – say around 20 cm / 8 in thick, and a quantity of boughs of spruce, &c., bent over the tops, 15–20 cm / 6–8 inches in thickness.

Archduke Charles – light rose, margins almost white, changing to brilliant crimson; a profuse bloomer; moderate grower. One of the best changeable roses. Unique.

Rubens – flowers blush, lilac, and crimson; changeable; very large, full, and cupped.

Virginale – flowers flesh-colour, of medium size; full, globular; requires forcing to bring out.

Evergreen Roses

These are the progeny of *R. sempervirens*, which abounds throughout Europe in a wild state, and, like the Ayrshire, are employed as climbing and weeping roses. Their beautiful dark-green leaves grow on to the depth of winter, which has procured them the name, although, strictly speaking, they are deciduous. They are mostly trees of vigorous growth and abundant bloomers, adapted for pillar-roses; their small, but very double flowers, hanging in graceful cymes of fourteen to twenty on a branch. They require much thinning in the pruning season; the shoots left being merely cut at the points, the others cut close to the base.

Donna Maria – pure white, of medium size; full and cupped; a choice variety.

Félicité perpétuelle – flesh-colour, changing to creamy white; produced in graceful trusses drooping from their own weight; a superb sort.

Fortune's five-coloured – creamy white, striped with carmine.

Fortune's double yellow – bronze and yellow; large and very distinct.

Moss-rose

The Moss-rose above all others requires a warm rich soil, with an airy exposure; moisture and shade also seem essential to preserving the mossy character; but this moisture must not partake of the stagnant nature. The roses should be lifted annually or biennially, and replanted with some rich fresh compost at their roots. The following list gives a few of the best moss-roses:

A feuilles luisants – flowers delicate, pink-blush on the circumference; of medium size: full and globular; blooming freely in dusters, with shining leaves.

Old Moss – flowers pale rose; very large and full, well massed and globular; very beautiful. Thrives as a standard.

Eclatante – flowers deep pink: well massed, large, and double. Thrives as a standard.

Panachée Pleine – flowers white or flesh-colour, occasionally streaked with rose; of medium size, cupped, and very double. To bring out the streaks, plant in rather poor, but fresh soil, as turfy loam, giving a very little manure.

Pompon, or de Meaux – flowers blush, pale pink, centre small; full and cupped.

Perpetual Roses

Barome Prevost – bright pale rose.colour; glossy; a very large, full, and compact flower; free grower, blooming freely from June till November.

Geant des Batailles – dazzling crimson, the nearest approach to scarlet in this class; very free grower, and one of the most abundant bloomers, flowering from June till December.

La Reine – brilliant glossy rose-colour, shaded with lilac, and sometimes with crimson; cupped and very large; has the appearance of a true perpetual cabbage, but much larger.

Pompon Roses

The beds for these delicate roses, where they are confined to one variety, should be small, as should be the garden. Whatever the soil, the beds will be improved by its being removed to the depth of 45–60 cm / 1½–2 ft, and replaced with a layer of stones and brick and lime rubbish, for drainage. If the natural soil is pretty good, it may be returned, after mixing it with a portion of decomposed cow-dung; adding a little sand, the whole thoroughly blended together: rich vegetable mould full of fibre will do.

These roses are recommended to be on their own roots and planted in autumn. The stocks on which they are usually budded are too gross for their delicate structure, Plant them 40 cm / 15 in apart if it is intended to peg them down, so as to cover the bed; if they are to stand apart, 45 cm / 18 in will be better. In March, or early in April, when all danger from frost is over, they may be pruned. Use the knife sparingly; cut out all dead wood, and regulate the branches: this is all that will be required.

As the season advances, water them from time to time with weak liquid manure, removing all decaying leaves; and where they have bloomed in clusters, cut back to the next bud, from which they will again break, and bloom in the autumn, Short shoots, showing no bloom, should have the terminal buds pinched off on attaining the length of 13–15 cm / 5–6 in; the lateral shoots thrown out will probably bloom freely. During the winter keep the buds as dry as possible; they are even worth protecting from the cold rains.

Rosa Multiflora

Of this there are many varieties: it is a delicate rose, and often killed to the ground by the frost. Covered with mats, it shoots so early that it cannot endure the spring frosts. Grevillea, or Seven Sisters rose, is a vigorous climber of this family, blooming in clusters, of shades varying from rose to purplish crimson; the flowers change from crimson at first coming out, to pale rose and purplish crimson. Thatch over the pillar in November with green gorse or furze, which admits air and keeps off the severity of the frost; continuing this covering till

March, and then removing it by degrees, so as to inure the plant to the cold before full exposure to it. In this way, Alba, or Double White, a pretty pale flesh-coloured rose; the Double Red, and Hybrida, or Laure Davoust, a most elegant and beautiful hybrid, with large flowers and beautiful foliage, will bloom in perfection.

Tea Roses

The tea-scented Chinese roses form undoubtedly the most desirable group which has come under our notice. Their odour is delicious, and closely resembles the flavour of high-class tea; their colours are generally subdued in tint, being white, creamy-white, flesh-colour, and yellow, except where they have been hybridized with others of more brilliant colours.

To grow this group in perfection requires considerable knowledge of their habits as well as care; they are peculiarly adapted for pot-culture. In the open ground they all require a rich well-drained soil, close pruning, and the means of protection from frost in winter. As ornaments to the conservatory they are unsurpassed. The following is a list of the hardier tea-scented roses.

Gloire de Dijon – fawn, tinted with salmon and rose; small, fragrant, and of vigorous growth.

Goubault – bright rose, the young bud, opening a rich deep crimson as the sepals open; very large, double, and expanded.

Niphetos – creamy-white, approaching to lemon, the centre lemon-colour; magnolia-like; large, full, and globular; a beautiful rose.

Original – creamy-white, centre salmon-buff; large and full.

Pauline Plantier – white, tinged with lemon; globular and full.

Safrano – saffron-yellow to apricot-colour in the bud, changing to pale buff; cupped, large, and double.

Weeping Roses

Weeping Roses are roses of vigorous growth, and should be worked on stems 120 cm / 4 ft and upwards in height. In the first pruning they are cut close in; and to have one bud only is an advantage: the shoots are thinned out as with standards, shortening back the others to give vigorous growth.

The nature of the stocks, whether the dog-rose or the Manetti be selected, limits the height to which weeping roses may be grown; but there seems to be no reason why either of them should not attain the height of 3–3.5 m / 10–12 ft, with a proportionate thickness. In this case the chief support must be provided by a strong stake of wood or iron to which the stock may be fastened, while the head is extended outwards and directed downwards. For this purpose light wire hoops, of sufficient circumference, will be found very useful.

SAGE

This useful garden herb is a salvia, which is a very extensive genus in botany. All the kinds should be grown in a light rich soil, and are propagated by cuttings, the division of roots, and seed.

SALSIFY

This may be sown about the end of April or beginning of May. It is best to sow this seed in drills 40 cm / 15 in apart, or thereabouts, and thin to 15 cm / 6 in in the row. The roots of the plant are usually boiled and eaten.

SAPONARIA

Of these charming little plants it is impossible to speak too highly; they carpet the ground with their pretty little star-shaped flowers during the summer and autumn months. For edgings they are unequalled, bearing cutting back, if necessary, for a late autumn bloom; in beds they produce a fine effect, while in ribbons, the pink, rose, and white make a striking combination. S. ocymoides flowers so profusely in the spring and early summer months as literally to present to the eye a sheet of rosy pink: a fine rock-plant.

Saponaria Calabrica (true) – rich deep pink, 15 cm / ½ ft, hardy annual.
S. Calabrica rosea – rose, 15 cm / ½ ft, hardy annual.
S. C. alba – pure white, 15 cm / ½ ft, hardy annual.
S. ocymoides – rose-pink, 8 cm / ¼ ft, hardy perennial.

SCARLET RUNNERS

These may be planted at any time from April to late in July. The seed should be dropped about 10 cm / 4 in apart, and if a line be selected along the two sides of a walk in the kitchen-garden, a very pretty shady avenue may be made. Plant stakes 2–2.5 m / 7–8 ft high in the row where the beans are; set two or three stakes to the yard, and bend them over at the top to form arches. In the spaces between the stakes place pea-sticks, to which the runners may at first be trained. The stakes should be tied together by wands arranged longitudinally, one along the top and one halfway up each side. When this framework becomes covered with scarlet runners, a very pleasant shady walk will be formed. With a little care in manuring and watering, the runners may be kept green and in bearing till killed by the autumn frosts. The runners will blossom and bear much more freely if the old beans are all removed, and they are not allowed to ripen seed. A mixture of the white Dutch runner with the scarlet runner gives to the avenue a very pretty effect.

SCIZANTHUS

A genus of extremely beautiful and strikingly effective plants, if well grown, combining with elegance of growth a rich profusion of beautiful flowers. For flower-beds and borders all the varieties are desirable, but for single specimens, either for conservatory decoration or the centre of beds and vases, *S. Grahamii* are the most useful, producing a splendid effect. Valuable for indoor decoration during the winter and spring months; they succeed best in a rich soil. Those just named are half-hardy annuals, but all the other varieties are hardy annuals.

SCORZONERA

This is sown, and eaten, in the same manner as salsify. To have it large, it should remain over the second season.

SNOWDROP

This is one of the most elegant and interesting of spring flowers: it may be had in bloom indoors at a very early period; its swan-white blossoms contrasting beautifully with the rich hue of the crocus, &c. A row of snowdrops is often very effective in juxtaposition with a row of blue crocuses. October is the best month for procuring and planting them, although they may be inserted much later.

SNOWFLAKE, or LEUCOJUM

Of all our early spring flowers few can excel the Snowflake. The very early variety is greatly superior to *L. aestivum*. To ensure a fine display of blossom, the roots should be well-manured as soon as they have done flowering.

Leucojum vernum (spring Snowflake) – pure white, tipped with green; blooms in February or March.

L. aestivum (summer Snowflake) – white; a pretty snowdrop-like flower, which blooms readily in aquariums, fountains, and small fishponds early in May.

SPINACH

☛ PREPARATION OF THE SOIL: The ground for a summer crop of spinach cannot be too rich, and should be heavily manured and trenched deeply: a rather strong loamy soil is to be preferred. For the winter crop, however, a light and sandy soil is the most suitable, but this also should be deeply trenched, and in unfavourable localities a sheltered situation should be chosen. In wet, undrained

177

soils, or those of a very strong tenacious nature, it may be advisable to sow the winter crop on raised beds, for spinach is very impatient of ground saturated with wet in winter, and under such conditions will not stand severe frost. The spring and summer crops are often sown between the rows of other crops, as peas, celery trenches, &c.; and there can be no objection to this practice, save the injury which may be done to the ground by treading it, when wet, in gathering the spinach. Crops sown in this way should be cleared off as soon as done with, and the ground forked up. If the soil is not moderately rich, a slight dressing of well-decayed manure should be applied; but this should be kept some distance under the surface.

🖛 TIME AND MANNER OF SOWING: For the summer crop sow early in March, and at intervals of three weeks or a fortnight, until the middle of July, in quantities according to the demand. The round-seeded varieties are the best for summer crops. The winter crop should be sown from the middle of August to the beginning of September. The prickly-seeded is the hardiest, and should be partly used for this crop. All the crops should be sown in drills, from 2.5–5 cm / 1–2 in deep, and from 30–45 cm / 12–18 in apart, scattering the seed thinly, and covering with the finest of the soil. When the ground is dry, the drills should be well soaked with water before sowing. If the seed is steeped for twenty-four hours before sowing, it will germinate sooner; but this should be done only when the ground is hot and dry.

🖛 AFTER-MANAGEMENT: The winter crop should be thinned as soon as the plants are strong enough to draw, so as to leave them about 20 cm / 9 in apart in the row; but the summer crops soon run to seed, and need not be thinned to a greater distance in the line than 8 cm / 3 in. Some growers recommend a liberal use of manure-water for the summer crop, and this doubtless increases the size of the leaves; but it must not be depended upon to prevent the plants running to seed for more than a few days; and while the weather is hot a succession should be provided for, by making frequent sowings. Keep the ground between the lines free from weeds, and in an open state by frequent deep hoeings.

STOCKS or MATHIOLA

The stock Gilliflower is one of the most popular and important of our garden favourites; its delicious fragrance, brilliant and diversified colours, profusion and duration of its bloom, make it invaluable for flower-beds and borders, for edgings and pot-culture.

The 10-week stock (*Mathiola annua*) is the most universally cultivated; it usually blooms ten or twelve weeks after being sown, grows from 15–40 cm /

6–15 in high, and when cultivated in rich soil and occasionally watered with very weak guano-water, throws out an immense quantity of lateral spikes of bloom, so that a plant forms a perfect bouquet: it would indeed be very difficult to surpass the grand effect produced by these exquisite floral gems.

The Imperial or Emperor, sometimes called perpetual stocks – They are half-hardy biennials, hybrids of the Brompton, growing 45 cm / 18 in high, and of a robust branching habit. Sown in March or April, they make splendid 'autumn-flowering stocks,' and form a valuable succession to the summer-blooming varieties. Should the winter prove mild, they will continue flowering to Christmas. Sown in June or July, they flower the following June, and continue blooming through the summer and autumn months.

The Brompton and Giant Cape are generally called winter stocks, on account of their not flowering the first year: the former is robust and branching, the latter possesses the characteristic so much esteemed by some, viz., an immense pyramidal spike of bloom. These are half-hardy biennials.

The intermediate stock is dwarf and branching. It is of great value in filling flower-beds for an early summer display. Half-hardy biennials.

☞ TO SELECT DOUBLE FLOWERS: Reject from the seed-bed all those plants which have a long tap-root (these will almost invariably prove single), and reserve for bedding only those which have the largest quantity of delicate fibres at the roots: experience shows that these, in general, prove double.

SUNFLOWERS or HELIANTHUS

Hardy annuals. A genus of plants remarkable for their stately growth and the brilliancy and size of their noble flowers; they are eminently adapted for dispersing in shrubbery borders. Round the margins of lakes, ponds, and wherever plants of this character are required, this genus will be found extremely effective; some of the varieties, as H. Californicus and H. Californicus striatiflorus, are particularly adapted for mixed flower-borders and large beds in conspicuous situations. They grow freely in any rich soil.

SWEETCORN

☞ PREPARATION OF THE SOIL: Select a warm, sunny and open situation, and trench deeply, adding a liberal dressing of well-rotted manure.

☞ TIME AND MANNER OF SOWING: Sow in pots in April, or in the open ground in May, but, except in very favourable localities, the plants succeed best if raised under glass and planted out when the weather becomes warm and settled.

If raised in pots, be careful to keep the plants strong and stocky, hardening them by giving air freely on fine days.

AFTER-MANAGEMENT: When planted out, water freely until the roots have got hold of fresh soil, and also in dry, hot weather. Keep the surface of the ground free from weeds, and mulch every fortnight. The ears, if cut when silk-like fibres appear, make a delicious vegetable.

SWEET-WILLIAM or DIANTHUS

Hardy perennials. A splendid free-flowering garden favourite, producing an unusually fine effect in flower-beds, borders, and shrubberies.

TARRAGON

This is the *Artemisia Dracunculus*, the leaves of which are so much used in France for salads, chicken dishes, and flavouring vinegar.

THUNBERGIA

A genus of slender and rapid-growing climbers, with extremely pretty and much-admired flowers, which are freely produced, either when grown in the greenhouse or in a warm situation out of doors: they delight in rich loamy soil. All the varieties are half. hardy annuals, except *T. coccinea*, which is a green-house perennial, and blooms in clusters.

Thunbergia alata (Black-eyed Susan) – orange, rich brown eye.

TOMATO

An admirable vegetable, there is, undoubtedly, some little difficulty in our climate in fruiting and ripening tomatoes to perfection; but the following directions, if attended to, will generally be found to succeed — Sow the seeds in pots in very rich light mould in March or April, and place them in a cucumber-frame, or other gentle heat. When the second leaf appears, repot the plants either singly or at most two or three together, keeping them near the glass and well watered. In May remove them to a cold frame for the purpose of hardening them before they are planted out, which should be done as soon as the fear of spring frosts is over, and the earlier the better. The best situation for tomato-plants is against a south wall fully exposed to the sun. The plants should be well watered with liquid manure to keep up a rapid growth. As soon as the blossom-buds appear, watering should cease. Stop the shoots by nipping off the tops, and throw out all those sprays that show little signs of fruit, exposing the young fruit as much as possible to the sun and air, only watering to prevent a check in case of very severe drought, of which the state of the plant will be the best index. In a very dull, wet, cold autumn, even with the greatest care, the fruit will sometimes not ripen as it ought; but in this case it may frequently be made fit for use by cutting off the branches on which full-grown fruit is found, and hanging them in a warm dry greenhouse or elsewhere to soften and ripen.

TRITOMA or RED-HOT POKER

An exceedingly showy free-flowering plant, with long graceful leaves and majestic flower-spikes, 90 cm–2 m / 3–7 ft in height, crowned with densely-flowered spikes of bloom, which are produced during the autumn months, 46–70 cm / 18–27 in long.

☛ CULTURE: Dig and well work the soil to the depth of 2 or 3 ft, adding plenty of rotted manure. The crown of the plant should not be more than an inch and a half in the soil; for winter protection surround the plant with 5 cm / 2 in of sawdust, firmly trodden. Remove this early in May: from then till the plant is in bloom, weak liquid manure must be applied in large quantities, especially during dry weather.

Tritoma glaucescens – rich scarlet.
—*T. grandis* – bright scarlet, tall and late.

TROPAEOLUM

Half-hardy annuals. A tribe of elegant-growing, profuse-flowering, and easily-cultivated climbers, combining with these important qualities great richness and brilliancy of colour, with finely-formed and beautifully-marked flowers. For pillars and rafters, in the greenhouse or conservatory, they are invaluable; for covering trellises, verandahs, and bowers out of doors, they are of equal importance. When used for bedding, they should be regularly and carefully pegged down, interlacing the shoots, and occasionally removing the large leaves.

We may remark that all the 'Lobbianum' varieties bloom beautifully through the winter months in the greenhouse or conservatory, so that where cut flowers are in demand they will be found an invaluable acquisition. Grow freely in light rich soil.

TULIPS

There is a peculiarity belonging to tulips which does not, so far as we are aware, belong to any other flower. The seedlings, in their first bloom, generally produce flowers without any stripes or markings, all the upright portions of the petal being self-coloured, flowering for years without any such variegations, when they are called breeders. After some years they break out into stripes: if these are liked, they are named; but they have multiplied in the breeder state, and may have been distributed in all directions, each person possessed of one which has broken using the privilege of naming it; hence many, with different synonyms, are one and the same thing.

The perfection of soil for tulip-culture would be 8 cm / 3 in of the top of a rich loamy pasture, the turf of which has lain by till thoroughly rotted, and which has been repeatedly turned and picked: the decayed vegetable matter will suffice without other dressing. The tulip-bed should run north and south, with drainage perfect, but without stones or rubbish at the bottom. The bed may be dug out 120 cm / 4 ft wide and 75 cm / 2 ft 6 in deep, and the compost previously prepared filled in till it is a few inches above the bed, the centre being 5 cm / 2 in higher than the sides. Giving a few days for the bed to settle, rake all smooth, leaving the bed 8 cm / 3 in above the path. On this the tulips are placed in seven rows across the bed, and 6 inches apart in the rows. They are pressed in a little; soil is then placed upon them, 8 cm / 3 in above the crown of the bulbs, so that the bed being raised in the centre, the middle row will be covered 10–13 cm / 4–5 in.

When planted and covered, they may be left until the leaf-buds begin to peep through the ground.

As frost approaches, while giving as much air as possible, they should be protected against it by mats or other shelter, but not longer than is necessary; otherwise they get drawn up weakly. In February they begin to appear, when the ground should be stirred, all lumps broken, and pressed close round the stems. As the spikes begin to open, they form a receptacle for the wet, and the frost must not then be allowed to reach them. When the colours begin to show, in order to protect their bloom, shelter them from the sun, taking care that no more air than is absolutely necessary is excluded. By the end of June the stems will have turned brown or yellow. As soon as the leaves begin to decay, the bulbs may be taken up, dried, and stored away.

The best time for planting is the last fortnight in October, or early in November – Tulip-seed may be sown either in spring or autumn, and in the soil already described; it should be saved from the best flowers only. The small offsets should be planted by themselves and labelled, in similar soil to that already described. Breeders such as we have described may be grown in any soil.

Tulips are divided into Roses, Byblomens, and Bizarres. Roses have a white ground, and crimson, pink, or scarlet markings. Byblomens are those having a white ground, and purple, lilac, or black markings. Bizarres have a yellow ground, with any coloured marks that present themselves. Self-tulips are those which are of one colour, such as white or yellow, showing no inclination to sport into other colours.

Early Tulips

For the purposes of winter and spring gardening, early-flowering tulips, double and single, are even more indispensable than the hyacinth, narcissus, and crocus. Their extreme hardiness, certainty of blooming, and the absence of all difficulty in their cultivation, distinctly entitle them to a preference in the choice of occupants for the spring flower-garden.

Early Single Tulips

No section of tulips display so great a variety of delicate, striking, and attractive colours. Of Selfs, there are beautiful scarlets, crimsons, whites, and yellows; of parti-colours, snow-white grounds, striped and feathered with purple, violet, crimson, rose, puce, and cerise, and yellow grounds, with crimson, scarlet, and red flakes and feathers.

Culture in ornamental vases and other elegant contrivances should be the same in every respect as that recommended for the hyacinth. Culture in pots is also the same as that of the hyacinth, except that three bulbs should be planted in a 10- or 13-cm / 4- or 5-in, and five in a 15-cm / 6-in pot. Those intended for early blooming should be forced as soon as the shoot appears.

Culture out of doors precisely that of the hyacinth, except that the bulbs should not be planted more than 10–15 cm / 4–6 in apart, when an effective display is desired, though many persons plant them 15–20 cm / 6–8 in from each other.

In beds the crown of the bulb should be 8 cm / 3 in under the surface, and should the weather be severe, a few branches placed on the bed will be found ample protection.

☛ TIME OF PLANTING FOR OUTDOOR DECORATION: The early part of November, or as soon after that period as convenient. We have planted the tulip as late as January, and have had a splendid display. We do not, however, recommend keeping the bulbs so long out of the ground.

Early Double Tulips

In pots the varieties of this section are very attractive, but as a rule they are better adapted for outdoor than indoor decoration.

Parrot Tulips

The parrot tulip has a singularly picturesque appearance; the flowers are large and the colours brilliant, so that when planted in flower-borders and the front of shrubberies they produce a most striking effect. When grown in hanging baskets, and so planted as to cause their large flowers to droop over the side, the effect is remarkable and unique.

TURNIPS

☛ PREPARATION OF THE SOIL: A somewhat light, sandy, but deep rich soil, is most suitable for turnips, and is indeed essential to secure bulbs of mild and delicate flavour. If the summer crops sustain any check during their growth, they are apt to be stringy and high-flavoured. Select, then, a deep light soil, manure it heavily, and trench to a depth of 60 cm / 2 ft, early in autumn. If ground must be used for the summer sowings which was not trenched in autumn, this should be done before putting in the seed.

☛ TIME AND MANNER OF SOWING: Sow a small breadth of the early Dutch, for the chance of a crop, upon a south border, or in a warm, sheltered situation, early in March; and as this sowing is liable to run to seed soon, put in a small quantity of the same variety about the middle of the month, and again early in April, sowing a small breadth of the Strap-leaf at the same time; afterwards sow at intervals of three weeks or a month till July, and for a winter supply from the beginning to the middle of August. On light warm soils, in favourable localities, useful-sized bulbs may be obtained from sowings made easy in September. The Orange Jelly is one of the best varieties for autumn sowing. All the sowings should be made in shallow drills 30–45 cm / 12–18 in apart: 30 cm / 12 in will be sufficient for the early and late sowings. Scatter the seed very thinly and evenly, and cover it lightly with the finest of the soil. In summer, when the ground is dry, the drills should be well watered before sowing, and if the seed is steeped in water for 24 hours, this will hasten germination.

☛ AFTER-MANAGEMENT: Thin out the plants us soon as they are sufficiently strong to draw, so that they may stand 15–20 cm / 6–9 in apart in the row. If fly makes its appearance – and this is generally very troublesome during summer in warm localities, dust the plants over with quick-lime early in the morning, while the leaves are moist with dew. Repeat this operation as often as may be necessary. Keep the surface of the ground open and free from weeds by frequent stirrings with the hoe.

VALERIAN

Perennial plants suitable for rockeries.

VERBENA

One of the most useful of bedding plants, a native of South America. The named varieties are infinite; every year adds many novelties to the list. The plants seed freely, and are of easy cultivation by cuttings; they also root rapidly by being pegged down. The following management has been recommended by a very experienced gardener:

'I have tried many different sizes of pots and pans for verbenas. I have found nothing so useful or successful as a score of cuttings in a pot. The pots are filled one-third full of drainage, 2.5 cm / 1 in of rough leaf-mould over it; then fill to within 3.5 cm / 1½ in of the top with equal parts of loam, leaf-mould, or peat and sand, finishing with 1 cm / ½ in of sand; insert the cuttings in the usual manner, making sure that the base of the cutting is made firm. Water level – a point of great moment in excluding the air from the part where roots are to be emitted, as in as in the future watering of the cuttings, and the work is finished. Verbenas are also best left in the store or cutting-pots until February; and, unlike calceolarias, if enough are kept over the winter for stock, spring-struck plants are best both for growth and flower.

VERONICA or SPEEDWELL

The evergreen shrubs of this genus, when well grown, are amongst the most valuable of autumn-blooming plants. Their handsome spikes of flowers, which are produced in great profusion and in succession for months, make them invaluable for conservatory and sitting-room decoration, and for prominent positions out of doors, where with a dry subsoil and somewhat sheltered situation, the plants will generally stand the winter uninjured. The miniature annual varieties *V. Syriaca* and *alba* make very pretty small beds and edgings during the summer and autumn, but in spring they are much more effective; we therefore recommend their being sown in autumn for the decoration of the spring garden.

VINCA

This is the classical name of the common periwinkle, and of its class there are many beautiful varieties. They grow in any soil, and look well on rockeries. Under the name Vinca also are included many choice greenhouse evergreens, as remarkable for their shining green foliage as for their handsome circular flowers. Plants raised from seed which has been sown early in spring will be found useful for the ornamentation of flower-beds and borders in warm situations.

Vinca rosea – rose, 60 cm / 2 ft.
— *alba* – white, with crimson eye, 60 cm / 2 ft.
Vinca alba pura nova – pure white, 60 cm / 2 ft.
— *lutea nova* – pure white with yellow eye, 60 cm / 2 ft.

VINES

It is certain that our moist and cloudy climate is not favourable to the ripening of the grape; its cultivation in the open air, therefore, requires great care; and in many seasons the most skilful management will fail to bring it to perfection. Nevertheless, the graceful trailing habit and beautiful foliage of the vine render it highly ornamental on the walls of a house; and for this it is worth cultivating, with the prospect of some fruit in favourable summers. It is also certain that in former days vineyards of considerable extent were cultivated, some remains of which are still found in Gloucestershire.

The vine is propagated by cuttings and by layering. Cuttings, made early in March or the latter end of February may be planted about the middle of March. The cuttings must be shoots of last year, shortened to about 30 cm / 12 in, or three joints each; and if they have an inch or so of last year's wood at the bottom, it will be an advantage. They may be planted either in nursery rows until rooted, or planted at once where they are to remain, observing in the latter case to plant them in a slanting direction, and so deep that only one eye or joint is above-ground, and that close to the surface.

Vines are propagated by layering of the shoot of last year, or of a part of the branch, laying them about 10–13 cm / 4–5 in deep and covering them with soil, leaving about three eyes above the ground; they are also layered in large pots, either by drawing the branch through the drainage-hole and filling the pot with soil, or by bending the branch and sinking it 10–13 cm / 4–5 in in the soil and pegging it down there; it may then either be grown as a potted vine or, when fully rooted, transferred to its permanent place on the wall or vine border; in the latter case the soil of the border it should be dug out for 90– 20 cm / 3–4 ft, as directed for other wall trees, a solid concrete bottom formed, with thorough drainage to carry off the water, and the border filled in again, first with bones and other animal remains, then with lime rubbish where that is available, and the surface with good loamy soil. In this soil the vine should be planted, the roots being previously trimmed and spread out horizontally, so as to radiate in a half-circle from the crown of the stem. Under such an arrangement as this the vine comes rapidly into bearing.

When the vine is approaching a bearing state, and the leaves have fallen, a general regulation of the shoots becomes necessary. In every part of the tree, a proper supply of last year's shoots, both lateral and terminal, should be encouraged, these being the principal bearers to produce next year's fruit. All irregular and superabundant shoots should be cut out, and with them all of the former year's bearers, which are either too close to each other or which are too long for their respective places. Where it is not desirable to cut out the branch entirely, prune it back to some eligible lateral shoot, to form a terminal or leading branch. Cut out also all naked old wood. The last summer's shoots thus left will in spring project from every eye or bud young shoots, which produce the grapes the same summer. The general rule is to shorten the shoots to three, four, five, or six eyes or joints in length, according to their strength, and cutting them back from 1 cm / ½ in to about 0.5 cm / ¼ in at every eye, the strongest branches being limited to five or six joints, except where it is required to cover a vacant space on the wall.

When left longer, the vines become crowded, in the following summer, with useless shoots, and the fruit is smaller in consequence. This pruning should be performed early in spring, even as early as February: in pruning at a later period, when the sap has begun to ascend, the wound is apt to bleed when the thick branches have been cut off. A second pruning should be performed about the middle of May, when the grapes are formed and the shoot has attained a length of 60–90 cm / 2–3 ft: at this time pinch off the shoot about 15 cm / 6 in above the fruit and nail it to the wall in such a way that the fruit may be in contact with it. About midsummer a third pruning should take place, when all the branches should be gone over and the fruitless ones, not required for next year's wood, removed. A vigorous vine will require a fourth and final pruning in August, when the long shoots from the previous stoppings must be shortened back again, and all leaves lying too much over the bunches of fruit removed; taking care to prune, however, in such a manner that there is always a succession of young branches advancing from the lower part of the stem properly furnished with bearers, as well as a sufficient supply of young wood to replace the old as it becomes unserviceable.

The pruning finished, let the branches be nailed or tied neatly to the wall or trellis, laying them regularly 15–25 cm / 6–10 in apart. Vine-pruning may be performed any time during the winter months, when the weather permits; but the sooner the work is done the better. The young shoots of last year produce shoots themselves the ensuing summer; and these are the fruit-bearers, which are to be trained horizontally or upright, according to the design of the tree.

In May the vines will shoot vigorously, producing, besides bearing and succession shoots, others which must be cut away, and bearing and other useful branches nailed or tied up close to the wall before they get entangled with each other; and all weak and straggling shoots: especially those rising from the old wood, should be cleared away. Much of this summer pruning may be effected by pinching off the young shoots with the finger and thumb while they are young and tender. This should be continued during June and July. Many small shoots rise, one mostly from every eye of the same summer's main shoots laid in a month or two ago: these must be displaced, in order to admit all the air possible to the advancing fruit. All new shoots whatever should now be rubbed off as they appear, except where: they are required to cover the wall. In August, even these must be rubbed off, being utterly valueless even for that purpose. During this month, the fruit itself requires attention. Where the branches are entangled, or in confusion, let them be regulated so that every branch may hang in its proper position. All the shoots that have fruit hanging on them, and where they are ranging out of bounds, may be stopped, and where the grapes are too much shaded during August and September, remove a few of the leaves which intercept the light and heat. They should now have all possible aid of the sun to enrich their flavour. It will be necessary now to protect them from birds, wasps, &c., by bagging the best bunches in gauze or paper bags. In October, the bunches are ripe to burst-ing, and ready to gather. Bear in mind that success depends on well-ripened wood – a short-jointed branch, ripened under an August sun, being a fruitful bearer of highly-flavoured fruit, and for this purpose a light porous earth is preferable to more tenacious clay soils. When the bunches of grapes are formed, pinch off the leading point of the growing shoot one joint above that from which the bunch proceeds. After the young points have been stopped, each joint below the stopping will put forth a side-shoot. These are termed lateral shoots. This stopping is continued till the stoning period commences. This process occupies six or eight weeks, during which the growth of the fruit remains stationary.

During the swelling of the berry, the fruit begin to acquire flavour, and the buds plumpness and firmness. Henceforth they must have all the sunlight possi-ble. To obtain this, all the lateral spray and others which shade the larger leaves must be stripped away, leaving the larger leaves exposed to the sun; for the fruit receives its flavour through the agency of the leaves. Spur-pruning consists of carrying up one leading shoot to the whole extent of the house or wall, either at one year's growth, or two or three, leaving spurs or lateral shoots to develop themselves at regular intervals on the stem. This is usually the result of three years' growth, the cane being allowed to make a third of the length the first year, a second third the second year, and the remaining third during the third year.

There will thus be five branches the first year, and fifteen the third year. The subsequent pruning is confined to pruning each of the laterals back to the last eye at the base of the shoot.

Long-rod pruning consists in establishing a stump with three strong branches or collars, from each of which, in its turn, a shoot springs, which, by a regular system of pruning, is worked in successive lengths, the one running the whole length of the rafter, the second half the length, and the third, recently pruned back, is to produce the renewal-shoot.

☛ SORTS: Early Black ripens in July in situations where the Black Hamburgs fail. Miller's Burgundy, known by its white downy leaf, is very early and hardy. White Sweetwater is early sort, with a fine large berry, but sets badly. White Muscadine, excellent for all purposes.

Black Hamburg ripens out of doors in fine seasons, but is very capricious in colour. White Frontignan is a fine early grape, sweet but insipid. Muscat of Alexandria requires artificial heat to ripen, but is one of the richest grapes in cultivation. West's St Peter and the Cannon Mill grape are both favourites for house-culture.

VIOLETS

The common violet, *V. odorata*, is a native of our own island. It is found wild, both purple and white. Violets may also be grown in pots, by placing two or three runners or offsets in a pot in May, and keeping them in the frame slightly shaded from the hot sun in summer. Loam and leaf-mould suit them admirably. Russian violets, and sometimes the Neapolitan, will flower all the winter. True violets flower in March and April.

The pots should be examined at all times when the weather will permit. Weeds and decayed leaves must be removed, and a little water given when the soil is dry. Care must be taken to wet the leaves as little as possible. In March and April, if the plants have been properly managed, they will produce abundance of flowers, and consequently will require more moisture than during winter.

For summer and autumn flowering, runners should be laid in pots in February, and kept moist, and planted out separately in April.

VIRGINIA CREEPER

A favourite plant for covering an ugly wall or shed. Its flowers are very insignificant; but this defect is amply compensated for by its beautiful leaves, which assume a most brilliant scarlet colour in autumn. Its growth also is very rapid: by some persons it is known as the Five-leaved Ivy.

VISCARIA

There are several varieties of pretty little annuals so named, suitable for borders, small beds, and single lines.

Viscaria oculata – 20 cm / ¾ ft, pink, dark eye.

WALLFLOWER

For spring gardening these hardy perennials are as indispensable as the crocus or the tulip, and from the delicious fragrance of their beautiful flowers they are especial favourites. On account of their variety, much interest is excited in raising them from seed.

XERANTHEMUM

Hardy annual. A showy class of everlastings; the flowers, gathered when young, are valuable for winter bouquets: require a rich soil. They are best sown mixed.

Xeranthemum album – 60 cm / 2 ft.
X. atropurpureum, fl. pl. – purple, very fine double variety, 60 cm / 2 ft.

YUCCA

These are popularly known as Adam's Needle. They are perfectly hardy plants, of quaint appearance, forming striking objects in garden scenery. Y. recurva has graceful drooping leaves. They grow best in a dry sandy loam, and will succeed well if planted on rockeries, to which they impart quite a tropical aspect.

ZAUSCHNERIA

A handsome Californian perennial plant, in bloom from June to October, with a profusion of beautiful tube-shaped flowers: succeeds best in dry gravelly soil.

ZINNIA

Half-hardy annuals. A grand genus of autumn-flowering plants, combining the greatest richness and diversity of colour with unequalled profusion and duration of bloom. We recommend the seed being sown early in March, so as to have strong stocky plants to put out in June; they should be planted in the richest soil and the warmest situation possible.

Zinnia elegans, fl. pl. – mixed, saved from splendid double flowers, 45 cm / 1½ ft.
Z. mexicana – yellow, flushed with orange up to the centre of each petal; habit dwarf, bushy, and free-flowering, 30 cm / 1 ft.

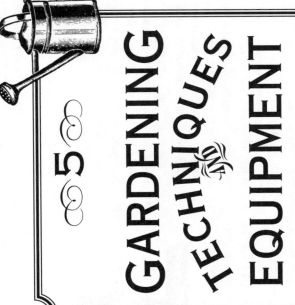

5

GARDENING TECHNIQUES AND EQUIPMENT

Instructions on how to take cuttings, lay out a vegetable bed, mulch a new border, sow seeds for best results, and much more.

BUDDING

GRAFTS of this description present the following characters; they consist in raising an eye or bud with a piece of the bark and wood, and transferring it to another part of the same plant, or any other plant of the same species. Budding is chiefly employed on young shoots or trees from one to five years old, which bear a thin, tender, and smooth bark.

The necessary conditions are that the operation takes place when trees are in full growth, when the bark of the subject can be easily detached from the liber (inner bark), and it may be performed generally from May to August. The buds adapted for the operation should present well-constituted eyes or gemmae at the axil of the leaf; if they are not sufficiently so, it is possible to prepare them by pinching the herbaceous extremity of the bud; thus producing a reflux of the sap towards the base; and in about twelve days' time the eyes will have become sufficiently developed: then detach the bud from the parent tree. Suppress all leaves, only reserving a very small portion of the petiole, or leaf-stalk [a] (see diagram, above).

Having fixed upon the intended stock and bud, take a sharp budding-knife, and with a clean cut remove the bud from its branch, with about 5 mm / ¼ in of the bark above and below [a]: remove all the wood without disturbing the inner bark of the eye; for it is in this liber, or inner bark, that the vitality lies. Now make a cross-cut in the bark of the intended stock, and also a vertical one, T, and shape the upper part of the shield, or bud [c] so as to fit it exactly (see diagram, left).

Having fitted the parts correctly, raise the bark of the stock gently with the budding-knife, and insert the bud; afterwards bandage lightly above and below the eye, bringing the lips of the bark of the stock together again over the bud by means of the ligature, in such manner that no opening remains between them, and, above all, taking care that the base of the eye is in free contact with the bark of the stock.

Some weeks after, if the ligatures seem to be too tight, they may be untied and replaced with smaller pressure. When the operation takes place in May, the scion will develop itself as soon as the suture is completed. In order to provide for this, cut the head of the stock down to within 2.5 cm / 1 in of the point of junction immediately after the operation.

When the operation takes place in August, the head is never cut till the following spring, when the scion begins to grow. If the same practice as in earlier budding were followed, the consequence would be, that the bud would develop itself before winter; and, having no time to ripen its new wood, it would perish, or at least suffer greatly. When the buds begin to grow, they require to be protected from strong winds; otherwise they would be detached from the stem. This is done by driving a stake [a] firmly into the ground, attaching it by a strong cord to the stem of the stock above and below the junction [b] and [c], as in the diagram, and tying the shoot of the young scion firmly to the stake above [d], protecting it by a bandage of hay or other substance, to prevent the bark being injured.

The shoots selected for budding or grafting, whether for fruit- or rose-trees, should be firm and well-ripened: watery shoots, or watery buds, are valueless. For grafting, the branches should be of the preceding year, well ripened under an August sun – *aoûté*, as French fruitists say.

The stock should be in a state of vegetation slightly in advance of the graft; otherwise the flow of the sap is insufficient to supply the wants of the scion. In order to provide for this, the graft may be removed from the parent branch a little before the operation, and buried under a north wall: there it remains stationary, while the stock is advancing to maturity.

CANES

I F YOUR plants need support to prevent damage by winds and rain it is a good idea to use garden canes. Bamboo is the common choice, being very straight, light and strong. Hazel branches are a good alternative, as is any other very straight and inflexible cane. Delphiniums, lilies, sunflowers, larkspur, &c., are all plants that are commonly staked. It is better to take preventative action early, when the plant is about 40 cm / 15 in, so as to train the plant around the stake. With plants growing from bulbs, stake from the time of planting. Choose a day when the soil is moist to make it easier to insert the canes, being careful to wear gloves to avoid splinters, and push each stake 10-15 cm / 4–6 in into the ground using both hands to avoid snapping. Use a fine hacksaw to cut your canes to the required length.

Other ways to use canes include using a series of shorter canes in a circle, where the canes are tied to each other and to the plant, with the plant overhanging the edges and opened up for maximum air and light inside; and in a wig-wam shape. If the plants are on prominent display, it might be worth considering using proprietary green-wire structures which are more easily camouflaged.

CUTTINGS

CUTTINGS in general may be considered as of two kinds – matured wood, and young green shoots. The former, whatever they may be, strike readily, and with very little care. An American plan, which is very successful, is to lay them in slightly-damped moss, or to drop them lightly into a wide-mouthed bottle, having a piece of damp sponge at the bottom and a covering of muslin over the top. In either of these methods a callus is soon formed, and the cuttings readily throw out roots. Cuttings of young green shoots, however, require a very different treatment. Put silver-sand about 2.5 cm / 1 in deep into shallow pans (common saucers answer every purpose), and in these plant the cuttings. Then pour carefully upon the sand enough water to make a thin sheet about it. The lower leaves of the cuttings are to be removed before planting, and the stalk fixed firmly into the sand before the water is poured on. These tender young green shoots, or cuttings, will be better for a little shade and heat. A piece of thin muslin or tissue-paper will provide the former, and heat may be had by placing the pan of cuttings over a basin of hot water, refilled twice a day. These cuttings will be rooted and ready for potting off before the water in which they are grown has dried up.

Cuttings of all sorts of geraniums for bedding the following year should be struck early: from the last week in July to the end of the first week in August is very good time. They should be taken in dry weather, when the parent plant has had no water for some days, and they should be kept to dry twenty-four hours after they have been prepared for potting. They may be potted four or six in a pot, according to sizes. It is essential that the pots be well fitted with drainers, that the soil be light and sandy, and that it be pressed tight round the joint of the cuttings, which should be buried in it. When filled, the pots may be sunk in the ground on a south border, and well watered in the evening, when the sun is off. If they grow too freely before it is time to take them in for the winter, the top shoots should be broken off, and in this way they will make strong bushy plants.

To preserve cuttings from frost where there is no greenhouse, dig a pit about 120 cm / 4 ft deep, strew the bottom well with ashes, and sink the pots in the same. Over it place a common garden-frame, bank up the outsides with straw and a coating of earth.

DAISY-FORK

This is a useful little tool for removing daisy roots from lawns: it is fitted with two metal prongs, and acts as a lever by means of a long or short handle.

DRAINAGE

THE object of draining is not only to get rid of superfluous moisture, but also to prevent the little there may be from remaining stagnant. It should, therefore, be the first care of the florist to make drains from the highest part of the ground to the lowest, 90 cm / 3 ft from the surface, dug the shape of a V; and if there be no outlet at the lowest part, to dig a hole into which all these should lead, even when there is no apparent means of getting rid of the water. At the bottom of these drains a row of common 5-cm / 2-in earthen pipes may be placed, end to end, and covered up again with the soil. These are too deep to cause any danger of disturbance in ordinary operations; and the effect is to let air into the soil, if there be no surplus moisture; and to prevent the lodgment of water anywhere.

This will be rendered still more obvious by the accompanying diagrams, which prove the beneficial influence exercised by drainage upon the soil. They are highly-magnified sections of soil in three different conditions. Under the microscope, soil is seen to be made up of numerous distinct porous particles. Fig. 1 represents it in a perfectly dry state; both the soil and the channels between being quite dry. Fig. 2, on the other hand, represents a soil perfectly wet; the particles themselves are full of water, and so are the channels

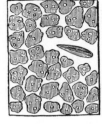

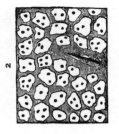

3

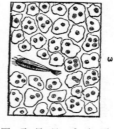

between them. In fig. 3 the particles are moist, while the passages between them are filled with air. The diagrams show that soil in the condition exhibited in figs. 1 and 2 was totally unfit for the germination of seed. In fig. 1 there is no water, in fig. 2 there is no air; in fig. 3 both are present, in the proportions favourable to the growth of seeds, and these are requisite to insure the vigorous growth of the plant throughout all its stages; fig. 3, therefore, is the condition of soil desirable for all cultural purposes, and exhibits that congenial admixture of earth, water, and air, that plants delight in, and which efficient drainage only can provide.

DUTCH HOE

A hoe with a blade attached as in a spade, used by pushing rather than pulling.

EDGING

Sometimes gardens are laid down on a mixed plan of grass and gravel. When each bed is edged with brick, stone, tile, or cement, these edgings are occasionally surrounded with from 60–120 cm / 2–4 ft of gravel, succeeded by the same or a greater width of turf. Flagstones are also used for this purpose instead of gravel, as well as to subdivide groups of figures close to the dwelling-house. Beds on grass, however, unless much elevated above the surface, are most effective without any edgings whatever; although, in certain situations, raised beds, with massive edgings of stone or rustic-work, look well. For beds on gravel, an edging of some kind becomes imperative. Of all living edgings box is the best; thrift, sedums, and saxifrages of various kinds, and that wonderful weed which was designed to banish grass from our lawns (*Spergula miliſera*), follow each other in value and adaptability for this purpose. Ornamental stone, tile, brick, or cast-iron edgings, are probably better than any living edging whatever. These can neither harbour insects, exhaust the soil, nor look patchy through dying off; and although perhaps more expensive in the first instance, the first expense is the only one. They can be purchased on very reasonable terms, and of varied and elegant designs. Whatever edgings are used, they must vary in height and thickness with the size of the beds they define. Nothing can be in worse taste than a heavy massive edging surrounding a small delicate pattern, or vice versa.

On sterile, uncongenial soils, it has been recommended by Mr Loudon and others to enclose all the flower-beds with a brick wall to a depth of 60–90 cm / 2–3 ft, so that the soil could be entirely removed at pleasure. Ornamental wire-work often makes a very effective edging for different beds.

EDGING PLANTS

There are many plants adapted for garden edgings. Among these we may enumerate *Buxus sempervirens*, thrift, cuttings of *Iberis saxatilis*, daisies, both white and red, the variegated alyssum, feather-grass, &c.

FRUIT-GATHERERS

U NDOUBTEDLY, the human hand is the best and safest of all fruit-gatherers; but when bunches of fruit grow at the extremities of slender branches quite out of reach, as is not infrequently the case, some additional assistance appears requisite even when steps and light ladders are at hand.

It is constructed thus: [a] is an oval piece of board; [b] a handle of any convenient length, to which the board is firmly fixed; [c] wooden pegs fixed in the oval frame. These pegs are about 15 cm / 6 in long, and 3–3.5 cm / 1–2 in apart – just wide enough, indeed, to allow the fruit-bearing twigs freely to pass through them. The application, of course, is obvious. The teeth act as a comb, and at the same time form a receptacle, by means of which the fruit may be safely conveyed to the basket; for, the rack being drawn over the twigs with the teeth upwards, the fruit is readily gathered into it.

Another very simple, useful, and inexpensive fruit-gatherer may be made as follows: [a] is a hoop of light iron rod; [b] a net-bag appended to it, after the manner of a landing-net; [c] three teeth set with a curve just a little higher than the hoop. These teeth may be made of the same wire as the hoop; but they should be covered with cloth or some soft material to prevent bruising the fruit; [d] is a wooden shaft or handle, which may be extended to any

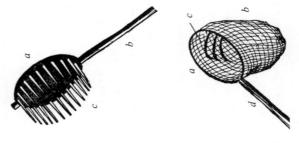

length, after the manner of a fishing-rod. In this case, it is desirable that the teeth should be set at such an angle with the rim, and the rim at such an angle with the shaft, as to insure the fruit falling into the net.

GRAFTING

Gardening ingenuity has invented many kinds of grafting: we shall describe a few of these processes, in order to explain their principle. Select a suitable stock, whose height will be according to the purpose for which it is intended; also a graft, which should be from an early branch of the previous year's wood which has ripened under an August sun, so that the wood has been thoroughly constituted before the early frosts set in.

It should also be selected so that the graft is in the same state of vegetation with the intended stock. Where the texture of the wood is less advanced in the graft than in the stock, the latter intercepts the descent of the pulpy sap, and forms the bulging on the stem which is observable on so many trees; when the case is reversed, the swelling occurs in the branch above the graft; for the principle of the union is, that the pulp from the scion descends to the point of junction, where, being excluded by the ball of grafting-wax, which surrounds it, from the light and air, it forms woody fibre in place of the roots which it would have formed in the soil; in the mean while, the sap from the stock rises into the graft, where it is elaborated into pulp by the action of the leaves, and returns again, but in a more consistent state.

It is necessary, therefore, where the graft selected is in a more advanced state of vegetation, to detach it from the parent stem, and bury it in the ground, under a north wall, until both are in a similar state: the graft will here remain stationary while the stock is advancing.

In gardening nomenclature, the term 'stock,' or 'subject,' is applied to the tree on which the operation is performed; that of 'graft,' and sometimes' scion,' to the portion of the branch which is implanted in it.

Cleft- or tongue-grafting In cleft- or tongue-grafting, the crown of the stock is cut across, and a longitudinal wedge-shaped slit [a] is made about 10 cm / 4 in long, according to the size and vigour of the intended graft: this cleft is kept open by a wooden wedge until the scion is prepared. The scion is then selected, having a bud [b] at its summit; and the lower part of it is shaped with the knife so as to fit the slit in the stock [c]. The double-tongue graft only differs from the first in having two grafts in place of one; and it is preferable, when the size

of the stock permits of its use; the wound heals more quickly, and the chances of success are greater than in the single graft.

In placing the graft, it is to be observed that the top, whether single or double, should incline slightly inwards, as at [d] thus leaving the lower extremity slightly projecting, as at [e] in order that the inner bark of the graft and stock may be in direct contact with each other. Finally, bind the whole, and cover it over, from the summit of the stock to the bottom of the cleft, with clay or grafting-paste.

DOUBLE GRAFTING In double grafting, where they both take, it is necessary to suppress the least vigorous as soon as the wound is completely closed, especially in the case of standard trees; otherwise the head gets formed of two parts completely estranged from each other. During the first twelve days after the operation, protect the head from the action of the air and the heat of the sun by some kind of shade. A paper bag answers very well for this purpose, protecting it at the same time from the attacks of insects; and when they begin to grow, protect the graft from being disturbed by the wind, or by birds lighting on it, by attaching it to some fixed object.

When the young scion begins to grow, it is necessary to suppress all buds which develop themselves on the stem, below it, beginning at the base, and upwards to 2.5–5 cm / 1–2 in long.

THE BERLEMBOISE GRAFT A very neat mode of grafting. Cut the crown of the stock at a long bevel, leaving only about 2.5 cm / 1 in at the top square, cutting out an angular piece to receive the graft, and operating in all respects as in the former instance. When the stock is not large enough to receive a graft on each side, this mode is preferred, as forming the neatest union, as well as the most rapid; for all the ascending sap is thus drawn to the summit of the bevel on which the graft is placed.

THEOPHRASTES GRAFT A graft, honoured with the name of Theophrastes, is sometimes practised on trees having healthy roots, where it is desired to improve the fruit. Having cut the stem of the tree itself horizontally, or selected

199

a single branch to be operated upon, about 50 cm / 20 in from the principal stem, three vertical cuts are made in the bark, at equal distances from each other, about 3 cm / 1 in long. Having selected three or more grafts [a] and shaped their lower extremities into a tongue somewhat like the mouthpiece of a tin-whistle, with a neck or shoulder at the upper part, then introduce a graft under the bark of each vertical cut, raising the bark for that purpose with the spatula of the grafting-knife, and placing each graft in such a position that the inner bark of the graft is in immediate contact with the inner bark of the tree. When neatly arranged, bandage the whole, and cover with the grafting-paste.

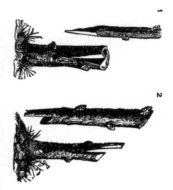

1

a

2

SLIT-GRAFTING In place of the vertical cut through the whole of the stem, in this process a triangular cut is made in the side of the stock, as in figure 1; the lower end of the graft is then cut so as to fit exactly into the gap made, so that the inner bark, or liber, meets in contact at all points: this done, it is covered with clay or grafting – paste, and bound up until amalgamation takes place.

A strong and efficient mode of grafting is represented in the second cut, figure 2. Make an elongated bevelled cut in the proposed stock from left to right; make another vertical wedge-shaped cut, 8 cm / 3 in long, from left to right, leaving a narrow shoulder at the top on the left side, and terminating in the centre of the stock, so as to resemble that in the engraving. Take the intended graft, of the same diameter as the stock, and shape its lower extremity so as to fit into the cleft thus made; bind up in the usual manner, and cover the joint with grafting-paste. This forms a very strong and very useful graft in species which unite slowly.

HERBACEOUS GRAFTING consists in choosing branches still in active growth. Pines, walnut-trees, oaks, and other trees which are multiplied with difficulty by other processes, are easily produced by this one. The mode of operating differs slightly, according to the species. In the case of pines and resinous

trees, when the terminal bud of the subject [a] has attained two-thirds of its growth, make an horizontal cut at [d]; then make a slit downwards to the point where it begins to lose its herbaceous character in the ligneous consistence of the tree; stripping the part of its leaves, and leaving only a bud or two at the top to attract the sap. The graft [b] is now prepared, having a cluster of young buds at its summit, and its lower extremity shaped to fit into the slit, where it is so placed that the upper part projects over the cut in the stock. It is now covered with grafting-clay and bound, beginning at the top, below the bunch of leaves left on the stock, so as to avoid disturbing the leaves, and working downwards. This done, break off, 2.5 cm / 1 in or so from their axils, the branches [c] of the stock below the graft. When operating on delicate species, it may be desirable to envelop the graft in a covering of paper, to preserve it from the over dry atmosphere or the heat of the sun, for ten or twelve days after the operation. Five or six weeks after grafting, the union will be complete, and the bandage may be removed, or at least relaxed; and when the suture is perfect, the leaves at [d] may be removed, otherwise they will originate buds and branches from the old tree.

In other species proceed as follows: Towards the end of May, when the terminal bud of the tree is in a state of active vegetation, make an incision, crossing the insertion of the petiole of the third, fourth, or fifth leaf, as at [b], penetrating half the diameter of the stem; the choice of the particular leaf depends upon its state of vegetation as compared with the proposed scion. If the axil of the leaf [a] is examined, it will be observed that it has three eyes, or gemmae, the centre one being most developed: it is between the axis of the central eye, at [b] and one of the lateral ones, that the oblique cut is to be made, stopping in the centre about half an inch blow the axil of the leaf. The graft [c] consists of the fragment of a branch of the same diameter as the stock, and in the same state of vegetation; it is cut to the same length as the prolongation of the stem [d]; it is wedge-shaped, fitted to the slit into which it is inserted, bound, and covered with some grafting-paste. The leaf [a] is left on the stock to draw the sap upwards for the nourishment of the graft. The leaf of the graft [e] assists in the process by absorb-

ing it to the profit of the young scion. The fifth day after the operation, the central eye [a] is suppressed; five days later, cut the disk of the leaf at [f] reserving only the median nervure, rubbing off at the same time the eyes at the axil of these leaves, repeating the same suppression ten days later. At this time, also, that is twenty days after the operation, cut the disk of the terminal leaf [a]. These several suppressions will force the sap progressively from the roots into the graft. Towards the thirtieth day the graft enters on its growth: at this time remove or relax the bandage, protecting it by a paper coronet from extreme drought and the sun.

SIDE-GRAFTING In side-grafting it is not essential, as in other cases, to amputate the head of the stock, the graft being attached to the side, as its name indicates. Having made a cross-cut into the bark of a tree, as at [d] and a vertical incision in the bark from its centre, thus marking a cut in the form of a T, each cut penetrating to the liber or inner bark; having also prepared the scion [a] by a longitudinal sloping cut of the same length, as [b–c] and raised the bark with the spatula of the grafting-knife, the graft is introduced, and the whole bandaged in the usual manner. This kind of graft is particularly useful in replacing branches on fruit-trees which are necessary to complete the symmetry of the tree for horizontal training.

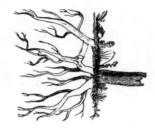

ROOT-GRAFTING In root-grafting the roots are operated on as the stems have hitherto been. Although it is by no means in common use, this mode of grafting is very convenient on some occasions. Having laid bare the roots to be operated on, shape the graft [a] by cutting its lower extremity into a shape resembling the mouthpiece of a tin whistle, with a tooth or shoulder [b] in its upper part. Cut the root across as at the dotted lines, and make a vertical cut in the separated part to receive the tongue of the scion, with an opening also corresponding to the tooth in the scion. Bring the scion and vertical cut together, so that all the parts cut meet and cover each other, meeting just below the last bud on the scion. This root being already fixed in the soil, will serve to multiply plants which do not even belong to the same species.

SHIELD-GRAFTING Shield-grafting is also usefully practised on the root in some cases even where the stock and scion are not of the same species. To discover the larger and best roots, trace them with the finger, and graft upon it in the spring, leaving the spot [a] occupied by the cushion uncovered. In the following spring, when the graft has pushed forward, separate the root from the parent tree. We thus obtain 'N': a new individual.

CIRCLE-GRAFTING These grafts are composed of one or many eyes or buds, carried by a ring of bark including the liber. They are applied generally to the multiplication of certain large trees, as the walnut, chestnut, oak, and mulberry. Towards the decline of autumn, as the sap returns to the roots, choose a mild day, free from rain. From the tree to be operated on, select a branch of the same size as the scion, having well-formed eyes. Upon this branch raise a ring of bark [a] without detaching the branch from the tree, making two circular incisions all round it, and making another vertical incision afterwards on one of its sides, and remove it gently detach from the intended stock another ring of bark of the same size, and place the ring of the graft in its place at [b] and the ring of the stock on the place whence the scion was taken; bind up and cover the joinings with grafting-paste. In the following spring, if the graft has taken, cut the head of the stock immediately above the rings, which will favour the development of the buds which they carry.

Another application of this mode of grafting is practised. When the spring sap is about to rise, cut the head from the tree to be operated on, and remove a ring [a] from the top [b]. Choose a tree of exactly the same size, on which the operation is to be performed; detach from it a ring furnished with two or three eyes, as [c], and of the same length. Adjust this cylinder carefully in

the place of the ring detached, making it coincide exactly at its base with the old bark, and cover the whole with grafting-paste. Of all these grafts this is the most solid, and least subject to be disturbed by the wind; but even this requires protection, so that it is not shaken in its place till complete suture has taken place.

APPROACH-GRAFTING In approach-grafting, supposing the stock to be planted, and the scion in a pot, as in the engraving next page, make a longitudinal cut in the stock, of such extent as to reach the medullary canal at [a], and leave a corresponding notch in the scion at [b]; but in such a way that in the scion it is less deep at the base [b]; while, on the contrary, the cut in the stock is less deep at the summit [c]. Bring the two cuts in contact, so that the liber, or inner skin, of each meets the other; then bind them. The consequence of these unequal incisions will be, that in separating the head at the point [d] of the graft, and a in the stock, there will be less deformity left in the tree.

In the preceding examples of approach-grafting, the parts of the branch operated upon should be of the previous year's growth at least. It is sometimes desirable, however, to apply the principle to branches of the same year's growth. Accident may deprive a tree of the branches

necessary to its symmetry, and a year's growth be saved by applying an herbaceous or green graft to supply the deficiency, if there happens to be a lower branch of the same tree available for the purpose. Let us suppose that a void exists at [e e e], on an otherwise healthy peach tree, and that side branches, or fruiting spurs, are required at these points to balance the tree and restore its symmetry, and that a lower branch from [f] is available to supply them any time between June and August. Supposing the shoot to have attained sufficient length, an incision is made in the branch, about 5 mm / ⅕ in long, with a cross-cut at each extremity, deep enough to penetrate to the inner bark; the bark is raised from the wood on each side of the longitudinal cut by means of the spatula at the end of the budding-knife. A thin slice is now cut out of the shoot [f], on the lower side, and opposite to a leaf-bud, corresponding in length with the incision on the branch. The parts thus laid bare are brought together, the lips of

GRAFTING TOOLS

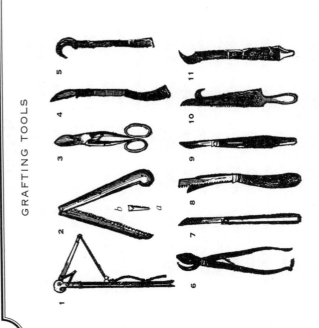

1. Averancators, 1.8 m / 6 ft long. 2. Folding pruning handle with tooth, a b.
3. Bow-slide pruning-shears. 4 / 5. Gooseberry pruning-knife, straight
and hooked blade. 6. Hand-sliding pruning-shears. 7. Pruning-knife, with
straight blade and smooth spatula. 8. Pruning-knife and saw.
9. Budding-knife, buckhorn handle, with ivory spatula added. 10. Gentleman's
improved pruning-saw, with billhook. 11. Grafting-knife, with strong
curved blade serving as a chisel, with spatula added.

raised bark brought over the shoots, and the parts are again bound together. The process is continued as often as is deemed necessary, or the length of the shoots will permit, taking care that in each case a leaf-bud is left above the point of union, and that it is left uninjured by the ligature, but leaving eight or tell days between each operation.

In the following spring the union will be complete; but it is better not to separate the grafts till the second spring.

At this time cut each shoot which has furnished the graft immediately below the ligature, and submit each of the new shoots to the usual training.

HOTBEDS

To MAKE a hotbed, let a quantity of stable-dung be got together, proportioned to the size of the frame: two double loads for a three-light frame are usually allowed for the body of the beds; but it is as well to add an additional load if the bed is required to last some time.

The dung should be turned over four or five times during a fortnight, and wetted, if dry. This preparation is most important; the inexperienced operator, unless he would run the risk of destroying his plants at the beginning, should follow it to the letter; for, unless the material has been well worked before the bed is made, it is apt to heat too violently, and burn the roots of plants. An equal quantity of leaves mixed with stable-dung may be used with advantage: the leaves give a sweeter and more moderate, as well as more lasting heat.

When the material is ready, measure the frame, length and breadth, and mark out the bed, allowing 30–50 cm / 12–18 in more each way than the length and breadth of the frame. At each corner of the bed drive a stake firmly into the ground, and perfectly upright, to serve as a guide to build the bed by; then proceed to build up the bed, shaking up the dung well and beating it down with the fork. The whole should be equally firm and compact, so that it is not likely to settle more in one part than in another. The frame and windows may now be placed in the centre, but the windows left off, so that the rank steam which always rises from a newly-made hotbed may escape.

This is the usual way of making a hotbed; there is, however, another which is very effective, and greatly economizes the manure. The trimmings and prunings of trees may be tied up into fagots, and with these the walls of a pit should be built, the exact size of the frame: on this the frame rests. The fagots are fixed by means of stakes driven through them into the ground, the walls being about 120 cm / 4 ft high. After the frame is put on, the mixture of dung and leaves is thrown in and well beaten down. The dung is piled nearly up to the glass, to allow for sinking: in other respects, the management is the same as for an ordinary bed. The advantage of this plan is, first, it requires a trifle less manure; secondly, the heat from the linings penetrates through the fagots under the bed, and is found more effective.

When the bed is made, the frame and windows put on, and the rank steam passed off, which generally takes five or six days, let a barrowful of good loamy soil be placed under each light; by the next day this will be warmed to the temperature of the hotbed, which will now be ready for use.

The heat of the manure is not lasting; consequently, the bed will require watching. It is advisable to have a thermometer in the frame, and as soon as the heat gets below 21°C / 70°F, apply a lining of fresh dung, which has been prepared as the body of the frame, to the front and one side of the bed; and when this again declines, add another to the back and the other side. The bed can be kept at a growing heat for any length of time by this means, removing the old linings, and replacing them by fresh.

In covering the windows, during frosts or rough winds, it is advisable to avoid letting the mats, or what not, hang over the sides, as there is often danger of conducting rank steam from the linings into the frame.

KEEPING HENS

K EEPING hens in the garden is an easy way to enjoy the delights of the fresh-est eggs. Hens are very entertaining companions, and can help keep weeds down if you let them range free in an enclosed garden, and provide an excellent source of manure for healthy plant propagation. Hens will also provide excellent pest control. In smaller urban gardens, they can happily exist on a small area of land, and provide the family with a sustainable source of food whilst becoming a focus of fascination for children.

If possible take a friend or contact who is already keeping hens when you are purchasing the stock, run and hen house of your choice. Start small to build up your confidence in keeping hens and you will benefit.

HOW TO GET STARTED

It is advisable to start with a minimum of three hens, and if adding to the coop in future, add in groups of three or more. Hens have a 'pecking order', and if you decide to increase the numbers it is a good tip to keep a second run next to the existing one for a time, so that the birds can see each other and get used to their new companions before being integrated.

THE HEN HOUSE

There are a huge variety of commercially available hen houses to choose from, but it is always important to purchase one which has a window. It is recommended that the window of the chosen should be positioned facing south to maximise first and last light. The house should have sufficient darkened space for the birds to feel comfortable when roosting. Smaller houses, including the popular 'Eggloo' are now a very practical solution for keeping hens in the urban kitchen garden.

TRADITIONAL RUN

This is advisable for a larger garden or extended paddock. It is suggested that between 6–8 m² / 6–9 sq yds be allowed per bird for an ideal run. This area can be reduced by as much as 50% per bird if the run has a central division which will allow for one side to be rested whilst the other is in use.

TYPES OF HEN

Jersey Giant, Light Sussex and Rhode Island Reds are all recommended breeds. The Araucana lays blue-shelled and Madama Bluebelle dark brown eggs. Try to buy birds from a recommended breeder, check the stock is clean and free of disease before you buy and try to buy stock which has been vaccinated.

FEEDING THE BIRDS

Pelleted food is preferable, as there is less waste and scatter, which will encourage vermin or other birds, both of which could be carriers of disease. A handful of mixed corn fed in the late afternoon is an excellent way to attract the hens and will encourage tame behaviour, whilst the corn fed at this time of the day will also be digested slowly, keeping the hens comfortable through the night. Do not feed corn in the morning as part of a mixed feed – the hens will pick it out and its digestion at this time of day will interfere with egg production.

A 2% solution of cider vinegar can be added to the hens' water supply, boosting their immune systems and keep a check on internal parasites.

It is essential to supply flint grit for your hens, without which they will have difficulty in feeding. Leave a small pile once a month and they will take what they need.

EGGS

Delightful as hens can be, it is the lay that matters, and it is advisable to keep a record of egg production and feed, so that you can adjust the feed mix if there are any problems. The average hen will produce an egg every 24 hours.

A CLEAN HOUSE IS A HAPPY HOUSE

Always think of the hen's home environment as your own. Keep to a regular cleaning out and disinfection programme, making sure that the nest boxes and dust baths are regularly deloused and the house is treated against Red Mite. Check the hens for signs of lice or mites, and seek advice from a vet or breeder at the earliest opportunity if signs of any disease are spotted.

PREDATORS

The fox is the single most likely predator, although cats come a close second. Basic hen wire is not strong enough to deter a hungry fox from breaking into a run and a stronger mesh can be purchased from all good garden centres or iron-mongers. Keep an eye out for any signs of rats or mice and be sure to lay bait or trap at the earliest sign of infestation.

LAYING OUT A GARDEN

THIS subject being far too extensive to be fully discussed in these pages, our observations had better be confined to a garden of a single acre. Here about two-thirds should be devoted to lawn, flower-garden, and shrubberies, and one-third to kitchen-garden, exclusive.

In the plan: 1 is the house; 2, the conservatory; 3, clump of American plants, consisting of some rhododendrons, ledums, and heaths; 4, roses; 5, flower-beds, with coniferae in the centre; 6, flower-beds; 7, jardinette, with fountain; 8, borders planted with Alpine plants; 9, vines or ornamental climbers; 10, pears, cherries, &c., trained against the wall; 11, verandah with climbers; 12, carriage-drive; 13, arches over path for climbing roses and other ornamental climbers; 14, fernery; 15, turf lawn; 16, shrubberies; 17, summer-house; 18, flower-beds, with deodars in the centre, surrounded by turf; 19, shady walk; 20, flower-border fronting conservatory; 21, flower-border fronting shrubberies; 22, melon-ground and compost-yard; 23, back entrance, wide enough for carts to enter; 24, range of three forcing-pits; 25, vinery and forcing-house; 26, tool-house; 27, frames; 28, manure-bed; 29, garden entrance.

The kitchen-garden being thoroughly drained, trenched, and manured, and the walls in order, the following will be its first order of cropping: – [a] Jerusalem artichokes; [b] gooseberies: [c] raspberries; [d] red, white, and black currants in rows; [e] strawberries, seakale, rhubarb, and globe artickokes; [f] a

row of plum-trees, asparagus, horseradish, and more strawberries; [g], pot-herbs, potatoes, and peas; [h] a row of pyramid apple-trees, parsnips, carrots, and turnips; [i] cabbages, celery, broad beans, scarlet runners; [k] pyramid pear-trees, scarlet runners, broad beans, cauliflower, and early broccoli. On the south border, plums and cherries.

The following is an illustration of a convenient villa garden. Where it can be so arranged, the garden should be an oblong square; here 90 m / 100 yds from east to west, and 65 m / 70 yds from north to south, about the proportions laid down in the accompanying plan. This allows the vegetables to range from north to south, which is always to be preferred, otherwise they get drawn to one side by the side-light of the sun. – [1] The site of the house; [2] the conserva-

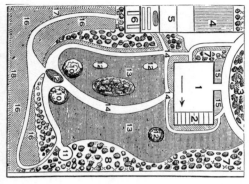

tory; [3] a clump of trees and shrubs fronting the main entrance; [4] coach-house and stables; [5] tool-house; [6] manure- and frame-yard; [7] flower-borders and shrubberies; [8] ferns and American plants; [9] rose clumps; [10] circular beds for hollyhocks, dahlias, and other free-blooming plants in summer, and thinly planted with evergreens to relieve the naked-ness in winter; [11] arbour; [12] flower-beds; [13] lawn; [14] paths; [15] beds for placing out flowers in pots; [16] kitchen-gardens; [17] peach-wall; [18] east wall for plums, cher-ries, and pears.

It is sometimes advantageous to have buildings and even groups of large trees contiguous to gardens. Where these are situated to the north, they not only break and turn aside the cold winds, but concentrate the heat of the sun; they also preserve the crops during winter. Buildings have this advantage over trees, that they afford the shelter without robbing the soil of the food necessary for its crop. In the accompanying plan it will be observed that the whole frontage north of the house is laid out as lawn, and to the south, that the breadth of the house and offices is disposed in the same way; a single winding path running through it. East of the house lie the conservatory and offices, sheltered by a belt of shrubbery, which runs round the whole lawn. The kitchen-gardens occupy the north-west side of the ground, and adjoining, at the southern extremity, are vineries, forcing-houses, and orchard-houses.

LEVELLING GROUND

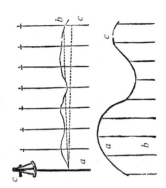

F OR levelling extensive tracts of country, a theodolite, which is a spirit-level raised on three legs and furnished with a telescope, is the instrument employed. A quadrant is also frequently used for the same purpose, and for determining the level of drains, &c. The following diagram and remarks are taken from Loudon's *Self Instruction for Young Gardeners* –

'Suppose it were required to run a level through the ground indicated [AB], from the point [A]. Provide a few staves proportioned in length to the work in hand, and let them have crosspieces to slide up and down; then, having firmly fixed your staff in the ground, to which the quadrant is attached at the point [a], set the instrument in such a position that the plumb line shall hang exactly parallel to the perpendicular limb of the quadrant: the upper limb will then be horizontal.

This done, direct the eye through the sights, and, at the same time, let an assistant adjust the slides on each staff so as exactly to range with the line of vision. Then suppose the height [a–c] to be 150 cm / 5 ft downwards from the upper side of the slide upon each staff, so shall the dotted line [a–b] represent the level line required. Suppose the operation had been to determine a cut for a drain, to have a fall of 8 cm / 3 in in every 6 m / 20 ft, the distance between each staff in the above figure may be supposed to be 6 m / 20 ft; then 1.6 m / 5 ft 3 in would have to be measured down the first staff, 1.65 m / 5 ft 6 in down the second, 1.7 m / 5 ft 9 in down the third, &c. The dotted line [a–b] would then represent the line parallel to the bottom of the intended drain.'

Where hills or mounds are to be thrown up, stakes should be inserted of the desired height, and a line stretched across their tops to show the conformation of the surface, as in the cut. These stakes, in all garden operations, should range 3–6 m / 10–20 ft apart, 5 m / 15 ft being a good average: they are not only necessary for ascertaining the levels, but enable the utmost ease and certainty as to the result.

One of the chief things to be attended to in levelling is to retain all the best soil for the surface. If judgment is exercised in the performance of the work, the surface-soil can generally be passed over on to the new level without the intervention of carts or barrows.

This will be obvious from the section shown opposite, in which [a] is the desired level, [b] an open trench to get rid of the worthless subsoil, and [c] the section of the next ground to be levelled. Of course, the surface-soil would be thrown from [c] into the trench [b], up to the level of the line [a]; the subsoil would then be carted or wheeled where it was wanted, and the same process be repeated throughout the entire section. The new level would then be furnished with a depth of 60–90 cm / 2–3 ft of good soil, fit for all cultural purposes.

MANURE

Collecting and preparing manure, and transporting it where it is wanted, are operations that should be attended to when other operations become impossible. The waste, not only of liquid, but solid manure, in this country, is enormous. Everything that has ever been endowed with life, and all the excrements proceeding from them, are available for manure. Their nature, qualities, influence, and the mode of their application, may be endlessly varied; but all alike possess a power of enriching the earth. The hard texture of bone or wood fibre may render it desirable to subject them to chemical action, or the influence of fire, to render them more speedily available to the wants of plants; but these hard substances possess the elements of plant-food in common with the soft constituents of plants and animals.

When fire is used to break down or soften woody fibre, it should be applied so as to char, and not to burn it. Charring is effected by covering the heap of wood to be operated upon with turf or earth, so as almost entirely to exclude the air, and thus insure slow combustion. Almost any vegetable refuse,

FERTILIZERS

Guano
Willow or Rape Dust
Ammonium Sulphate
Bone Dust
Dried Blood
Vegetable Compost
Wood Charcoal

including roots of weeds, can be charred; and this charcoal, saturated with urine, is one of the best fertilizers. It may be usefully drilled in with seeds, in a dry state. The scourings of ditches, decayed short grass and weeds, half-rotten leaves, soot, and every bit of solid manure that can be got, should be collected and thoroughly mixed together. The excrements of most animals are too rank and strong for flower-garden purposes, applied in a pure state; by mixing, however, the bulk of the manure may be quadrupled; it will be sooner available, and much more valuable.

MATS FOR FRAMES

As a substitute for garden-mats, which are expensive, and often not warm enough for protection, against frost, a very durable and efficient mat may be made of the long stout reeds which are used by thatchers and plasterers, and which, in the parts of the country in which they are grown, may be bought.

Cut the reeds into lengths of 140 cm / 4½ft for the width of the mat; work them in bunches about 3 cm / 1½ in thick, the bunches to be tied together with strong cord, in three places, each with a single tie: the mat will thus present a succession of rolls of reeds strongly tied together, forming a strong warm covering for frames and pits.

The mat can be made of any length that may be required, and if rolled up and stowed away in a dry place, will last for years.

MULCHING

This operation consists in spreading a layer of stable-dung over the roots of trees or plants, and in times of drought watering through it. After a time the dung may be forked into the soil.

NAILING

This is a difficult operation, for nailing is no ornament, and the less it shows itself the better. The gardener's skill must be exerted to conceal his nails and shreds as much as possible. Strips of leather or black tape have a neat appearance, and afford little harbour for insects. Fruit-trees should be nailed close on to the wall; ornamental shrubs, &c., merely fastened in for the sake of support.

NETTING

NETTING is extremely useful for many gardening purposes, to protect blossom from frost and fruit from birds. It may also with very good effect be suspended beneath both wall and standard trees to catch any falling fruit. Netting of very fine mesh may be used successfully to keep off the attacks of wasps and flies.

PACKING FRUIT

AS THE fruit approaches the ripe state, nets or mats stretched on short stakes should be suspended beneath, each having a lining of dry moss or lawn-grass, not to supersede hand-picking, but to guard against accidental falling. When a gathering is to take place, a shallow basket should be selected, covered with a layer of moss or leaves, and each fruit as it is removed from the tree should be deposited in it.

Packing delicate fruit for short journeys requires much care. Let us recommend for this purpose a box sufficiently deep to hold two tiers of fruit, and no more, and pack these with the following precautions: The box being ready, and a quantity of well-beaten and dry moss, or dried lawn-grass in the absence of moss, being provided, wrap each fruit, with the bloom untouched, in a piece of tissue or other equally soft paper, and pack them pretty closely with moss until the first layer is completed, then make it perfectly level by filling up with moss, placing an inner lid over the tier; make a second layer in the same manner, and put on the lid in such a way that the fruit, without being exposed to pressure, will nevertheless remain steadily in place.

PEGS FOR BEDDING PLANTS

VARIOUS expedients are resorted to by gardeners to peg down the different sorts of bedding-plants – verbenas, petunias, &c. Some use ladies' hair-pins, and some use small pegs made of hazel or other wood. Galvanised wire pegs are very durable.

PLANTING

THE season for planting may be from September to March. Many arguments may be brought forward in favour of the month of November, if the weather be open and free from frosts. Spring is always a busy season in the garden; digging, sowing, grafting, and pruning are then in full operation.

The pear loves a siliceous (sandy) earth, of considerable depth; plums flourish in calcareous soils, and the roots seek the surface; the cherry prefers a light siliceous soil; and all cease to be productive in moist, humid soils. The apple accommodates itself more to clayey soils, but does best in a loamy soil of moderate quality, slightly gravelly. In preparing stations, therefore, suitable soils should be supplied to each. The station is prepared by digging out a pit about 90 cm / 3 ft square, and the same depth, in ground that has been well drained. In the bottom of this pit lay 25–30 cm / 10–12 in of rubble or lime rubbish, the roughest material at the bottom, and ram it pretty firmly, so as to be impervious to the tap-root: the remainder of the pit is filled in with earth suitable to the requirements of the tree. When the surrounding soil is a tenacious clay, the root of the young tree should be spread out just under the surface, and rich light mould placed over them, forming a little mound round the roots; but in no case should the crown be more than covered: deep planting is the bane of fruit-trees.

The stations being prepared, the trees require attention. It is necessary to prune the roots, by taking off all the small fibres, and shortening the larger roots to about 15 cm / 6 in from the stem; if there be any bruise, the root in which it occurs should be removed entirely, by a clean sharp cut. Two or three spurs are sufficient: but if there be more good ones, they may remain, after careful pruning. The roots may be laid in milk-and-water or soap-suds, a few hours before the trees are planted. The process of planting will differ, according as the trees are intended to be dwarf, standard, pyramid, or wall-trees. With dwarf, standard, or espalier, place the tree upright in the centre of the station; spread the roots carefully in an horizontal direction, and cover them with prepared mould to the required height, supporting the young plant with a strong stake, driven firmly into the ground, and tying the stem to it with hay, or something that will not bruise; press the soil gently, but firmly, over the extended roots, having first cut away the tap-root. Then mulch the place. This process, called mulching, consists in spreading a layer of short half-rotten dung 15 cm / 6 in thick round the stem, in a radius 15 cm / 6 in beyond the extremity of the roots; the mulch spread evenly with the fork, and gently pressed down by the back of the spade, or, if exposed to the wind, pegged down to prevent its being blown away. In the case of a wall-tree, let the root be as far from the wall as convenient, with the stem sloping to it, the roots being extended and covered in the same manner with the soil.

The nature of the soil is to be regarded, and the tree planted at a greater or smaller elevation above the level of the surrounding soil accordingly: where the subsoil is a stiff clay, the mound in which it is planted should rise 20–30 cm / 9–12 in; in a warm dry soil, a very gentle elevation suffices. The roots should be planted in the richest mould; and various expedients may be used to keep them moist and cool, and free from canker. The mould requires to be pressed gently round the roots with the hand, so that the soil may be closely packed round them: with these precautions, no fear need be entertained of productive fruit-trees being obtained.

POTTING

This is one of the most important of gardening operations. Adapt the pots to the size of the plants as near as possible – or rather, to what the plant is expected to be – as allowance must be made for growth of the root as well as the plant. Let the pots be perfectly clean. Effectual drainage of the pots does not consist so much in the quantity of drainage, as in the arrangement of it. A potsherd should be placed over the hole: some pieces of pot, broken rather small, over that; and these again covered with a layer of peat-fibre or rough earth. This gives efficient drainage, and need not occupy more than 4 cm / 1½ in and a half of the pot. Hard-wooded plants should be potted rather firmly; soft-wooded should be left rather loose and free.

PRUNING

The pruning of fruit-trees is performed at two seasons – winter and summer. Winter pruning should be performed while vegetation is entirely at rest – the period which follows the severest frosts, and which precedes the first movement of vegetation, that is to say, the end of February or the very beginning of March, in ordinary years. If trees are pruned before the strong frosts of winter set in, the cut part is exposed to the influence of the severe weather long before the first movement of the sap takes place, which is so necessary to cicatrize the wound, and the terminal bud is consequently often destroyed. Equally troublesome are the wounds made during frosts: the frozen wood is cut with difficulty; sometimes the cuts are ragged, and do not heal; mortality attacks the bud, and it disappears. To prune after vegetation has commenced, except summer pruning, is not

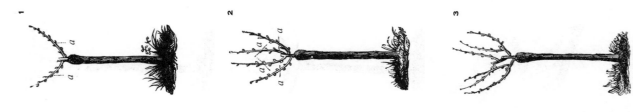

to be thought of; therefore let all chief pruning be done in February, if the frost has disappeared.

The implements required in pruning are a hand-saw, a pruning-knife, a chisel and a mallet. For garden trees the knife is the most important: it should be strong and of the best steel, with a considerable curve, so as to take a good hold of the wood. The manner of operating is far from indifferent. The amputation should be made as near as possible to the bud, but with: out touching it; the cut should begin on the opposite side, and on a level with its lower part, made at an angle of 45°, and terminate just above the bud.

If it is necessary to cut away a branch altogether, a small portion of it should be left on the stem, and the cut should be a smooth and bevelled one, presenting the smallest possible extent of wounded surface. If made with the saw, it should be made smooth with the knife or chisel, and covered with grafting-paste.

The first object in pruning it standard tree is the formation of its head. The first pruning must take place at the end of the first season after grafting, when the scion has made its growth, as represented in figure 1, when two shoots have sprung from the graft. To form a full round head, the two shoots should be pruned in to [a, a]. The year after the tree will present the appearance represented in figure 2; or, if three shoots have been left the first year, and the whole three headed in, in the following year they will appear as in figure 3, each shoot having thrown out two new branches. The one tree now presents a head of six, and the other four shoots. At the end of the second year both are to be headed back, the one to the shape indicated by the crossing lines, [a, a, a, a], the other as nearly as possible to the same distance from the graft.

Another year's growth will, in each instance, double the number of main shoots, which are now eight and six respectively, as represented in figure 5. If a greater number of shoots appear, or if any of them seem badly placed, their growth should be prevented

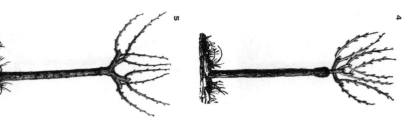

by pinching off the tops when young, and pruning them clean off when the tree has shed its leaves. The time for pruning is any of the winter months between November and February before the sap begins to stir. Those trees which have produced six shoots should be pruned exactly like those with eight, to form a compact head, as in figure 4; and when the standard tree has acquired eight main branches by these various prunings, it has attained its full formation, and with a little care may easily be kept in shape.

When a standard tree has reached its bearing state, the object of the pruner is the production of fruit. If the branches are well placed, let them have free course, and they will throw out bearing-spurs at the extremities. Little more need be said on the subject, except that all unproductive wood, crowded sprays, and decayed branches, that cross each other, should be cut out, the tree kept open in the centre, and the open cuplike form rigorously maintained. These remarks apply chiefly to apples, pears, and other trees which bear their fruit on spurs: where their habit is different, it will be noticed in treating of them specifically. These spurs will in time become long and scrubby, with many branches, as in figure 6, where we see a spur with many branches getting further and further away from the main branch. To bring it back to its proper position, cut away, neatly, the upper shoot at [a], and the side-shoot at [b], cutting out, also, the central shoot, when the small bud will push out and form blossom-buds the following year.

When a tree is very vigorous, the buds will break strongly and run into wood too strong to form blossom-buds. The remedy in this case is to break the young shoot near the third bud from the main branch, leaving the broken part hanging down. The time for this operation is about the middle of March. The broken part, while it droops, nevertheless draws up a portion of the wood-sap. The following winter, when the buds are turned into blossom-buds and become fruitful, the hanging shoot should he neatly pruned away, when a fruitful bearing-spur will be formed.

REGENERATING FRUIT-TREES

I T FREQUENTLY happens that grafted fruit-trees, some at one period of their age and some at another, cease to assimilate themselves with the stocks upon which they have been worked. This is to be seen by a thickening of the tree just about the place where it has been worked. This thickening, which in some parts of the country is called a burr, is always to be regarded as an effort of nature to throw out new roots and preserve life, and should be treated accordingly. If the tree has originally been worked, and the burr consequently shows itself at some distance above the ground, a large box should be provided, and placed round the burr, in such a way that it may contain a quantity of soil, into which the tree can strike out its new roots.

This soil should be a light loam, and always kept moist. In the second or third year, new roots will have been formed, and the tree may safely be separated by a saw from the old stock, and let down into the earth beneath. When the tree has been worked close to the surface, a place about a yard square may easily be built up with bricks or tiles, and filled with light soil 8–10 cm / 3 – 5 in over the burr, to receive the new roots. In this way the writer has preserved two small trees of the Sturmer pippin, which he found fast dwindling away, the stocks on which they were worked not having power to sustain them. By a somewhat similar process, the healthy branch [b] of a favourite tree may be preserved by layering it in a box or pot [a] as in the diagram.

Another operation, the object of which is to utilize the roots and stem of the old tree, is connected with the foregoing.

The final cause of the languishing state of these trees being the absence of vigorous young shoots and the imperfect organization of the cambium and liber, and, finally, the abortion of root-fibres in consequence, the tree can only be restored to health by the production of more healthy and vigorous organs; and this may be done by concentrating the whole energy of the tree on certain points. Amputate the principal branches, [A] (see diagram), about 18–20 cm / 7–8 in from their base at [c], the branches [b] being left entire for the present, the amputations being so made that the branches left are not required to carry out the new system of training to be adopted, passing, in all cases, the four largest branches. These branches are retained for the present, it being doubtful if the tree has strength to develop upon the old bark the new buds necessary to fulfil the functions of the roots; for if the buds perish, and there is no outlet for the rising sap, the tree dies. By preserving these branches, their leaves and shoots provide against such accidents. To facilitate the issue of buds on the tree, the hard dry bark should be removed by a plane, and its place covered by a coating of chalk and water, a covering which will stimulate the vital energy of the living bark, and protect the tree from the sun's rays.

Following this operation, we shall find that the sap concentrated on only a few branches acts with great energy upon the cellular tissues of the bark nearest to the summit of the cut branches. It determines towards these points the formation of buds, which soon develop vigorous branches. Towards the middle of June, choose such shoots as are best suited to form the principal branches for horizontal training; such would be [c d e f g h] in the diagram. The others must be cut towards the middle of their length.

The year following, in the spring, train the principal branches according to the plan laid down; for example, in the fan shape, as in the engraving, break the tender branches close to their junction with the stem or main branch, and, during the summer, pinch the leading shoots off, so as to convert into fruit-spurs the shoots not intended to form main branches.

In the following spring the tree will be as represented above. At this time, the branches [b] left for precaution, may be entirely suppressed, the several cuts being covered with grafting-paste. These new suppressions increasing the energy of the young branches, they will henceforth grow with great vigour, and will soon replace the ancient tree.

In the same proportion in which the stem is operated upon, so must the roots be. As soon as buds begin to appear upon the portion of the branches left, the

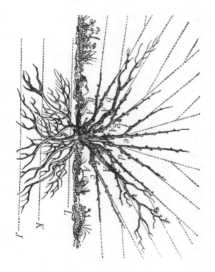

leaves which are developed send towards the roots a quantity of ligneous fibre and corticle, or wood-fibre. In its course towards the roots, this sap meets with beds or layers of cambium and liber, through which they extend themselves in a languishing state (since it is now deprived of the fluid which facilitated its passage), taking their natural direction, and penetrating the cells in the bark upon the roots, they give place to new organs, at once more nourishing, more healthy, and more vigorous than the old roots. If, after three or four years, a tree operated upon as we have indicated is transplanted, it will be observed that the lower half of the old roots, comprised between the lines [J] and [K], is decayed, and that young roots, comprising those between [K] and [L], have been thrown out. The tree has reached the state represented in the engraving, and is supplied with young, healthy, and vigorous roots, as well as more vigorous branches, with new layers of cambium and liber. It is, in reality, a new tree, which has taken the place of the prematurely old one, whose organs have ceased to live.

Analogous treatment to that which we have indicated for espalier trees may be followed with standards and pyramid trees; removing the objectionable branches 20–25 cm / 8–10 in from the stem, and placing a crown or cleft graft on each, if it is considered necessary, but taking care to leave a fourth of the old branches, till the branches cut down have thrown out young shoots. In the second year, the remaining branches may be removed altogether, the extremity of the severed cuts, when made perfectly smooth, being covered over with graft-ing-paste.

By these processes, it is possible, except in cases of complete decay, to restore the tree to its first vigour, especially in the case of pip fruit, as the apple and pear. In stone fruit, the success is less assured; and the application of graft-ing is had recourse to when it is desired to regenerate the tree, or to substitute an improved variety on an old but healthy stock. In this case, crown-grafting is adopted, and a graft placed at the extremity of each branch, which is cut down in the mean while, the development of young wood at the base of the tree, by short pruning, and pinching off the buds at the summit.

RIBBON-PLANTING

THE ribbon style in border-planting is very effective. As an illustration of it take the following arrangement: supposing there be room for five or six rows, each row 30–50 cm 12–18 in wide – a double row of *Lobelia speciosa* next the edging; followed by a row of verbenas – Mrs Holford's Snowflake, or any other white sort; these, again, followed by *Calceolaria aurea*, this by Tom Thumb geranium. If there be room for more rows, the above may be followed by *Salvia patens* (blue), *Coreopsis lanceolata* (yellow), a row of white phlox, and a back row of dahlias. These should graduate in height and colour. This is merely given as a sample of what may be done. There are many plants that may be used in the same way, as *Koenigia variegata*, isotomas, *Phlox Drumondii*, which are all dwarf, and suitable for front row; petunias; heliotropes, lantanas, &c., might form a second; ageratums, galardias, salvias, a third. Again, mirabilis, still taller; then dahlias and hollyhocks, tallest of all. Ribbons are also very pretty planted with annuals, as *Phlox drummondii*, stocks, asters, zinnias, xeranthemums, and sweet peas, all which graduate in height and vary in colour. These may be raised in frames in March and planted out in May, or sown in the open ground in May. Hardy annuals may be sown early in spring, and be allowed to flower, and then followed by bedding-plants or by biennials, which are best sown in May and planted out. Hardy herbaceous plants alone may keep a border perpetually lively, but are not well suited for massing. They should, however, be arranged with regard to height and colour. Pansies, daisies, primroses, selines, &c., being dwarf; pinks, cloves, carnations, veronicas, &c., taller; phloxes, various sorts of campanulas, chrysanthemums, &c.; starworts, rudbeckkias, &c., being tallest of all. Plants of this class flower at various times of the year, from early spring to late in the autumn. Where spring-flowering bulbs are mixed up with them, it is not advisable to plant them near the edge of the beds. Plant them far back; as they flower when the borders are comparatively bare, they are sure to be seen to advantage; and the long grassy leaves do not disfigure the borders after they have flowered. Late bulbs, as gladioli and lilies, being tall, should be placed far enough back to correspond with the other plants. A very good effect may be produced by planting a ribbon border or clump with plants of ornamental foliage. These look better than most people would imagine. The very commonest and cheapest of plants may be made use of, for instance, a front row of variegated arabis, which is a very common, hardy, herbaceous plant; second row, Henderson's beet, treated as an annual. This is a dwarf, and very bright crimson-coloured sort, and grows about 20–25 cm / 8–10 in high; third row, antenaria, or variegated mint; fourth row, *Perilla nankinensis* – annual; fifth row, ribbon-grass; sixth row, purple arack, Atriplex rubra. These graduate in height and colour, have a very pretty effect, and last the whole summer and autumn.

ROCKERIES

Few ornaments of a garden have a better effect than rockeries properly disposed; while at the same time it is also very useful. By means of it, not infrequently, an ugly corner may be turned to very good account, and very many plants will be found to flourish and do well upon rockeries which can hardly be kept alive elsewhere. It will be desirable that the work be constructed of the stone of the country, to give to it as natural an appearance as possible; but, in a general way, for rockeries which are intended to be covered with plants, any material that comes most readily to hand may be made use of. As a general rule, rockeries should never be raised on grass, but on gravel, or on a concrete foundation. It is also well placed around a pond. In the centre of a square gravelled plot, a tall piece of rockery is a very pleasing object.

It may be constructed by using the roots of old trees piled one upon another as a basis, which should be well covered with a good coating of fine loam. On this the stones may be built up, in any form that good taste may suggest, interstices, with more or less of surface, being left, which will in this way form beds for the different plants. The spring of the year is the best season for making rockeries, since the soil will have time to settle, and the stones to become fixed in their position before the next winter's frost. On the tall piece of rockery which has just been described may be planted almost every variety of hardy or half-hardy creepers – *Iophospermums, Maurandya callariensis*, the different sorts of periwinkle, &c.; while lower down, between the stones, cistuses, saxifrages, and sedums may be grown. The wild sedums of our different countries form most interesting collections when placed by themselves in a separate piece of rock-work; and so also do the wild ferns.

ROOT PRUNING

This is an important operation in gardening: it is performed by laying bare the roots 90 cm / 3 ft from the stem of the tree; then with a sharp axe, or chisel and mallet, cutting through a portion of the strongest roots, according to the requirements of the tree. If the tree is extremely vigorous, without producing fruit, two-thirds of the stronger roots cut through in this manner will probably restore it to a state of perfect bearing; the trench being filled up with fresh virgin mould, and the tree left at rest for a year. The proper season for root-pruning is the autumn, when the roots will send forth small fibrous spongioles, which elaborate the sap, and form blossom-buds. Should this operation fail to check the superfluous vigour of the tree, the roots may be again laid bare in the following autumn, and the remaining large roots then cut away, avoiding, as much as possible, all injury to the smaller fibres which have pushed out from the previous operation. Should the tree still present an over-vigorous growth, it must be taken up entirely, and all the strong roots pruned in, then re-planted, taking care that in re-planting, the tree is raised considerably above its former level – a severe operation but certain to be successful in reducing a tree to a fruitful state.

SEEDS

SEED SOWING

THE following observations upon the sowing of garden flower-seeds will generally ensure success. Too frequently good seed has to bear the blame of bad management.

PREPARATION, OR MODE OF SOWING SEEDS: In the majority of instances, the treatment recommended is the best in such situations where soil, locality, and other causes require care; for, in more favoured sheltered positions, the plants may succeed with more hardy treatment. Small seeds should only be lightly covered with soil, and if unusually dry weather prevail, a slight surface protection with moss or similar material is beneficial until the seeds have well germinated. The scale of humidity and temperature adapted to the germination of seeds and rearing of young plants is regulated by the temperature plants are capable of bearing in their mature growth. The hardier the species, the lower the average temperature required for germination, and vice versa, allowing for the artificial stimulus naturally required for establishing young plants in their primary stages of growth. The absence of surface – or bottom – heat may in some measure be compensated by early ventilation, if required; and, where compatible, closing up pits or houses with a high degree of sunheat and artificial moisture. As a uniformly modified degree of moisture in the soil is indispensable to the successful germination of seeds, it is important that the seed stores or pots should never remain parched or dry overnight: such omissions, when repeated often, prove injurious to the vital germs, and cause the eventual loss of the produce.

The following may very well serve as types of the different sorts of seeds. Martynia, abroma, and tropaeolum generally require peeling previously; coboea is best planted edgeways; geranium pricked in, leaving the feathery tailor pedicle out. Calceolaria germinates best without heat. Ipomoea and convolvulus, when very dry, or as old imported seed, often refuse to vegetate. They should be taken up and slightly cut on the surface, or on the edge, apart from the eye or vital speck (where it exists outwardly), which should be preserved from injury. Rhodanthe, and other seeds of similar character, should be well soaked in water before sowing. Cyclamen should be sown as soon as ripe. Ferns should be sown on the surface of rather coarse heath-soil, without further covering them. Place over a flat square of glass, or a bell-shaped one; place the pot in a dish, and keep the surface-soil uniformly moist and covered until the plant germs are well developed, after which very gradually admit air. Seeds of *Clianthus dampieri* should be sown singly, each in a small pot. Mistletoe seeds should be inserted within the bark, on the underside of the branches, to prevent the birds from feeding upon them.

In the sowing of exotic seeds in pots, especially those of a small and delicate structure, and those in which germination is slow and irregular, one very essential point consists in obtaining the most suitable quality of soil for surface-covering. Whilst it is important that the bulk of soil used in such operations should be well pulverized, and proportionately porous throughout, in order to admit of a free and quick growth during and after germination (which a too retentive and close quality is unfavourable to), it is still more important that the soil with which the seed is covered should not only be well pulverized but also rendered less retentive of moisture. For effecting this, where prepared soils are not at hand, that which is intended either as a mixture or otherwise should be passed through a suitable sieve, and also be thinly spread in the open air, or exposed to the influence of artificial heat until thoroughly dry or parched. In making use of the soil thus dried for covering seeds, it is best sprinkled with pure water, and passed through the hands until it admits of being easily spread. By thus reducing the retentive quality of the soil, it admits of a more uniform and healthy circulation of moisture during the first growth of the young seedlings, and, moreover, preserves the surface soil from becoming stagnant by the incipient germination of moss, &c., brought on in unprepared soils by repeated after-waterings. Two very important benefits arise from using a less retentive quality of soil for covering seeds: first, it admits of a proportionately greater depth of soil upon the seeds, while being equally pervious to the atmosphere; thus acting as a preserving medium in the case of small and delicate seeds exposed to extreme alternations of temperature; secondly, it dispenses to a great extent with the excess of sand in mixture, which is too often used in covering seeds generally. Beyond the requisite amount of it as a mechanical agent or force in modifying too retentive soils, sand only impoverishes in proportion to its bulk. The more nutritive the elements of soil for the growth of plants, the less they are subject to injury by extremes of temperature, other conditions being equal, and vice versa. In all cases where rare or delicate-bodied seeds, uncertain in their periods of germination, are covered with prepared soil, as described in the foregoing remarks, it is requisite that the pots or seed-pans thus sown should be carefully well watered immediately to settle the soil down to a uniform surface, suitable for after-waterings.

As all seeds lie dormant in the soil for given periods previous to the swelling of the inner substance, which is the first evidence of their fermentation, it is not safe to give successive heavy waterings for a short time after the first application, as referred to. Even the softest seeds should be but gradually moistened, and not repeatedly gorged with water, before they are able to digest or decompose it through the medium of living organs; and from this fact it is legitimately inferred that there should always be a due period allowed between the first repeated waterings of seeds, to admit of a healthy evaporation from the surface soil at each watering, especially where the material for covering seeds has been indiscriminately applied, without previous exposure to the ameliorating and purifying influences of sun and air.

Daily or alternate waterings are essential, when required, first by the gradual upheaving of the surface soil, and secondly, by the bursting or expansion of the seed-lobes above the soil. Water may always be given more freely with advancing growth to the most delicate germs, admitting a healthy evaporation or dryness of surface as the test of a further supply. The importance of uniform attention to watering may be best learnt by experience and observation; but the inexperienced cultivator may be reminded, that to omit a single watering overnight of young plant-germs from seeds, when in a parched state, often leads to the eventual loss of the whole, and, in many individual instances, is the incipient cause of constitutional debility throughout the entire life of the plant.

STORING SEEDS

In collecting seeds, the greatest care is required to have them ripe, and that the paper bags or envelopes into which they are put are correctly marked. All that is known of the parent plant should be added, if it other than a common kind, including the soil in which it is found. When collected, before packing away, the seeds should be carefully dried. When they belong to pulpy fruit, separate the grains from the pulp as soon as decomposition begins, and dry before placing them in bags.

SOILS AND COMPOSTS

ALL who have examined this question admit that the value of manures is in proportion to the nitrogen or phosphates which they contain, more especially the former; for nitrogen is almost synonymous with ammonia, that being the chief source of nitrogen for plants. The first and most important source of these elements is farmyard manure, which, in its fresh state, consists of the refuse of straw, of green vegetable matter, and the excreta of domestic animals. Horse-dung, varies in its composition according to the food of the animal; it is most valuable when they are fed upon grain, being then firm in consistence and rich in phosphates. Sheep-litter is a very active manure, and rich in sulphur and nitrogen; for if a slip of white paper, previously dipped in a solution of lead, be exposed to the fumes of fresh sheep-dung, the paper will be blackened; a sure test of the presence of sulphur.

Cow-litter is cooler, and less rich in nitrogenous matter; but it is rich in salts of potash and soda, and thus better adapted for delicate and deep-rooted plants. Swine's dung is still less nitrogenous and more watery, and full of vegetable matter; but the most important of all manures is the urine from the stables and drainings of the dung-heap, which is wasted daily to an enormous extent.

The composition of manure is a very heterogeneous mixture. It may be broadly viewed as a mixture of humic acid bodies fixed in alkaline salts, and nitrogenous bodies capable of yielding ammonia; and it becomes an important question how is its strength best economized. Some advocate the practice of allowing the compost-heap to be entirely decomposed into an earthy mass – thus permitting the whole of the ammonia to escape; others have gone so far as not to permit of any fermentation at all, stopping all action by continual turning. There are means, however, of fixing the ammonia and retaining it in all its strength, while the manure containing it is reduced to a state suited for assimilation as food for plants. It may be absorbed by gypsum or sulphate of lime, which, being cheap, is often mixed with the compost-heap for the purpose; the ammoniacal salts thus formed being afterwards decomposed by the vegetable organism, or by its agency combined with atmospheric influences.

STORING VEGETABLES

THERE are several sorts of vegetables which require storing for winter; – potatoes, carrots, beet, and onions are the chief of them. Potatoes do best when harvested in clumps in the open ground care being taken to protect them from rain and frost. A long ridge is the best form. The ground should be dry and thoroughly drained.

The potatoes should be heaped on a ridge, tapering from a base of 90 cm / 3 ft to 45 cm / 18 in, or less, at the top, separating the different sorts by divisions in the ridge. It is usual to cover this ridge with a thatch of wheat-straw, and then with 15–20 cm / 6–8 in of mould; but some authorities highly disapprove of this. McIntosh recommends the tubers being covered with turf, and afterwards with soil: and in the absence of these, laying on the soil at once without any litter. After having laid on 20–25 cm / 9–10 in of soil, thatch the whole over 3 cm / 1½ in thick, with straw, fern leaves, or any similar non-conducting material; 'the object being,' he says, 'first to exclude frost and wet, and, secondly, to exclude heat; for which purpose earth is not sufficiently a non-conductor of heat and cold.'

If the weather is fine when the tubers are taken up; and the potatoes are required for early use, much of this labour may be dispensed with; but if for spring and early summer use, the precautions will be found necessary.

Carrots, beet, and other similar root-crops should be taken up before the frosts set in: they may either be stored in a dry cellar, covered with dry sand, or after the manner of the potato.

It is probably unnecessary to add that in roots and tubers, as with fruit, all cut or bruised ones should be thrown aside: when the skin is cut, or a bruise exists, the elements of decay are soon introduced, and all others within reach contaminated. A dry day should be chosen for lifting them, and they should be exposed for a few hours before collecting into heaps, that the soil adhering to them may dry.

Onions should be lifted a little before they have altogether ceased to grow, the leaf turning yellow and beginning to fade will be the sign. As they are taken up, they should be placed in a dry, airy place, but without being exposed to the sun. If they are thinly spread out on a dry floor or shelf covered with sand, or on a gravel walk partially shaded in fine weather, they will do very well. As they dry, the roughest leaves should be removed; when dry, they should be removed to a warm dry loft, where they can ripen more thoroughly. When in a proper state for storing, they should be gone carefully over and separated, the smallest ones for pickling, the ripest picked out, as likely to keep longest: those with portions of leaves to them are best stored by stringing and suspending them from the ceiling of the room, which promotes ripening. The stringing is done by twisting a strong piece of matting or twine round the tails of each in succession, so that they may hang as close together as possible without forming a cluster; when they are hung up, they occupy very little room, and have a good opportunity of ripening.

TRAINING FRUIT-TREES

VARIOUS modes of training fruit-trees are in use among gardeners, but none are more graceful than the pyramidal form; and it is profitable as well as graceful, inasmuch as double the number of trees may be planted in the same space without crowding. This mode of training is extensively adopted in continental orchards, chiefly with pear-trees, but it is equally applicable for apples, cherries, and plums. The form is, of course, the result of pruning as well as training; and the commencement is from a young tree with a single strong leader, which may be obtained at any of the nurseries; though the best and surest way is to plant stocks where the trees are to stand, and graft them with suitable varieties for the purpose, taking care that one shoot only is allowed to spring from the graft. If they are procured from the nursery, plant them in properly prepared stations, supported by a strong stake driven firmly into the soil, and leave them for a year, in order that the roots may have a secure hold of the soil, and send up plenty of sap when growth commences, to push the buds strongly. We will assume that the young trees have plenty of buds nearly down to the graft; then, in the following autumn, cut off the top of the shoot at a, figure 1, with a clean cut.

At the end of the second year it will have made several shoots, and will probably, in many respects, resemble figure 2; but as we still require vigorous growth, it will be necessary to cut in again severely at [a] and [b, b]. The summer following, the side-shoots will spring forth with great vigour, spreading on all sides; and now the first foundation of the pyramidal form is laid, by extending the shoots horizontally, and tying them firmly to stake, so placed that the range of branches forming the bottom of the pyramid should project from the tree at nearly right angles, and at equal distances from each other. If they are too numerous, the superfluous shoots should be cut off. The third summer, if it continues in a healthy state, the tree will present the appearance of figure 3, with this exception, that the lower branches will be more

1

horizontal than they are here represented, in consequence of being tied to the stakes. If some of the branches have grown more vigorously than others during the summer, such shoots should be pruned into where the lines cross the branches. On the other hand, should others develop themselves feebly, they should be left at their full length, so that the descending sap, elaborated by the leaves, should deposit a larger amount of cambium. Strong shoots may also have their vigour modified by making an incision immediately below their junction with the stem, just before the sap rises in the stem; and if a desirable bud remain dormant, it may be forced into growth by making an incision just above it. Where a large vacancy occurs between the branches, then a side-graft should be inserted to fill up the space. The branches should again be cut at [a], and the fourth year will present the appearance of figure 4. It will then most likely begin to throw out fruiting-spurs: these should be carefully encouraged, for it depends on the number of spurs which a branch exhibits whether the tree is to bear a good show of fruit or not.

The tiers of branches, as they advance in height, should be regulated, so that every side is furnished with an equal number of branches. In the autumn of the year the tree will resemble figure 5. The pruning is now confined to shortening the leading shoots and the laterals where the lines cross (figure 5) the branches. The spurs should be carefully examined, and if any of them get long and branching, prune them in, as described and illustrated in figure 6. If any of them promise to be unfruitful, follow the method described in figures 1 and 2.

The fifth year the tree, continuing its progressive growth, presents the appearance of figure 6. It is now a tree of considerable size, and reqires, besides the regular annual pruning of the leading shoots and spurs, that the lateral branches should be cut in a line as nearly as possible to that indicated between [a] and [b] in figure 6. We see in the figure some short lateral shoots crowding towards the centre; all these, if present, should be pruned

away. After this, careful pruning is all the tree requires, taking care that the lower branches are not shaded by the upper ones, which is attained by pruning them at greater length than those above; for it is one of the great principles on which this mode of training has been advocated, that the trees should be so managed that the advancing tier of branches shall not interfere with the swelling and ripening of the fruit on the lower tier by overshading them. During every summer all superfluous shoots should be rubbed off as they appear, and all strong shoots in the spurs should also be stopped during that season, in order to insure vigorous action in the remaining buds, while the base of the pyramid is to be extended as far as is consistent with the development of fruit-bearing habits: and this will probably be best attained by making it a rule, that as soon as a shoot has extended 20–25 cm / 8–10 in, the point should be cut. By this practice the more powerful shoots are checked, and the weaker shoots encouraged. The advantages derived from this system of training may be stated as follows:

1. An increased number of trees in the same space.
2. The trainer has his trees more directly under control.
3. Increase of crops.
4. Ornamental and uniform appearance.

Any large and straight tree that has been allowed to grow in a wild manner, may, by grafting, be converted into the pyramidal form, like that illustrated in figure 7. By a process of this kind, following the directions already given for side-grafting, fine new varieties of fruit may be raised in a comparatively short period, and a comparatively life-less tree converted into an object of great beauty.

Another method of training the pear-tree, which has obtained some reputation with our French neighbours, was first practised by M. Verrier, chief gardener at Saulsaye, by whose name it is known. The tree is subjected to this training when it has attained a central stem and two lateral branches, as in

7

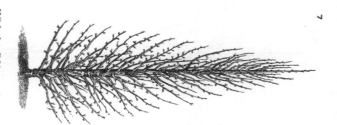

figure 8. In the autumn or winter pruning of the following year, the two side-branches are trained horizontally, as in figure 9, and pruned back to about two-thirds of their length, with a bud imme-diately below the cut. The stem itself is pruned back to about 45 cm / 18 in above the side-branches, taking care that there are three buds immediately below the cut – one on each side, well-placed, and a third in front to continue the cut. With the fall of the leaf in the following year the tree will be as represented in figure 10, with two horizontal shoots, a central stem, and two other untrained side-shoots. When the pruning season arrives, the same process of cutting back takes place, each of the new side-shoots being cut back to two-thirds of its length, the two lower branches to two-thirds of the year's growth, and the stem to within 45 cm / 18 in of the second pair of laterals, leaving three well-placed buds immediately below, as before, to continue a third pair of side-branches and the stem.

With the fifth year's growth the lower side-branches will have attained as much horizontal extension on the wall or espalier as it is intended to give them.

Having, therefore, nailed or tied them to the trellis, give the end of the shoot a gentle curve upwards. Continuing this annual process of cutting back after each year's growth, in some eleven years from the graft the tree will have covered a wall 3.5–4 m / 12–14 ft high, and 1.8 m / 6 ft on each side of the stem; each side-shoot, when it is within 45 cm / 18 in of the one immediately below it, receiving an upward direction, until the tree is as here shown. The stem, as well as the side-shoots, having reached the top of the wall, the extremities of the branches are pruned back every year to about 45 cm / 18 in below the coping, in order to leave room for the development of the terminal bud, which is necessary to draw the sap upwards for the nourishment of the fruit. After 16 or 18 years, a

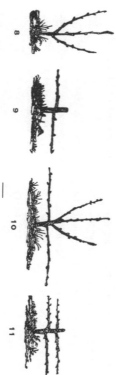

8

9

10

11

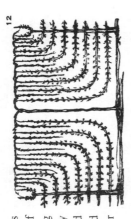

12

healthy tree, properly trained on this system, presents a surface of upwards of 18 m² / 60 sq ft of young fruit-bearing wood. The symmetry of the tree is pleasant to look at, and it is said to be admirably balanced for vegetation, and consequently for fruit-bearing.

One objection to this mode of training is, that the buds do not always occur at the right spot for projecting new side-shoots. When this is the case, the process of shield-budding is had recourse to in August. In other respects, the same principle of pruning is adopted as in pyramid-trained trees, the only modi-fication being the removal of the spurs thrown out between the tree and the wall. Another objection to the system is the time which must elapse before the wall is covered; but this is inseparable from any mode of growing apples and pears on walls, and may be met by planting vines between each, running a central rod of the vine to the top of the wall; stopping it there for the first year, and carrying a shoot on each side under the coping, with descending rods at intervals, calculated not to interfere with the side-shoots of the pear-tree.

TRANSPLANTING

I N TRANSPLANTING any tree or shrub, especially evergreens, be careful to preserve the same aspect; that is, keep the same sides to the north, south, east, and west, as before. This will greatly facilitate the speedy establishment of the plant in its new situation.

Transplanting is an important operation, and in a general way November is the best month for it. To save time, it is frequently desirable to transplant large trees and shrubs. The effect of ten or twenty years' growth is gained on any given spot at once. This is of immense importance in the lifetime of a man, and the practice of transplanting large trees is therefore popular and highly to be commended; neither is there much risk of failure, with proper caution and skill, and it is not so expensive as many imagine. With the aid of transplanting machines, trees of almost any size may be safely and expeditiously removed: in fact, these machines forcibly remove earth and roots, and all, with the minimum risk of failure. But even very large trees and shrubs may be safely moved with no other machinery than a few strong planks nailed on a harrow sledge. In this mode of transplanting, a trench is dug round the plant at a distance from the bole of two-thirds the diameter of the top, and to a depth of 60–150 cm / 2–5 ft, according to the age and size of the tree, character of the soil, depth of roots, &c., leaving a space of 60–90 cm / 2–3 ft at the back of the tree untouched. At the same time, the front, or part where the tree is intended to come out, should be approached at an easy angle of inclination, extending 60–90 cm / 2–3 ft beyond the circumference of the trench already begun. The earth is rapidly removed from the trench; the roots carefully preserved as you proceed. The size of the ball in the centre must be determined by the nature of the soil and size of the plant. Its size is of less consequence than the preservation of the roots.

As the removal of the earth proceeds, a fork must be used to separate the roots from the soil, and they should be carefully bent back and covered over until the work is finished. After excavating 30–90 cm / 1–3 ft beyond the line of the bole of the tree or shrub, according to its size, introduce into the vacant space a sledge or low truck; cut through the solid part at the back line, and the tree will rest on the machine. This should be furnished with four rings at the corners, through which ropes or cords should be fastened and firmly fixed to the bole of the tree. Of course, some soft substance, such as hay or moss, will be introduced between the bole and the cords, to prevent them chafing the bark. The tree is then ready for removal; the necessary horse or manual power can be applied: the plant will slide gently up the inclined plane, and may be conveyed any distance desired with facility. Sometimes it may be impossible to fix the cord through the back rings until the tree is out of the hole. In that, and indeed in any case, cords had better be attached to the top, and carefully held by men, lest a too strong vibration of the top should upset the machine, or topple the tree over. The hole destined to receive the tree should have an inclined plane on each side to enable the horses to walk through. When the ball arrives towards the centre of the hole, the horses stop. If the tree is not too heavy, the truck or sledge is prised up by manual strength, and the plant gradually slid off. If very heavy, a strong chain is passed under the ball, attached to a couple of strong crow-bars; the horses are applied to the other end of the truck, and the tree drops off into its place. The roots are carefully undone, and spread throughout the whole mass of soil as the process of filling-up goes on; three strong posts are driven in to form a triangle, and rails securely fixed to them across the ball to keep it immovable; the top reduced in proportion to the mutilation the roots may have suffered; the whole thoroughly drenched and puddled in with water and covered over with 10 cm / 4 in of litter to ward off cold and drought, and the operation is complete. If this operation is well performed, the loss will not average more than from 5–8 per cent. The principle involved in all planting is the same, and only of secondary importance to securing as many healthy roots as possible. The stability or immovability of both root and top comes next; for, if not attended to, every breeze that blows is analogous to a fresh removal. No sooner do the roots grasp hold of the soil than they are forcibly wrenched out of it again, and the plant lives, if at all, as by a miracle. The planting of young trees and small shrubs is so simple as scarcely to require instructions. Always make the hole considerably larger than the space required by the roots, whether few or many, so that they may find soft, recently-moved soil to grow in; and yet the soil must not be left too loose. If so moist as not to need watering, which will moisten and also consolidate the soil, it may be gently trodden down round the roots.

In reference to the proper distance at which shrubs should be planted, much depends upon the object in view. A safe rule, however, is to plant thick, and thin quickly: from 90–120 cm / 3–4 ft is a good average for small shrubs and trees. In three years, two out of three plants should be removed; and in planting it is well to introduce rapid-growing common things amongst choice plants, to nurse them up; only the nursing must not continue too long.

TRELLIS WORK

THIS may frequently be introduced with good effect in the mixed flower and kitchen-garden, to shut out buildings or unsightly objects. Small oak stands, or small larch poles, about 150–180 cm / 5–6 ft apart, and having the intervals filled with thin iron wires crossing each other, form the most durable trellis work. Against the walls of a house a very nice trellis-work may be made with a lacing of copper wire over nails of the same. This may be worked in any pattern and carried in any direction; to this wire the creepers may be tied when necessary; and in this way the walls of houses may be covered with flowers or evergreens, without injury to the brickwork from continual nailing.

TURF

THE appearance of a garden depends greatly on the quality of the turf and the way in which it is kept. Close cutting and continual rolling is the secret of good turf. On good soil little else is requisite; but on poor sandy soil the verdure must be maintained by occasional waterings with liquid manure and a dressing with guano or soot, if the lawn be not so near the house as to render such applications objectionable. Aerating the soil, by repeatedly spiking it 2.5 cm / 1 in below the surface, can be helpful. Worms should be encouraged, except where their casts might interfere with the function of the lawn, as for croquet, bowls, &c.

VENTILATION

WHEREVER, for gardening purposes, artificial heat is employed, artificial ventilation, as a matter of course, must be provided. To frames upon hot-beds, and to garden-pits, this ventilation may easily be given by lowering or lifting the windows. In glass houses some machinery is requisite on account of the height and the greater heaviness of the glass covering. The plan introduced by Mr Messenger is that generally approved.

Upright or side windows, 60 cm / 2 ft high, which run the entire length of the house, are made to open and shut by means of a rod of iron, which runs the whole length also. To this rod are attached shorter rods at intervals of 120–150 cm / 4–5 ft, with joints; the other end of the shorter rods being attached to the windows, both ends of the short rod working on a joint. To one end of the long rod is fixed a long screw, working in slings made to receive it. To this screw is attached a grooved wheel, which is made to revolve in an endless chain, acted upon by another grooved wheel, turned by a handle placed in some convenient part of the house. By the action of the screw, the long rod is drawn backwards or forwards, which acts upon the short rods, and opens or shuts the window to any required point. The same system of raising the windows may be applied to one or more of the windows, or to the whole, as may be necessary.

The system of ventilation adopted by Mr Messenger will be better understood by reference to figure 1, in which [b, b] are short rods, connected with the sling [a] at one end and the windows at the other. The dotted lines [d], represent the upright divisions which support the roof; [c], the screw-slings, in which the screw [f] is to work; [c] is a grooved wheel in which the endless chain is to work and turn the screw; in fact, this is its axis. The handle [h] is fixed to some convenient place on the front wall, being the mover of the whole apparatus. As the rod is moved from right to left, the short rods push the windows up and admit fresh air as they are acted upon: by reversing the screw, the opposite result is obtained. The ridge-ventilation is obtained in precisely the same manner; the

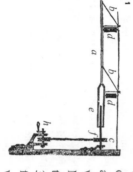

1

windows under the coping being pushed out or drawn down by turning a handle attached to a long endless chain on the end wall. The results of this system, to use Mr Messenger's words, are: 1. perfect ventilation; 2. non-interference with the plants; 3. no risk of broken glass by the windows falling down; 4. keeping out rain when the windows are open.

The roof of his houses Mr Messenger makes of very light rafters, only 8 cm / 3 in by 5 cm / 2 in, strengthening them by means of a tension-rod placed under each. These are firmly fixed at each end, and kept extended by means of two iron rods fixed in the rafters at equal distances from each other, and from the extremities. Between these rafters sash-bars are placed, which, when glazed and painted, are perfectly waterproof, and extremely light and elegant in appearance; the tension-rods being graceful, and the rafters light and airy, and yet strong enough for every purpose required. To his other patents, Mr Messenger has added a new principle of glazing for greenhouse and other roofs, which is perfectly waterproof, and air-proof also, without putty. With this invention the roof may be nearly flat; thus effecting a great saving in material.

The system of glazing patented by Mr Messenger is simple and ingenious: the upper surface of the sash-bar, of which we give a section, is an open gutter, and the glazing is performed by bending the edge of the glass over the edge of the gutter. The accompanying engravings will make more clear the principle of this mode of glazing. The gutters are made of either lead, copper, zinc, or iron, or the sash-bar itself can be made with a gutter on its surface. The mode of securing the glass down to the gutter is shown by the section, figure 2. It is done

2

by a screw passing through a brass plate and India-rubber, into the wood or metal bar; the India-rubber pressing slightly upon both sides of the glass, keeps it in its place. If the glass is very heavy, zinc or copper clips are used to prevent it slipping down. Figure 3 is a plan of the roof, showing the brass plates and shape of glass, which is so arranged as to convey the condensed vapour as well as the external rain into the internal gutter,

whence it escapes by a gutter attached to the wall-plate.

In the ventilation of the forcing-houses at Frogmore, an iron rod, which works on brass bearings or chains, runs the whole length of the house about a foot from the wall-plate. On this shaft, opposite each light, is a brass pinion working into a toothed quadrant attached to the bottom rail of each light. This shaft is turned by a handle, when the quadrants are either thrown out or drawn in, and the whole light thrown open or shut to the extent required. In the back wall of each intermediate light is a ventilating-frame, which is opened or shut by similar apparatus: above these frames over the glass is a corresponding number of open gratings. Flues or chambers in the wall open into the flues at the bottom,

3

while the grating covers the opening at top. When it is desired to thoroughly ventilate the house, the fan-lights being open, it is only necessary to turn the screw or worm, which is connected by the rod attached to the lever; and the lever being attached to the end of an iron shaft running the whole length of the house, the whole are thrown open at once.

WATERING

I N WATERING fresh-potted plants, it is important that the whole of the soil be effectually moistened, which can only be accomplished by filling up two or three times with water. No fear need be entertained of over-watering; if the plants have been rightly potted, all surplus water, beyond what the soil can conveniently retain, will drain away. Irregular watering is frequently the cause of failure in plant-culture, even with experienced growers. A certain amount of tact is necessary in giving plants, which have been so neglected, just as much water as they should have, and no more. In watering, much depends on the weather, and also on the season: plants require less in winter than in summer. The proper time to water them in winter is when they are in bloom, or growing rapidly – in summer, as soon as the least dryness appears; but a little practice will be more useful than a lengthy description. In giving air, it may be observed that all plants which are not tender, that is, all plants which are natives of temperate climes, may be exposed to the air at all times when the thermometer indicates a temperature above 40°, except in case of rough winds or heavy rains. Hardy plants may be exposed at any temperature above 4°C / 40°F; for, although frost will not kill them, it may spoil their appearance for a time. Plants in bloom should never be kept close, or exposed to wet or wind: the flowers last longest in a soft, mild atmosphere, free from draught. Plants should never be wetted overhead in cold weather, or, rather, while they are in a cold atmosphere; and never, except to wash off dust, should those having a soft or woolly foliage be so treated; but some plants, as the Camellia, Myrtles, Heaths, and others with hard leaves, may be plentifully sprayed, or watered overhead from a fine rose, in warm weather, especially when in full growth.

6

COMMON GARDEN PESTS AND DISEASES

Common-sense suggestions for getting rid of familiar pests and diseases without the use of modern pesticides and insecticides.

ANTS

Ants should not be removed from compost heaps, where they contribute to the composting process. However, if they are disrupting the garden, boiling water may be used to destroy the nest. Another solution is to mix borax, a white powder available from chemists, with sugar or jam and place as near the nest as possible. A thick barrier of petroleum jelly can be useful in preventing ants walking up, for example, fruit tree trunks or greenhouse shelving.

APHIDS

To deter aphids, make a garlic spray by infusing one or two whole heads of garlic in boiling water left overnight. Strain off the liquid and spray over the affected plants.

BLACK-SPOT

Prevention is much better than cure. Do not water roses from above so as to avoid spreading spores, remove and burn affected parts at once. Prune to allow light and air to circulate and spray with baking soda solution (1 tbsp baking soda, 1 tbsp horticultural oil and 4.5 litres / 1 gallon of water).

BOLTING

Bolting is triggered either by changes in temperature or the amount of light available. Prevent this by carefully following recommended sowing times, and taking measures to cushion any changes.

CHLOROSIS

Yellow or pale-green leaves indicate a lack of iron, usually due to inappropriately chalky soil. Dig in iron-rich organic matter such as bone-dust, blood or manure. If this cannot be eradicated, the plant may not be suitable for the soil.

CLUBROOT

Clubroot affects almost all the members of the brassica family. If your plants are stunted and wilting, examination of the roots may find them swollen and deformed. Clubroot thrives in waterlogged, acid soils, so ensure you have good drainage and apply lime to keep alkaline levels up. Once the spores have taken hold, the disease is spread very easily and can last for decades, so prevention is crucial. Immediately burn any plants that are affected and be careful not to spread the disease by foot or by tools.

DAISIES ON THE LAWN

To clear a lawn of daisies, there is nothing equal to the continued use of the simple daisy- or household table-fork. Several square yards of apparently the most hopeless grass can be cleared in a few days. The fork should be used in moist weather and the grass cut afterwards.

DANDELIONS

Cut the tops off in the spring, and place a pinch of salt on the fresh wound.

DOCKS

Docks, as dandelions, may be got rid of by cutting off the tops as soon as they appear, and placing a little salt on the wound.

DRESSING TO DESTROY INSECT'S EGGS

Stir one packet of pipe tobacco into a large full watering can and add one table-spoon of garden lime. Allow the mixture to settle, then spray the liquid over the infestation.

EARWIGS

To get rid of earwigs, place pieces, about four or six inches long, of the hollow stems of any plant, in a horizontal position, in different parts of the trees or

shrubs on which the earwigs appear. The earwigs will congregate in these, and maybe shaken out into boiling water and destroyed.

GREENFLY

Mechanical removal is the first resort. If this doesn't have much effect, fumigate with tobacco the plant infected, then douse with clean water. If it is not possible to fumigate, wash the plant with strong tobacco water or a litre of water in which a level teaspoon of eucalyptus oil has been added, using a soft brush. Repeat every week. Encourage birds and ladybirds.

GUMMING

To get rid of gumming in fruit-trees, cut out and burn any cankers, scrape the gum clear away, wash well the place where it has accumulated, and stop it with a compost of horse-dung, clay and tar.

MICE

There are three sorts of mice, all capable of doing more or less injury to the garden – the common house-mouse, and the short- and long-tailed field mouse. All are very destructive to newly-sown peas and beans, also to crocuses and other bulbs. To preserve peas and beans from injury by mice, soak them in vegetable oil and roll them in sand before planting. The most effective remedy is the mousetrap.

MILDEW

Spray the affected plant with a solution or decoction of the green elder leaves. Make this by taking a handful of elder leaves and pouring over boiling water. Cover and leave this until cool and then spray over the affected area. This is also effective in the prevention of aphid and caterpillar infestation.

MOLES

These troublesome intruders may be driven out of the garden by placing the green leaves of the common elder in their subterranean paths.

MOSS ON FRUIT TREES

Wash the branches of the trees wherever moss appears, with strong lime-water or brine.

MOSS ON GRAVEL AND PAVED WALKS

Sprinkle the walks and gravel with salt, ideally in dewy or damp weather. Be careful not to catch any plants with the salt.

MOSS ON LAWNS

All remedies are useless until the lawn is well-drained. When this is done, rake the grass with a sharp-toothed rake in different directions in order to drag out the moss.

PEST-AVERTING PLANTS

Plants such as mint, garlic, basil, chives, dill, onions and marigolds discourage pests when planted amongst your plants.

RED SPIDER MITES

Spray walls with a weak solution of water and garden lime to get rid of these troublesome pests.

ROOT FLIES

These affect carrots, parsnips, fennel and some herbs. Companion-planting with onions and garlic can help, as the flies are attracted by the smell of their favoured crop. Pay careful attention to sowing times and sow sparsely. The flies are deterred by strong winds and tend to fly low, so that a surrounding fence of polythene about 1 metre / 1 yard high can be useful. Affected plants should be burned, and the area cleared of grubs.

RUST

Avoid getting the leaves wet, and prune to maximise the circulation of air and exposure to light. Remove and destroy severely affected plants.

SAW-FLIES

Among the saw-flies, so called from the females possessing a saw-like apparatus at the extremity of the body, *Cladius difformis*, which is very destructive in gardens, measures 3 mm / ⅛ in in length, black and shining in body, with dirty yellowish-white legs. It feeds upon the leaves of various types of roses; the caterpillars are found feeling on them in the beginning of July, remaining in the pupa state a fortnight or three weeks when they appear as perfect insects.

Remove the larvae – if necessary, break off affected parts of the plant – immediately, and expose larvae for birds to eat.

SCALE

Small white insects that can be, if caught early enough, sprayed with a horticultural oil solution.

SLUGS

Grind up eggshells and sprinkle them around the base of each affected plant. Also try powdered ginger sprinkled at ground level – remember to reapply these treatments after rain. A tub of beer, submerged in soil up to the rim and kept topped up, attracts slugs which then drown.

SNAILS

To prevent snails they must be looked for, picked off by hand and killed. Make a thick paste with vegetable oil and ashes, and this will form an effectual barrier, over which no snails will attempt to pass.

THRIPS

Tiny insects causing silvery or yellowish mottling on leaves, these pests can be sprayed with a strong solution of garlic in boiling water plus 1 tbsp horticultural oil, left to cool. Avoid gardening in bright clothing, as this can attract and spread thrips.

WASPS

Where the wasps's nest is found in the ground, take a common wine bottle and rinse the inside of it with turpentine. While the inside of the bottle is still wet, thrust the neck of the bottle into the main hole of the nest. This is of course best done in the evening. The fumes of the turpentine will first stupefy, and then destroy the wasps, and in a few days the nest may be dug up. For large nests found inside properties or inaccessible areas it is recommended that professional help be sought.

WIREWORMS

If any bed or favourite plant suffers much from wireworm, a good trap may be made by placing small potatoes with a hole in them just under the surface of the ground, at different intervals. The wireworms will, in general, prefer this to any other food, and a daily examination will serve to entrap a great many of them.

WOODLICE

These insects are very destructive, especially to tender seedlings in a frame. Indeed, where woodlice abound, many persons are often under the impression that the seed has never come up at all, for it requires a magnifying glass to enable us to detect the minute stalks when deprived of their leaves. Woodlice congregate at the bottoms of pots in a hotbed and round the sides of the frame. They should be searched for every morning and destroyed by having boiling-hot water poured upon them.

WORMS IN THE LAWN

Although worms aerate soil and should normally be encouraged, their presence in certain lawns used for special purposes, such as croquet lawns, is a problem. In these cases, drying out the surface area by regular spiking, as well as raising the acidity of the soil, can help. Another solution is to mix lime with water in the proportion of 1 lb / 450 g of lime to about 3 gallons / 13.5 litres of water. Stir often, then allow to settle. Draw off the water from the sediment and apply freely to the lawn by watering can. The worms will come to the surface, and may be swept up with a broom. This operation is most effectual if performed in damp weather, as the worms then lie nearer the surface. It may be repeated till the worms disappear.

INDEX